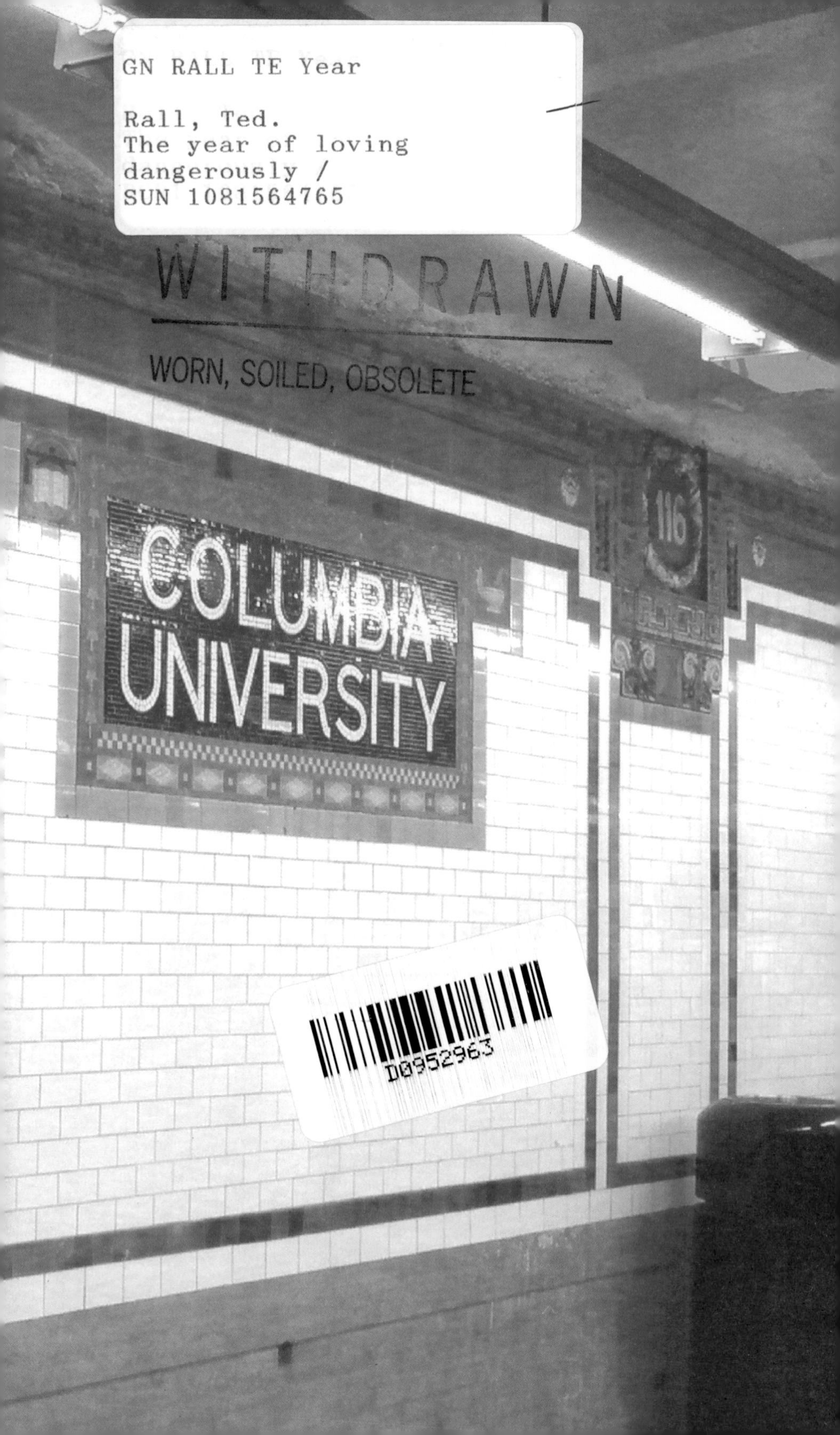
COLUMBIA
UNIVERSITY
116

THE YEAR OF LOVING DANGEROUSLY

Ted Rall, writer
Pablo G. Callejo, artist

Front and Back Cover Design: Mikhaela B. Reid

Ted Rall would like to thank: Jennifer Escott,
Merrilee Heifetz, Stephanie McMillan, Terry Nantier,
Mikhaela B. Reid, Martin Satryb, Cole Smithey.

Pablo G. Callejo thanks Ted and Terry for their patience
in waiting the three years I've taken to draw this book.
And to Eva, for the same reason. Gracias por estar
siempre ahí, mi amor.

ISBN: 978-1-56163-565-8 cl.
ISBN: 978-1-56163-566-5 pb.
©2009 Ted Rall & Pablo G. Callejo
Library of Congress Control Number: 2009934810

Printed in Hong Kong

3 2 1

ComicsLit is an imprint
and trademark of

NANTIER · BEALL · MINOUSTCHINE
Publishing inc.
new york

INTRODUCTION
by Xaviera Hollander

"The business of sex [has] a new relevance" since 9/11, I wrote in the bonus chapter to the reissue of my book "The Happy Hooker." Frightened people live for the moment. But sex never goes out of style. In my case, the intersection of sexuality and commerce goes back to my life as a "madam" in New York during the early '70s. Out of my arrest for promoting prostitution began a cottage industry that, in one way or another, exploits the uncomfortable realities that love and sex don't always happen at the same time and that cash sometimes steps in to fill the void.

It started with the publication of my 1971 memoir "The Happy Hooker," which sold 16 million copies. As the critics say, it "remains not only a classic taboo-buster, but one of the earliest flashpoints of sex-positive feminist writing to have emerged from the '70s sexual revolution." Four years later, they made a film starring Lynn Redgrave. There have been books, more movies, even an album. I produce plays. For 35 years, I wrote a column for *Penthouse* magazine titled "Call Me Madam."

My 2008 autobiographical "Xaviera Hollander, the Happy Hooker: Portrait of a Sexual Revolutionary" won the best documentary award at the Philadelphia International Film Festival and first prize at the West Hollywood International Film Festival. There's a musical in the works about my life as the Happy Hooker.

None of it would have happened if I hadn't run a place called the Vertical Whorehouse in 1970s New York.

New York had changed by the 1980s, when Ted Rall, cartoonist and future graphic novelist, found himself on the streets low on cash but rich in charm. The AIDS scare, police crackdowns and the puritan atmosphere of the Reagan years made the city a less sexy place. And yet Ted managed to do something countless women, and some men, have done from time immemorial,

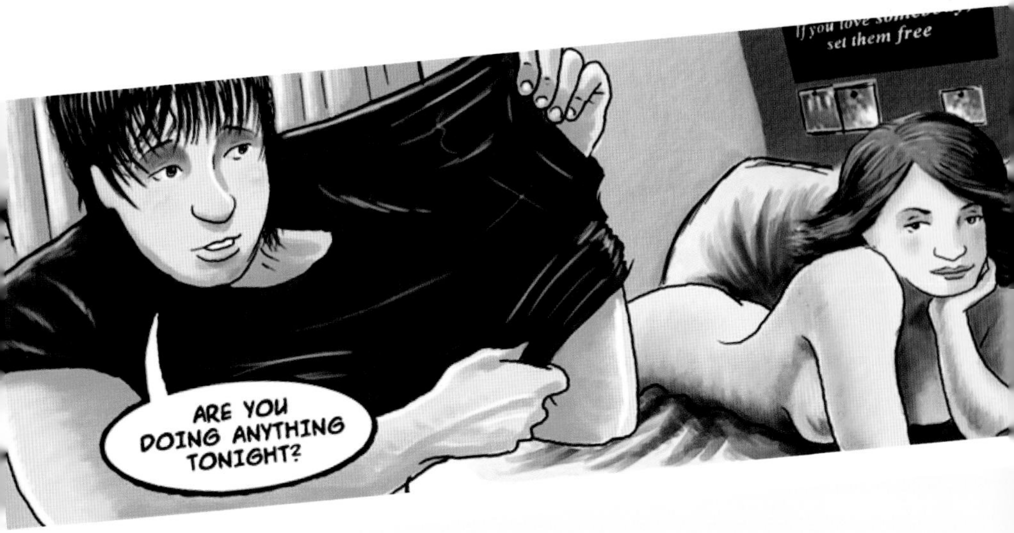
set them free
ARE YOU DOING ANYTHING TONIGHT?

especially during desperate times in urban centers: exploit his looks in return for financial reward.

Ted didn't take money for sex, but, in Manhattan, a place to spend the night is the next best thing to cash—and that's what he wanted, and consistently got, for over a year until he landed back on his feet. His is an unusual story for its honesty. But I'm willing to bet it's anything but uncommon in its frequency.

What makes "The Year of Loving Dangerously" interesting is that, unlike the work of many cartoonists, he is not a shoe-gazer. He is not socially awkward, writing about his inability to get a date, much less get laid on a Saturday night. Like my attitude as "The Happy Hooker," Ted didn't wallow in self-pity. To the contrary, he embraced life and sex, even when they came about in unconventional ways. He loved and respected women and loved every minute of his sexual adventures. He was not a cad. He was a lover. The fact that he did it to survive doesn't change that. "The Year of Loving Dangerously" may be the first sex-positive book written by a typical, well-adjusted, heterosexual American man.

Never listen to those who warn that a life of sexuality will ruin you. Nowadays I live in Amsterdam, where I run a fun Bohemian-style Bed and Brothel... oops, sorry... *Breakfast* and also spend time at a villa in Marbella, Spain, where I produce English-language theater for the culture-starved British ex-pat community.

And I am happily married to a wonderful man. I am 66 years old and have never been busier or happier. I feel great.

–Amsterdam, 2009

FOREWORD
by Ted Rall

There are two kinds of people: those who have empathy and those who don't. An empathetic person sees a homeless guy sprawled across a sidewalk and thinks "there but for the grace of God, or pure chance, or both, goes I." A self-righteous person judges. "If he had worked harder... laid off the booze... cleaned himself up... he'd be fine."

Because I usually fall into the first category, I don't begrudge a person born minus an empathy chip their lack of concern for the unfortunates. For one thing, the stone-hearted among us often have a point: how can a person so broke that he has to sleep outside justify spending ten bucks on a pack? For another, the ability to see oneself in another human being's failures isn't innate. It's taught. Change your parents, teachers, even the movies you've seen, and your ability to empathize may well change too.

Lacking empathy can be a valuable boon in life. At freshman orientation during my first week at Columbia, a dean told us new fish about our odds. "Look to your left. Look to your right. Look in front of you. Look behind you." We did. "Three out of four of those people won't be here on graduation day." He wasn't bluffing. I don't know if their policies have changed, but at the time, Columbia's engineering school prided itself on the fact that it admitted hundreds of the nation's brightest mathematical and scientific minds through its gates in early September of 1981, only to reduce seventy-five percent of them to the status of college dropouts by 1985—dropouts with five-figure student loan balances.

The odds were clear enough, especially to students required to study advanced statistics. Still, it would never occur to an eighteen-year-old who felt entitled, superior and arrogant that he (there were only a few dozen women in my class) would end up being one of those who would wind up failing out. Failing was for losers. Kids like that think of themselves as winners. And usually, it's an attitude that serves them well.

I was arrogant enough. But I wasn't stupid. "I'll probably be one of those three," I remember thinking. And so I was.

Queen Elizabeth II called 1992 her *annus horribilis*. Mine was 1984.

The inciting incident, the event that led to all the rest, took place during finals week of my first semester of junior year, in December 1983. Columbia's engineering curriculum accelerates dramatically in junior year, and I was scared enough to take my classes seriously. I had stopped skipping classes. I stayed up late studying.

One evening, while taking a shower, I noticed a wart growing on my chest. I didn't think much of it; I scheduled an appointment with the campus health clinic for the next day and went to sleep. I woke up in the middle of the night, covered with my own blood. The root of the wart, it turned out, had grown into an artery, which burst. I spent about a week in the hospital—finals week.

When I contacted my professors about making up my final exams, however, I learned that Columbia did not require teachers to allow make-up exams. No matter how legitimate the excuse—a death in the family, landing in the hospital due to a killer wart—professors had the option to refuse. Three of my professors did that. An F on the final meant an F in the class. I wound up on academic probation.

If a student on probation got nothing but As and Bs the following two terms, he would resume normal student status. One grade lower than a B-, on the other hand, and he would be expelled.

At a time like that, in a situation like that, the last thing you need is a guy like Michael T----.

The following term, spring 1984, I took T---- partial differential equations class. Apparently Professor T---- felt that my mastery of partial differential equations fell woefully short of his standards. He slammed me with a D. Which, considering that he gave out perhaps one or two As and Bs in a class with over a hundred students, wasn't bad. My dean of students asked him to reconsider. But he refused. There was a lot of that going around at the time, and it was the fatal blow to my academic career.

The dean told me not to worry, that he knew about my medical problems and wouldn't expel me. Then I got the expulsion letter. And then, to paraphrase Art Spiegelman's father in "Maus", my troubles truly began.

In the space of three months I got arrested, fired, expelled, dumped by my very-serious girlfriend and evicted. With less than twenty-four hours notice and eight bucks in my pocket, I wound up on the streets of Manhattan. I had nowhere to go, no one to turn to, and no way to make things better.

At least it was summer.

Who am I to judge the nicotine-addicted bum? The first night, I spent a third of my worldly assets on pizza. The second, another third on beer. Both of which turned out to be superb investments. Each night I met a woman. Each night I had a place to sleep. Those two events set me down a path that soon became a pattern. For day after day, week after week, and month after month, I ended up crashing at women's apartments, wondering whether I was shopping for Ms. Right less than for squatting rights in a magic box of Manhattan real estate. Exploring the intersection between sex and expediency was puzzling—and I'm still figuring out the summer of 1984 a quarter-century after the fact. But there's no denying that things worked out. I didn't sleep outdoors. And I got to know a lot of great women.

The first question about "The Year of Loving Dangerously" should be the first question asked of any book, or more precisely to the author of any book: Why? Why did you write it and why should anyone care?

First and foremost, "The Year of Loving Dangerously" is a chronicle of desperation, of how easy it is for anyone—even a white male attending an Ivy League school—to fall off the merry-go-round of U.S.-style laissez faire capitalism. It happens to thousands of people every day—the Coalition for the Homeless estimates there are currently 3.5 million homeless people in the United States—yet they keep their troubles to themselves. If poverty is a disease, it's one that carries more shame than syphilis. I want others, particularly those who are or have been in dire financial straits, to know that they're not alone. No one should take this book as evidence that things usually work out. To the contrary—such dire events *rarely* work out. The fact that they did for me (albeit with difficulty), for the time being, testifies merely to the fact that I lived to tell the tale. Which I very nearly did not.

"Year" is also something of a reaction against the fey, pathetic archetype that defines so many other cartoonists' personal narratives, in which guys—most of whom, truth be told, are actually reasonably attractive and charming—declaim their masturbatory nerddom to an uncaring world (which does care enough to buy their books and adapt them into Major Motion Pictures).

"Unlikeability and self-hatred are by no means anomalous traits in the protagonists created by today's younger male cartoonists, the 'young fogeys' whose relentless portrayal of unattractive qualities and male insecurities, often combined with extremely beautiful and technically accomplished artwork, does not always make for enjoyable reading," writes Elif Batuman in *The London Review of Books* in an overview of "books that weren't really designed with you in mind." "Some graphic novels give you the impression of being stuck in conversation with a self-hating man who constantly harps on about his most unappealing qualities, less in the hope that you will protest—if you do, he will start arguing with you—than to make you feel shallow for not liking him."

This book *was* designed with you in mind. Despite its non-linear chronology, the story and overarching themes are meant to be easily understood by anyone. You shouldn't need an MFA in order to understand a graphic novel. And it's anything but a request for pity.

Sure, 1984 was a horrible year, my worst ever. Day to day, I never knew whether I would live or die. But living on the edge feels real. I wouldn't trade my year of loving dangerously for the world.

—New York, 2009

Also Available by Ted Rall from NBM:
My War With Brian, $8.95
2024, $16.95 hc., $9.95 pb.
To Afghanistan and Back, $15.95 hc., $9.95 pb.
Generalissimo El Busho, $19.95 hc., $13.95 pb.
Silk Road to Ruin, $22.95 hc.

Edited by Ted Rall:
Attitude: The New Subversive Political Cartoonists, $13.95
Attitude 2: The New Subversive Alternative Cartoonists, $13.95
Attitude 3: The New Subversive Online Cartoonists, $13.95

Other Books by Ted Rall:
Waking Up in America
All The Rules Have Changed
Revenge of the Latchkey Kids
Search and Destroy
Gas War
Wake Up, You're Liberal!
America Gone Wild

Ted Rall Online: www.RALL.com

Also available by Pablo G. Callejo from NBM
With Rob Vollmar:
Bluesman, $24.95 hc.
The Castaways, $17.95 hc.

We have over 200 graphic novels available,
write for our color catalog:
NBM
40 Exchange Pl., Ste. 1308
New York, NY 10005
www.nbmpublishing.com

It's morning
in America

REAGAN
BUSH '84

I

A World Without Gravity

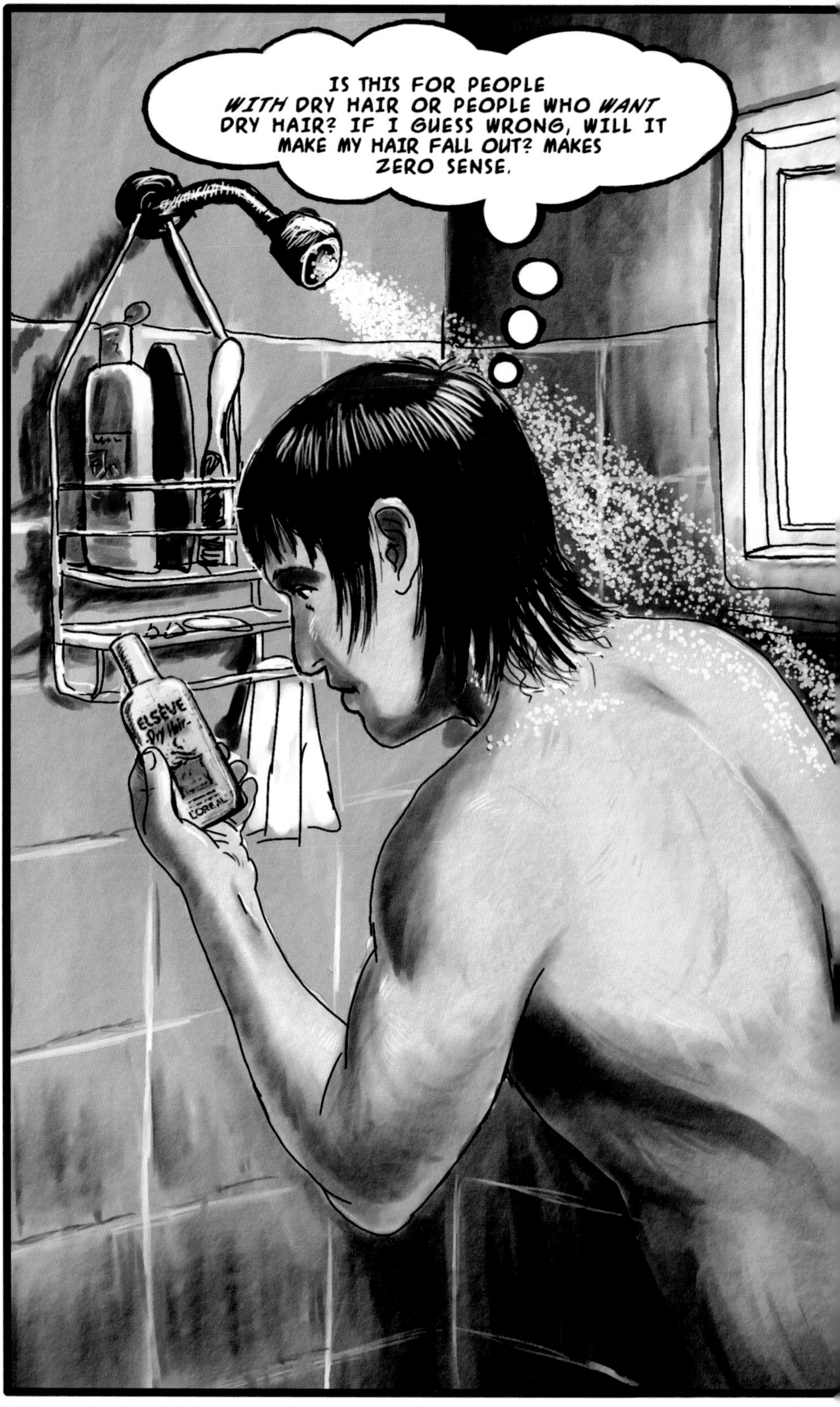
IS THIS FOR PEOPLE *WITH* DRY HAIR OR PEOPLE WHO *WANT* DRY HAIR? IF I GUESS WRONG, WILL IT MAKE MY HAIR FALL OUT? MAKES ZERO SENSE.
ELSEVE
Dry Hair
L'OREAL

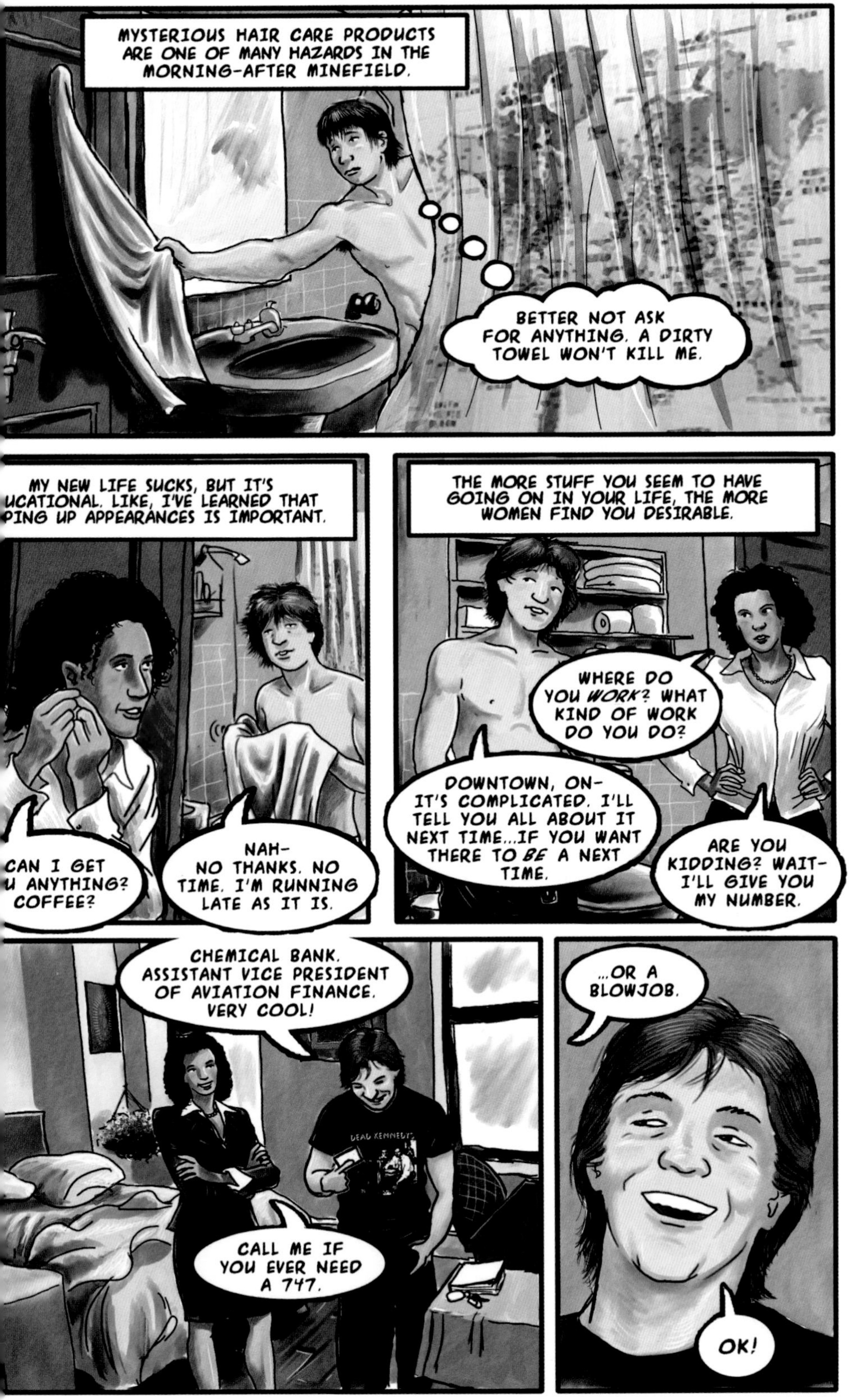
MYSTERIOUS HAIR CARE PRODUCTS ARE ONE OF MANY HAZARDS IN THE MORNING-AFTER MINEFIELD.
BETTER NOT ASK FOR ANYTHING. A DIRTY TOWEL WON'T KILL ME.
MY NEW LIFE SUCKS, BUT IT'S UCATIONAL. LIKE, I'VE LEARNED THAT PING UP APPEARANCES IS IMPORTANT.
CAN I GET U ANYTHING? COFFEE?
NAH- NO THANKS. NO TIME. I'M RUNNING LATE AS IT IS.
THE MORE STUFF YOU SEEM TO HAVE GOING ON IN YOUR LIFE, THE MORE WOMEN FIND YOU DESIRABLE.
WHERE DO YOU *WORK*? WHAT KIND OF WORK DO YOU DO?
DOWNTOWN, ON- IT'S COMPLICATED. I'LL TELL YOU ALL ABOUT IT NEXT TIME...IF YOU WANT THERE TO *BE* A NEXT TIME.
ARE YOU KIDDING? WAIT- I'LL GIVE YOU MY NUMBER.
CHEMICAL BANK. ASSISTANT VICE PRESIDENT OF AVIATION FINANCE. VERY COOL!
DEAD KENNEDYS
CALL ME IF YOU EVER NEED A 747.
...OR A BLOWJOB.
OK!

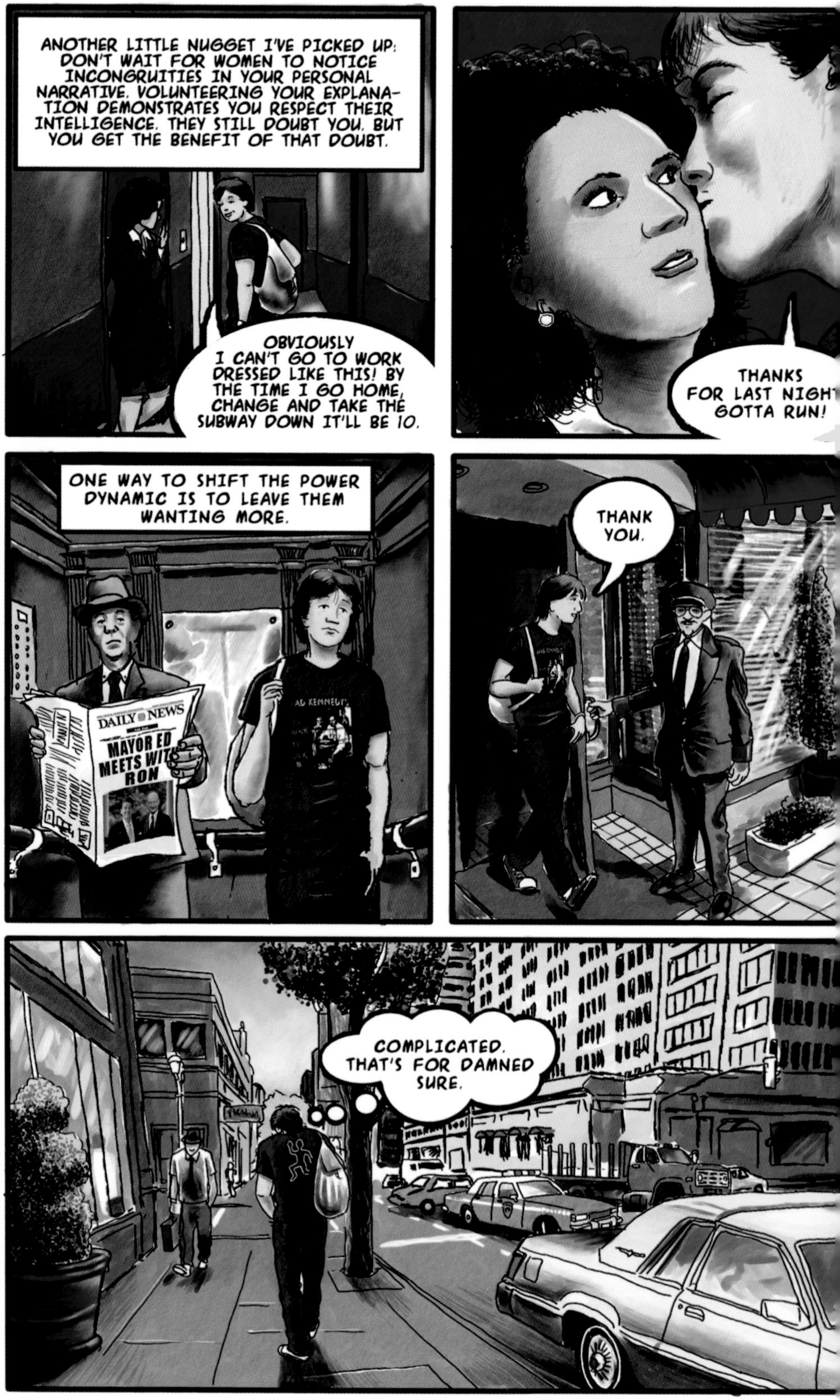
ANOTHER LITTLE NUGGET I'VE PICKED UP: DON'T WAIT FOR WOMEN TO NOTICE INCONGRUITIES IN YOUR PERSONAL NARRATIVE. VOLUNTEERING YOUR EXPLANATION DEMONSTRATES YOU RESPECT THEIR INTELLIGENCE. THEY STILL DOUBT YOU, BUT YOU GET THE BENEFIT OF THAT DOUBT.
OBVIOUSLY I CAN'T GO TO WORK DRESSED LIKE THIS! BY THE TIME I GO HOME, CHANGE AND TAKE THE SUBWAY DOWN IT'LL BE 10.
THANKS FOR LAST NIGHT GOTTA RUN!
ONE WAY TO SHIFT THE POWER DYNAMIC IS TO LEAVE THEM WANTING MORE.
DAILY NEWS
MAYOR ED MEETS WITH RON
THANK YOU.
COMPLICATED. THAT'S FOR DAMNED SURE.

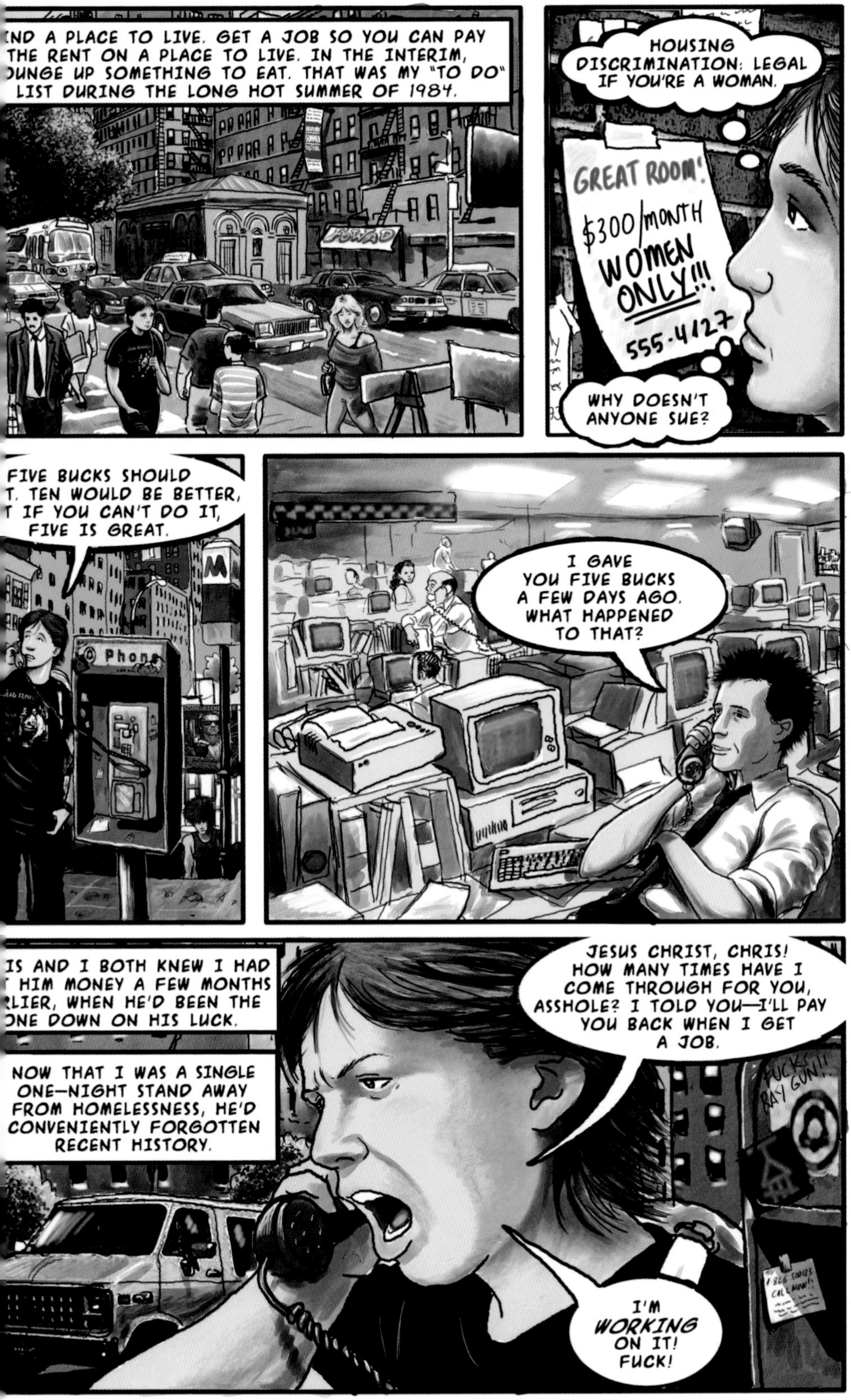

IND A PLACE TO LIVE. GET A JOB SO YOU CAN PAY THE RENT ON A PLACE TO LIVE. IN THE INTERIM, OUNGE UP SOMETHING TO EAT. THAT WAS MY "TO DO" LIST DURING THE LONG HOT SUMMER OF 1984.
HOUSING DISCRIMINATION: LEGAL IF YOU'RE A WOMAN.
GREAT ROOM!
$300/MONTH
WOMEN ONLY!!!
555-4127
WHY DOESN'T ANYONE SUE?
FIVE BUCKS SHOULD T. TEN WOULD BE BETTER, T IF YOU CAN'T DO IT, FIVE IS GREAT.
Phone
I GAVE YOU FIVE BUCKS A FEW DAYS AGO. WHAT HAPPENED TO THAT?
IS AND I BOTH KNEW I HAD T HIM MONEY A FEW MONTHS RLIER, WHEN HE'D BEEN THE ONE DOWN ON HIS LUCK.
NOW THAT I WAS A SINGLE ONE-NIGHT STAND AWAY FROM HOMELESSNESS, HE'D CONVENIENTLY FORGOTTEN RECENT HISTORY.
JESUS CHRIST, CHRIS! HOW MANY TIMES HAVE I COME THROUGH FOR YOU, ASSHOLE? I TOLD YOU—I'LL PAY YOU BACK WHEN I GET A JOB.
FUCK RAY GUN!!
I'M *WORKING* ON IT! FUCK!

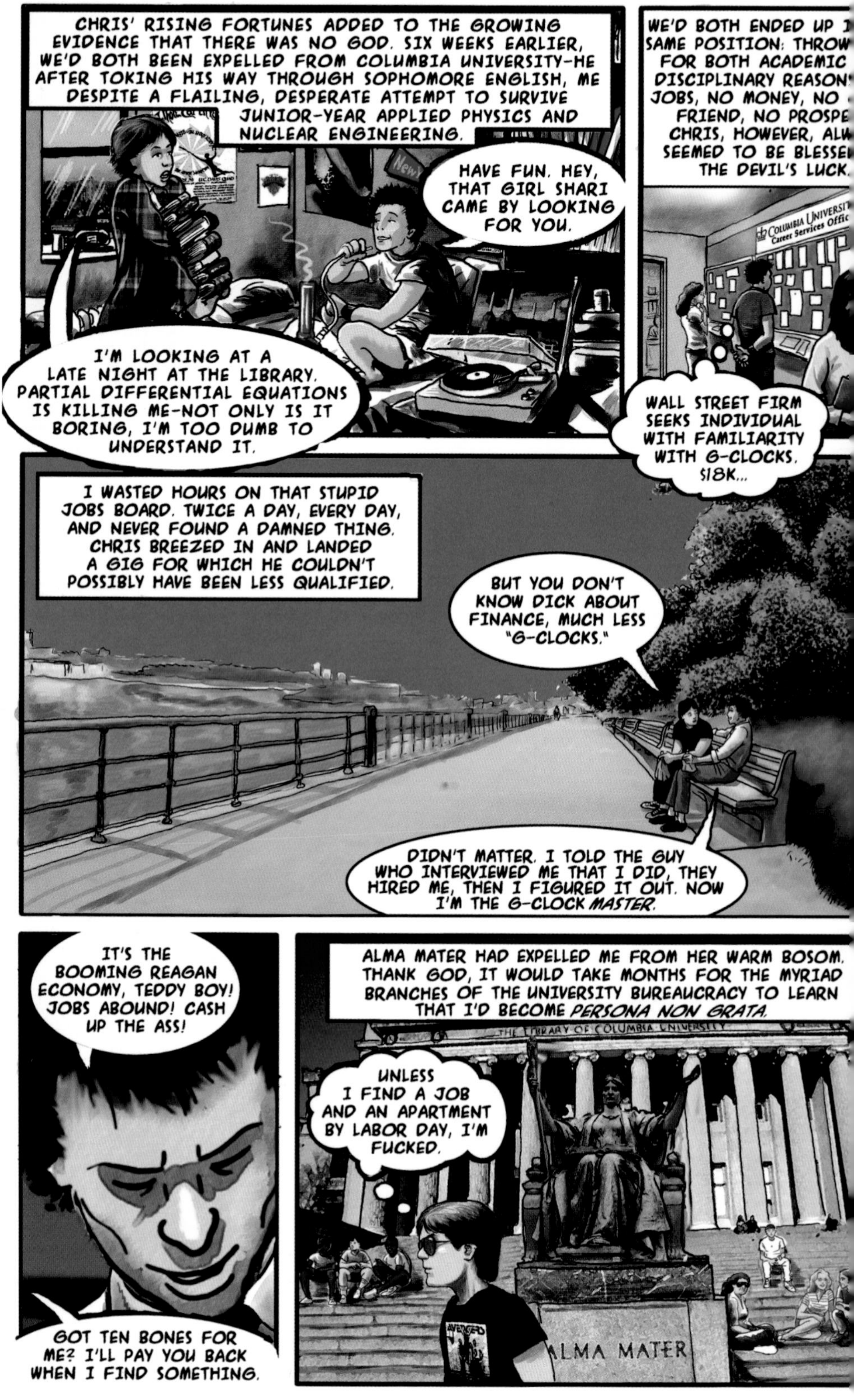
CHRIS' RISING FORTUNES ADDED TO THE GROWING EVIDENCE THAT THERE WAS NO GOD. SIX WEEKS EARLIER, WE'D BOTH BEEN EXPELLED FROM COLUMBIA UNIVERSITY–HE AFTER TOKING HIS WAY THROUGH SOPHOMORE ENGLISH, ME DESPITE A FLAILING, DESPERATE ATTEMPT TO SURVIVE JUNIOR-YEAR APPLIED PHYSICS AND NUCLEAR ENGINEERING.
HAVE FUN. HEY, THAT GIRL SHARI CAME BY LOOKING FOR YOU.
I'M LOOKING AT A LATE NIGHT AT THE LIBRARY. PARTIAL DIFFERENTIAL EQUATIONS IS KILLING ME–NOT ONLY IS IT BORING, I'M TOO DUMB TO UNDERSTAND IT.
WE'D BOTH ENDED UP I
SAME POSITION: THROW
FOR BOTH ACADEMIC
DISCIPLINARY REASON
JOBS, NO MONEY, NO
FRIEND, NO PROSPE
CHRIS, HOWEVER, ALW
SEEMED TO BE BLESSE
THE DEVIL'S LUCK.
COLUMBIA UNIVERSIT
Career Services Offic
WALL STREET FIRM SEEKS INDIVIDUAL WITH FAMILIARITY WITH G-CLOCKS. $18K...
I WASTED HOURS ON THAT STUPID JOBS BOARD. TWICE A DAY, EVERY DAY, AND NEVER FOUND A DAMNED THING. CHRIS BREEZED IN AND LANDED A GIG FOR WHICH HE COULDN'T POSSIBLY HAVE BEEN LESS QUALIFIED.
BUT YOU DON'T KNOW DICK ABOUT FINANCE, MUCH LESS "G-CLOCKS."
DIDN'T MATTER. I TOLD THE GUY WHO INTERVIEWED ME THAT I DID, THEY HIRED ME, THEN I FIGURED IT OUT. NOW I'M THE G-CLOCK *MASTER*.
IT'S THE BOOMING REAGAN ECONOMY, TEDDY BOY! JOBS ABOUND! CASH UP THE ASS!
GOT TEN BONES FOR ME? I'LL PAY YOU BACK WHEN I FIND SOMETHING.
ALMA MATER HAD EXPELLED ME FROM HER WARM BOSOM. THANK GOD, IT WOULD TAKE MONTHS FOR THE MYRIAD BRANCHES OF THE UNIVERSITY BUREAUCRACY TO LEARN THAT I'D BECOME *PERSONA NON GRATA*.
THE LIBRARY OF COLUMBIA UNIVERSITY
UNLESS I FIND A JOB AND AN APARTMENT BY LABOR DAY, I'M FUCKED.
ALMA MATER

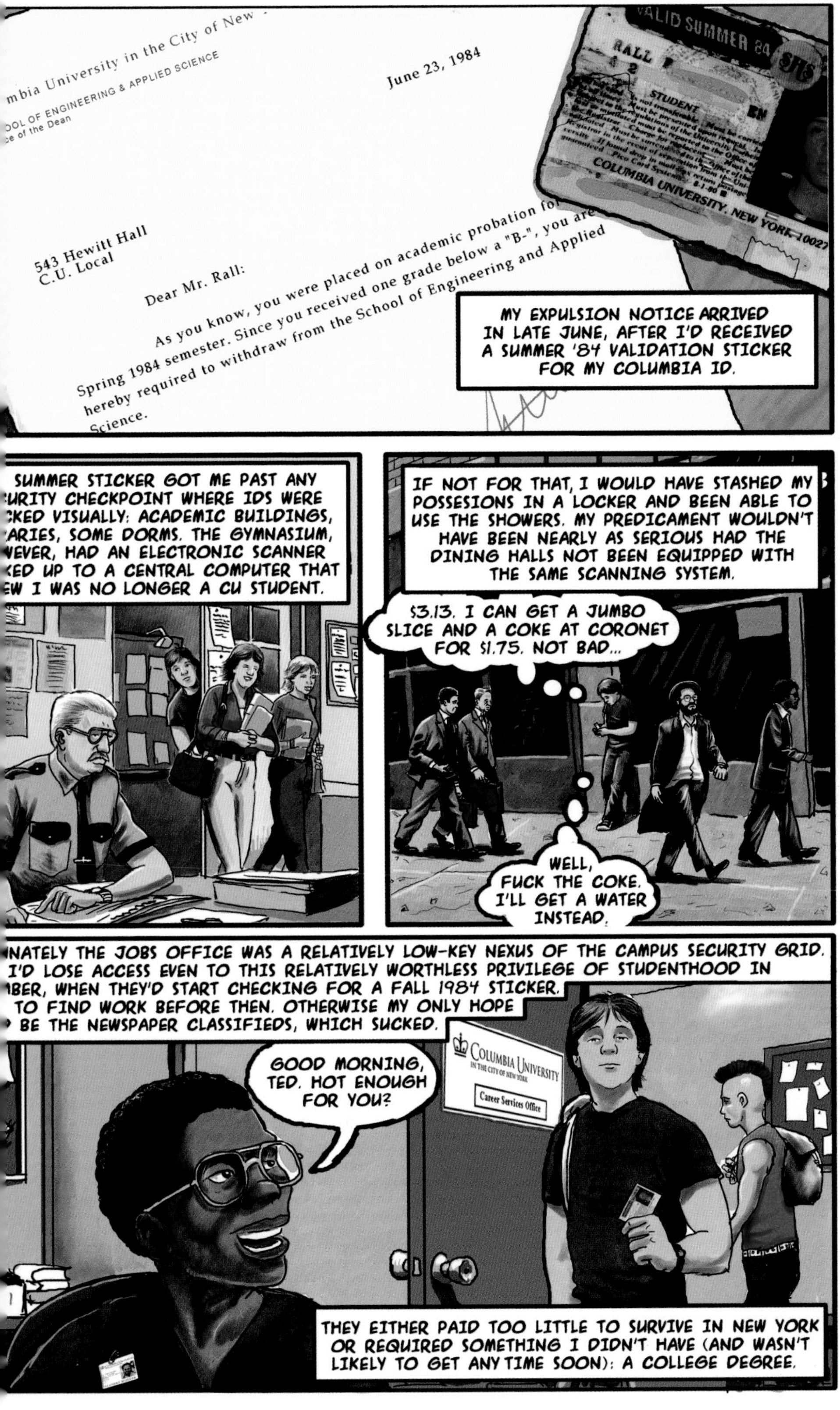
mbia University in the City of New
OOL OF ENGINEERING & APPLIED SCIENCE
ce of the Dean
June 23, 1984
543 Hewitt Hall
C.U. Local
Dear Mr. Rall:
As you know, you were placed on academic probation for
Spring 1984 semester. Since you received one grade below a "B-", you are
hereby required to withdraw from the School of Engineering and Applied
Science.
VALID SUMMER 84
RALL
STUDENT
COLUMBIA UNIVERSITY, NEW YORK 10027
MY EXPULSION NOTICE ARRIVED IN LATE JUNE, AFTER I'D RECEIVED A SUMMER '84 VALIDATION STICKER FOR MY COLUMBIA ID.
SUMMER STICKER GOT ME PAST ANY URITY CHECKPOINT WHERE IDS WERE CKED VISUALLY: ACADEMIC BUILDINGS, ARIES, SOME DORMS. THE GYMNASIUM, VEVER, HAD AN ELECTRONIC SCANNER KED UP TO A CENTRAL COMPUTER THAT EW I WAS NO LONGER A CU STUDENT.
IF NOT FOR THAT, I WOULD HAVE STASHED MY POSSESIONS IN A LOCKER AND BEEN ABLE TO USE THE SHOWERS. MY PREDICAMENT WOULDN'T HAVE BEEN NEARLY AS SERIOUS HAD THE DINING HALLS NOT BEEN EQUIPPED WITH THE SAME SCANNING SYSTEM.
$3.13. I CAN GET A JUMBO SLICE AND A COKE AT CORONET FOR $1.75. NOT BAD...
WELL, FUCK THE COKE. I'LL GET A WATER INSTEAD.
NATELY THE JOBS OFFICE WAS A RELATIVELY LOW-KEY NEXUS OF THE CAMPUS SECURITY GRID. I'D LOSE ACCESS EVEN TO THIS RELATIVELY WORTHLESS PRIVILEGE OF STUDENTHOOD IN BER, WHEN THEY'D START CHECKING FOR A FALL 1984 STICKER. TO FIND WORK BEFORE THEN. OTHERWISE MY ONLY HOPE BE THE NEWSPAPER CLASSIFIEDS, WHICH SUCKED.
GOOD MORNING, TED. HOT ENOUGH FOR YOU?
COLUMBIA UNIVERSITY
IN THE CITY OF NEW YORK
Career Services Office
THEY EITHER PAID TOO LITTLE TO SURVIVE IN NEW YORK OR REQUIRED SOMETHING I DIDN'T HAVE (AND WASN'T LIKELY TO GET ANY TIME SOON): A COLLEGE DEGREE.

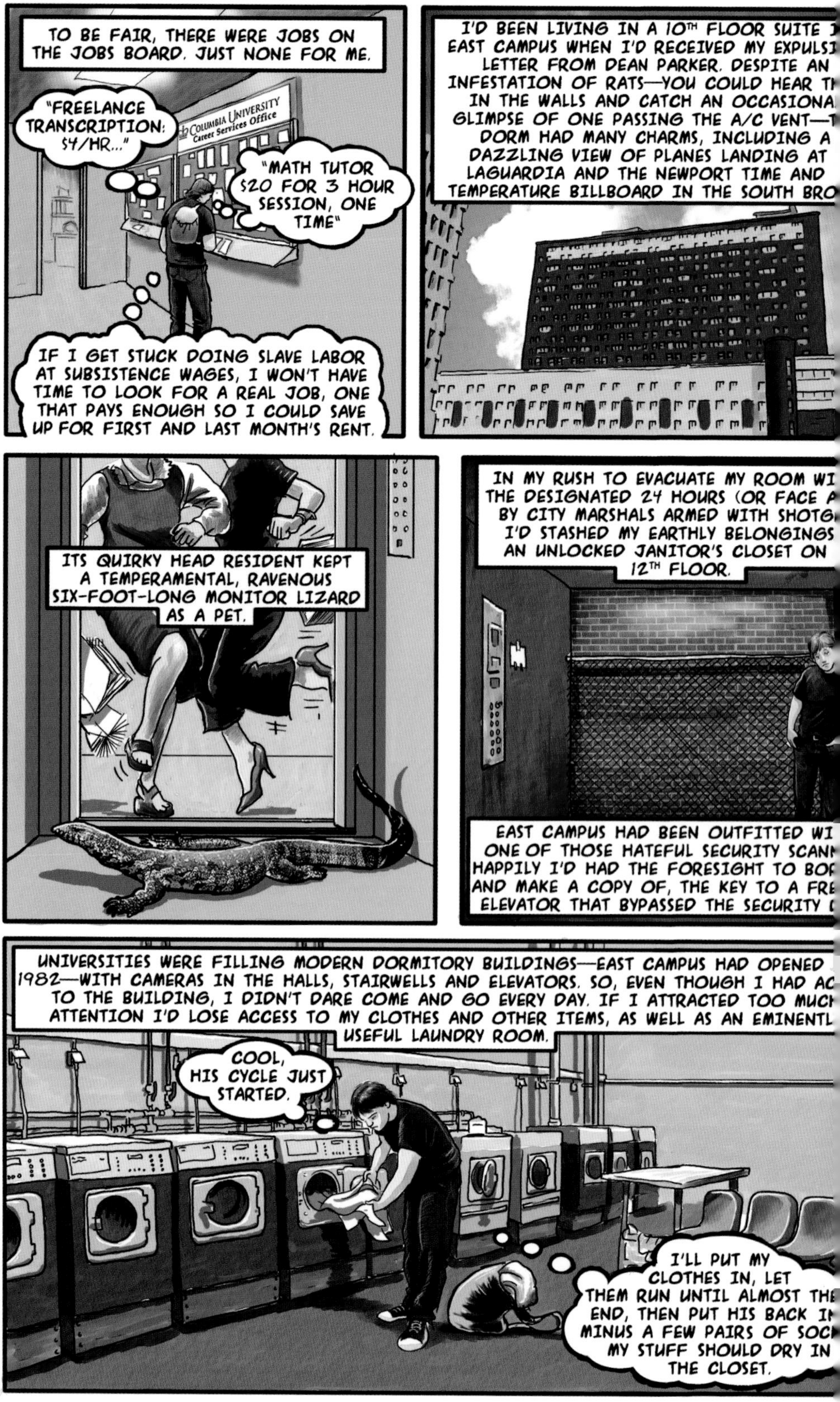
TO BE FAIR, THERE WERE JOBS ON THE JOBS BOARD. JUST NONE FOR ME.
"FREELANCE TRANSCRIPTION: $4/HR..."
COLUMBIA UNIVERSITY Career Services Office
"MATH TUTOR $20 FOR 3 HOUR SESSION, ONE TIME"
IF I GET STUCK DOING SLAVE LABOR AT SUBSISTENCE WAGES, I WON'T HAVE TIME TO LOOK FOR A REAL JOB, ONE THAT PAYS ENOUGH SO I COULD SAVE UP FOR FIRST AND LAST MONTH'S RENT.
I'D BEEN LIVING IN A 10TH FLOOR SUITE I EAST CAMPUS WHEN I'D RECEIVED MY EXPULSI LETTER FROM DEAN PARKER. DESPITE AN INFESTATION OF RATS—YOU COULD HEAR TH IN THE WALLS AND CATCH AN OCCASIONA GLIMPSE OF ONE PASSING THE A/C VENT—T DORM HAD MANY CHARMS, INCLUDING A DAZZLING VIEW OF PLANES LANDING AT LAGUARDIA AND THE NEWPORT TIME AND TEMPERATURE BILLBOARD IN THE SOUTH BRO
ITS QUIRKY HEAD RESIDENT KEPT A TEMPERAMENTAL, RAVENOUS SIX-FOOT-LONG MONITOR LIZARD AS A PET.
IN MY RUSH TO EVACUATE MY ROOM WI THE DESIGNATED 24 HOURS (OR FACE A BY CITY MARSHALS ARMED WITH SHOTG I'D STASHED MY EARTHLY BELONGINGS AN UNLOCKED JANITOR'S CLOSET ON 12TH FLOOR.
EAST CAMPUS HAD BEEN OUTFITTED WI ONE OF THOSE HATEFUL SECURITY SCANN HAPPILY I'D HAD THE FORESIGHT TO BOR AND MAKE A COPY OF, THE KEY TO A FRE ELEVATOR THAT BYPASSED THE SECURITY
UNIVERSITIES WERE FILLING MODERN DORMITORY BUILDINGS—EAST CAMPUS HAD OPENED 1982—WITH CAMERAS IN THE HALLS, STAIRWELLS AND ELEVATORS. SO, EVEN THOUGH I HAD AC TO THE BUILDING, I DIDN'T DARE COME AND GO EVERY DAY. IF I ATTRACTED TOO MUCH ATTENTION I'D LOSE ACCESS TO MY CLOTHES AND OTHER ITEMS, AS WELL AS AN EMINENTL USEFUL LAUNDRY ROOM.
COOL, HIS CYCLE JUST STARTED.
I'LL PUT MY CLOTHES IN, LET THEM RUN UNTIL ALMOST THE END, THEN PUT HIS BACK IN MINUS A FEW PAIRS OF SOC MY STUFF SHOULD DRY IN THE CLOSET.

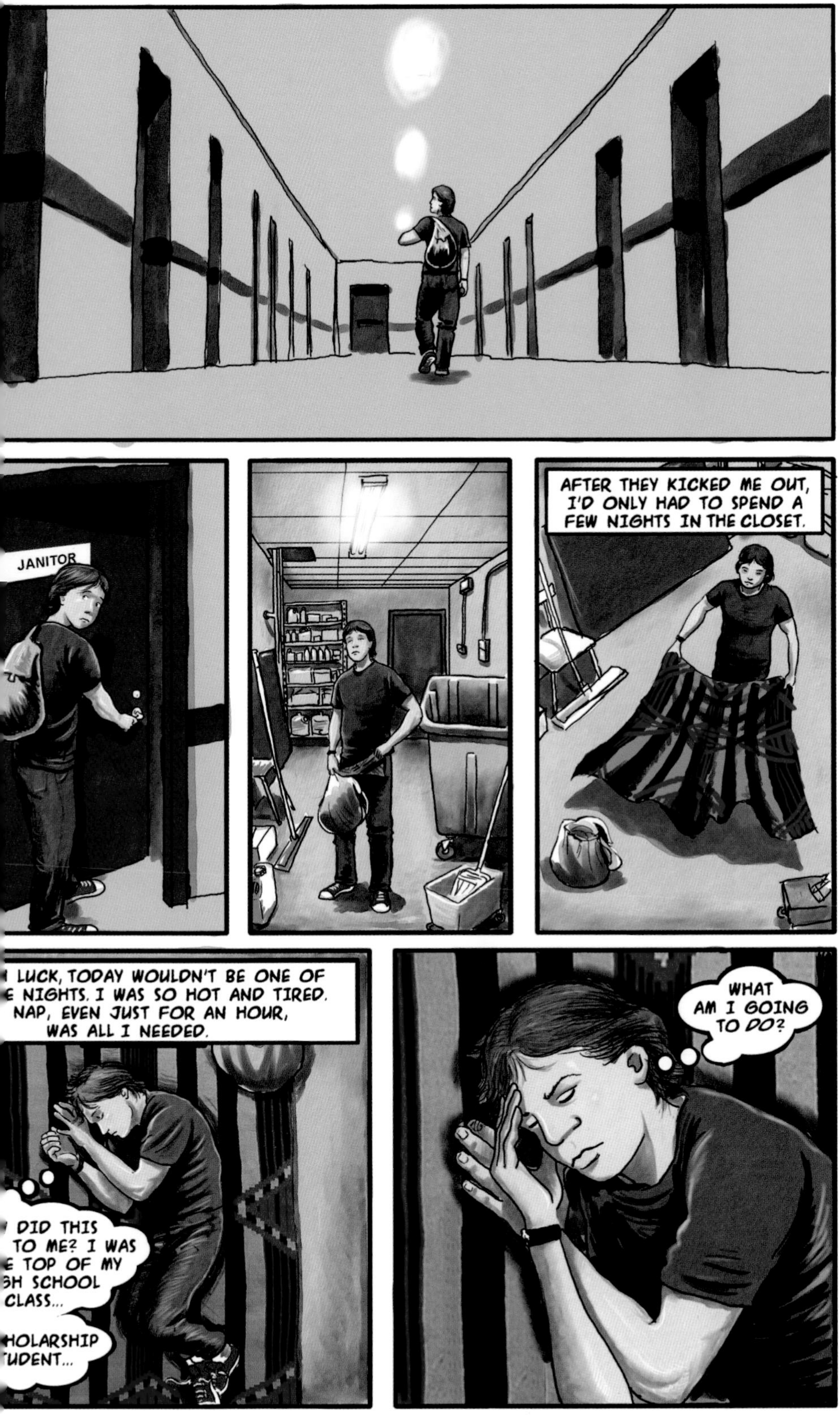
JANITOR
AFTER THEY KICKED ME OUT, I'D ONLY HAD TO SPEND A FEW NIGHTS IN THE CLOSET.
LUCK, TODAY WOULDN'T BE ONE OF
NIGHTS. I WAS SO HOT AND TIRED.
NAP, EVEN JUST FOR AN HOUR,
WAS ALL I NEEDED.
DID THIS
TO ME? I WAS
TOP OF MY
SH SCHOOL
CLASS...
HOLARSHIP
UDENT...
WHAT AM I GOING TO DO?

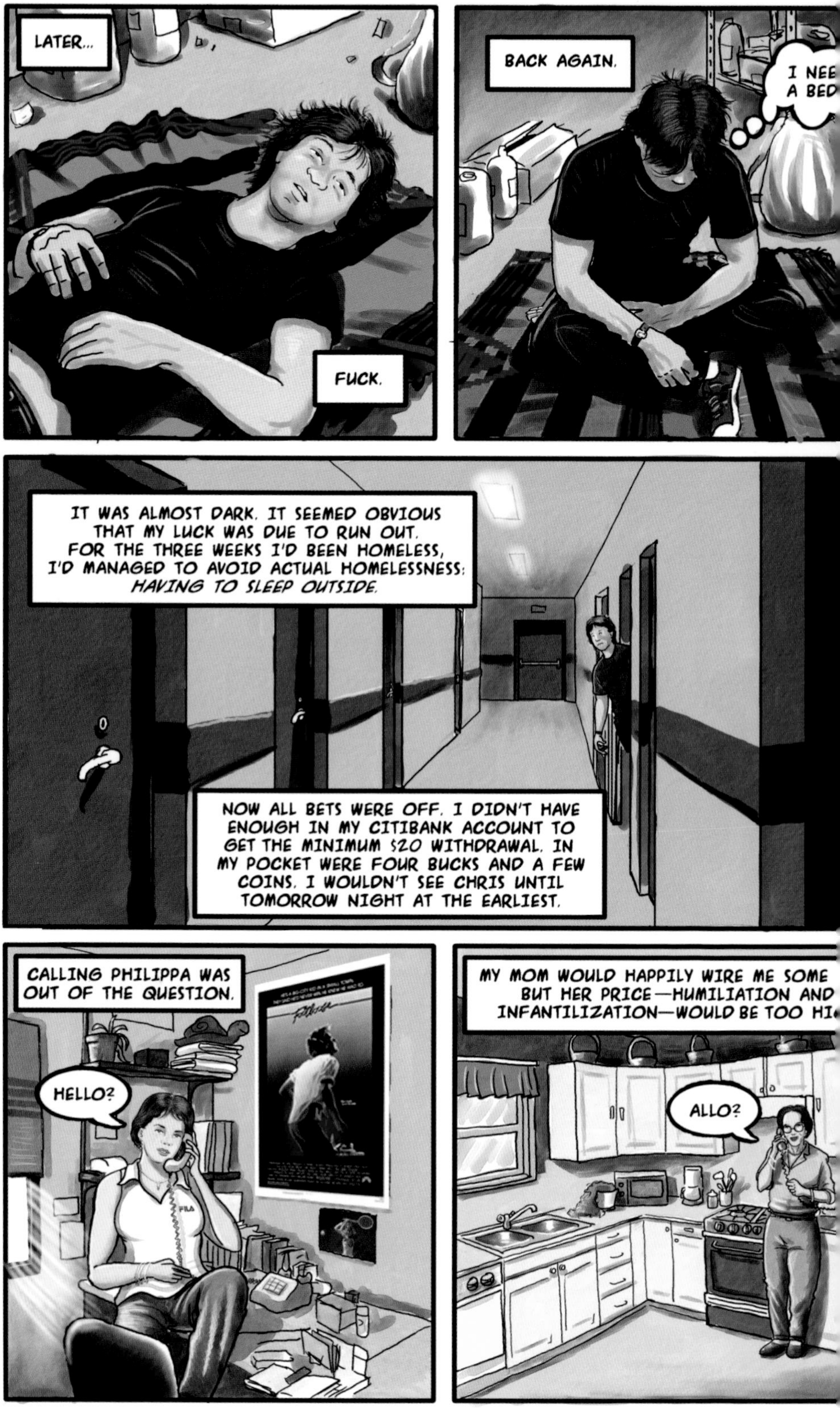
LATER...
FUCK.
BACK AGAIN.
I NEE
A BED
IT WAS ALMOST DARK. IT SEEMED OBVIOUS THAT MY LUCK WAS DUE TO RUN OUT. FOR THE THREE WEEKS I'D BEEN HOMELESS, I'D MANAGED TO AVOID ACTUAL HOMELESSNESS: *HAVING TO SLEEP OUTSIDE.*
NOW ALL BETS WERE OFF. I DIDN'T HAVE ENOUGH IN MY CITIBANK ACCOUNT TO GET THE MINIMUM $20 WITHDRAWAL. IN MY POCKET WERE FOUR BUCKS AND A FEW COINS. I WOULDN'T SEE CHRIS UNTIL TOMORROW NIGHT AT THE EARLIEST.
CALLING PHILIPPA WAS OUT OF THE QUESTION.
HELLO?
MY MOM WOULD HAPPILY WIRE ME SOME
BUT HER PRICE—HUMILIATION AND
INFANTILIZATION—WOULD BE TOO HI
ALLO?

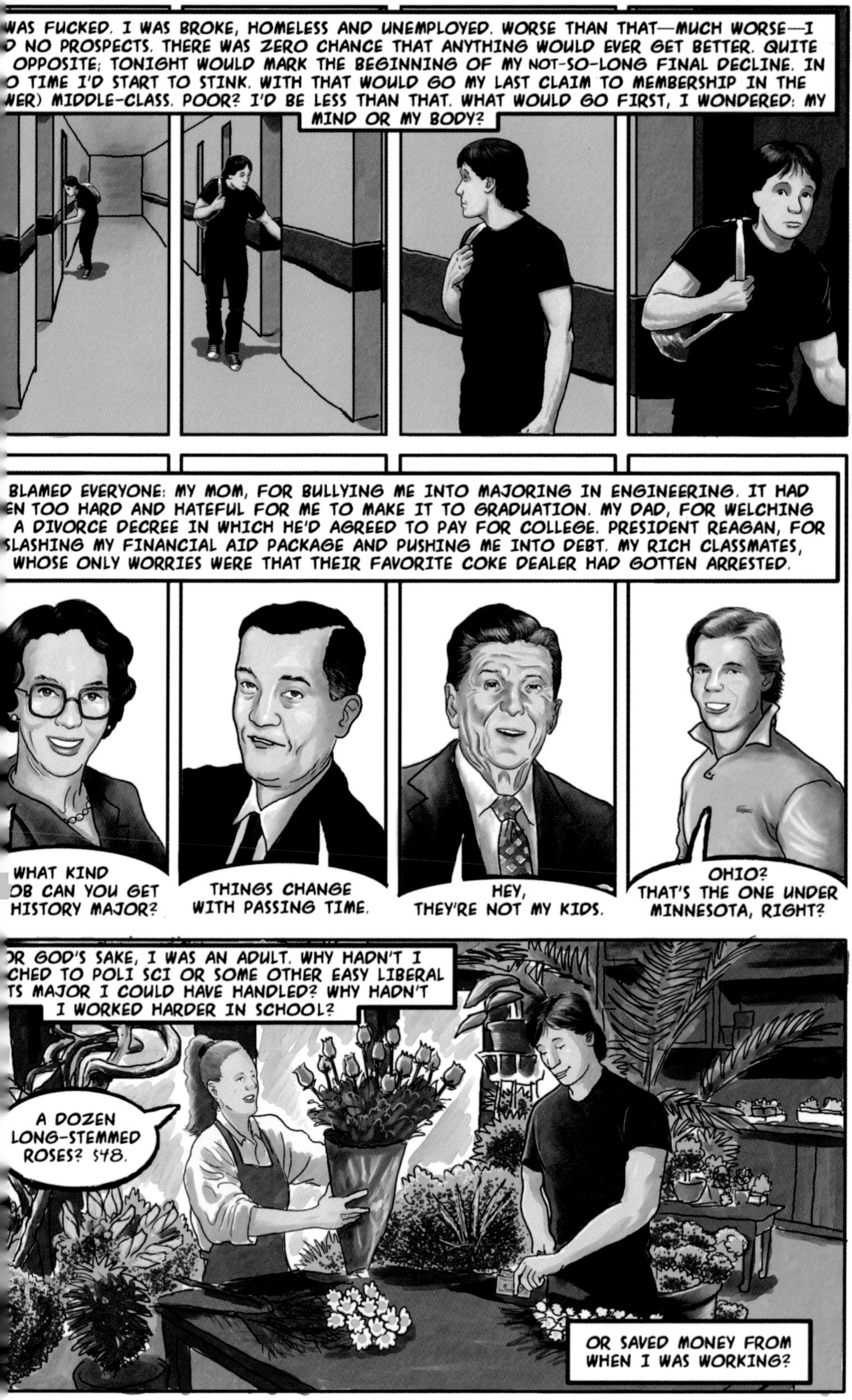
WAS FUCKED. I WAS BROKE, HOMELESS AND UNEMPLOYED. WORSE THAN THAT—MUCH WORSE—I
D NO PROSPECTS. THERE WAS ZERO CHANCE THAT ANYTHING WOULD EVER GET BETTER. QUITE
OPPOSITE; TONIGHT WOULD MARK THE BEGINNING OF MY NOT-SO-LONG FINAL DECLINE. IN
O TIME I'D START TO STINK. WITH THAT WOULD GO MY LAST CLAIM TO MEMBERSHIP IN THE
WER) MIDDLE-CLASS. POOR? I'D BE LESS THAN THAT. WHAT WOULD GO FIRST, I WONDERED: MY MIND OR MY BODY?
BLAMED EVERYONE: MY MOM, FOR BULLYING ME INTO MAJORING IN ENGINEERING. IT HAD
EN TOO HARD AND HATEFUL FOR ME TO MAKE IT TO GRADUATION. MY DAD, FOR WELCHING
A DIVORCE DECREE IN WHICH HE'D AGREED TO PAY FOR COLLEGE. PRESIDENT REAGAN, FOR
SLASHING MY FINANCIAL AID PACKAGE AND PUSHING ME INTO DEBT. MY RICH CLASSMATES,
WHOSE ONLY WORRIES WERE THAT THEIR FAVORITE COKE DEALER HAD GOTTEN ARRESTED.
WHAT KIND OB CAN YOU GET HISTORY MAJOR?
THINGS CHANGE WITH PASSING TIME.
HEY, THEY'RE NOT MY KIDS.
OHIO? THAT'S THE ONE UNDER MINNESOTA, RIGHT?
OR GOD'S SAKE, I WAS AN ADULT. WHY HADN'T I
CHED TO POLI SCI OR SOME OTHER EASY LIBERAL
TS MAJOR I COULD HAVE HANDLED? WHY HADN'T
I WORKED HARDER IN SCHOOL?
A DOZEN LONG-STEMMED ROSES? $48.
OR SAVED MONEY FROM WHEN I WAS WORKING?

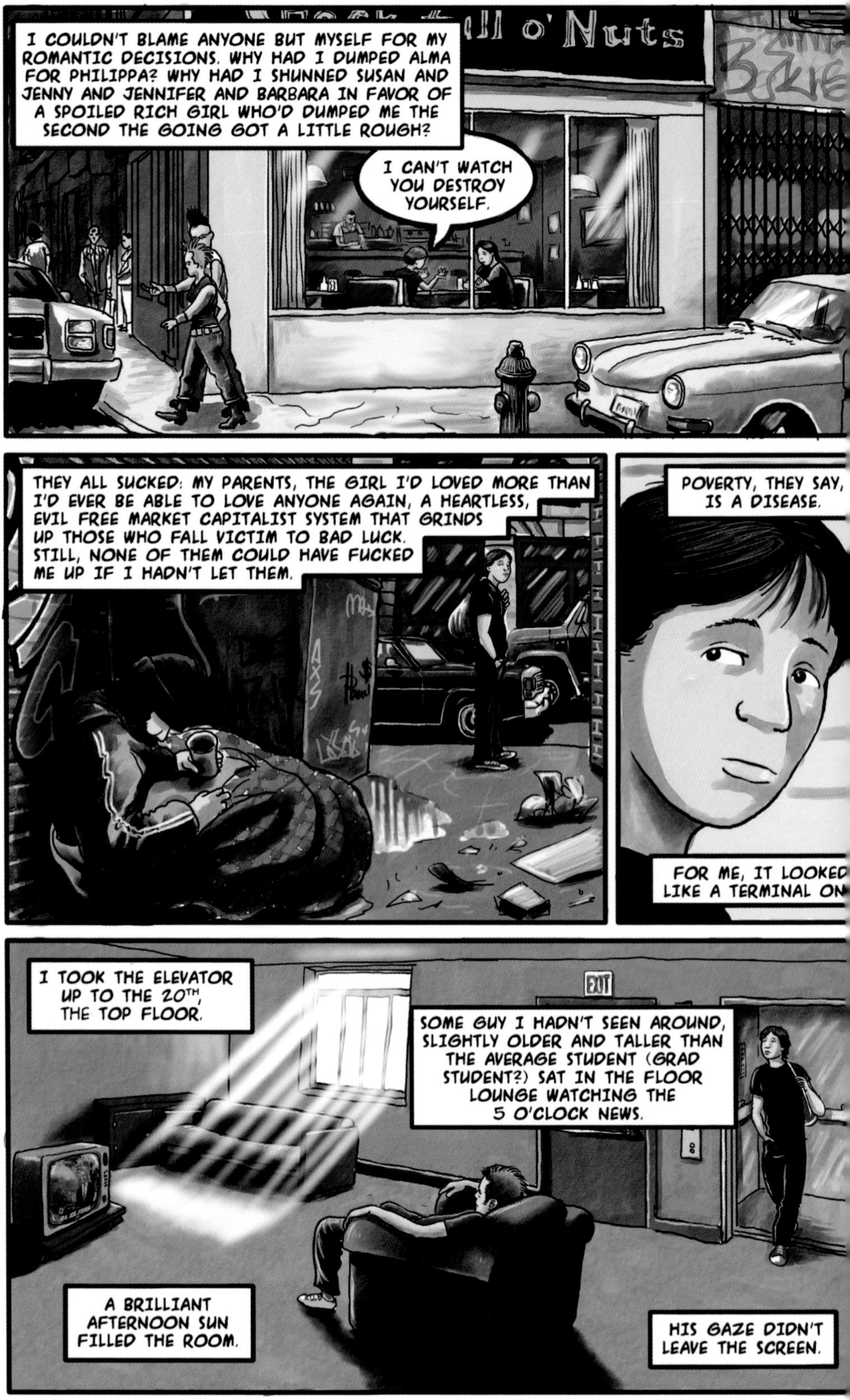
Ill o' Nuts
I COULDN'T BLAME ANYONE BUT MYSELF FOR MY ROMANTIC DECISIONS. WHY HAD I DUMPED ALMA FOR PHILIPPA? WHY HAD I SHUNNED SUSAN AND JENNY AND JENNIFER AND BARBARA IN FAVOR OF A SPOILED RICH GIRL WHO'D DUMPED ME THE SECOND THE GOING GOT A LITTLE ROUGH?
I CAN'T WATCH YOU DESTROY YOURSELF.
THEY ALL SUCKED: MY PARENTS, THE GIRL I'D LOVED MORE THAN I'D EVER BE ABLE TO LOVE ANYONE AGAIN, A HEARTLESS, EVIL FREE MARKET CAPITALIST SYSTEM THAT GRINDS UP THOSE WHO FALL VICTIM TO BAD LUCK. STILL, NONE OF THEM COULD HAVE FUCKED ME UP IF I HADN'T LET THEM.
POVERTY, THEY SAY, IS A DISEASE.
FOR ME, IT LOOKED LIKE A TERMINAL ON
I TOOK THE ELEVATOR UP TO THE 20TH, THE TOP FLOOR.
EXIT
SOME GUY I HADN'T SEEN AROUND, SLIGHTLY OLDER AND TALLER THAN THE AVERAGE STUDENT (GRAD STUDENT?) SAT IN THE FLOOR LOUNGE WATCHING THE 5 O'CLOCK NEWS.
A BRILLIANT AFTERNOON SUN FILLED THE ROOM.
HIS GAZE DIDN'T LEAVE THE SCREEN.

...PENED THE DOOR TO THE STAIRS. I SMILED AT A ...MORY: CHRIS LYING IN A ...L OF PUKE AND PISS AND ...EFIED SHIT IN THE SAME ...RWELL, 16 STORIES DOWN, ...T EVEN A YEAR EARLIER.

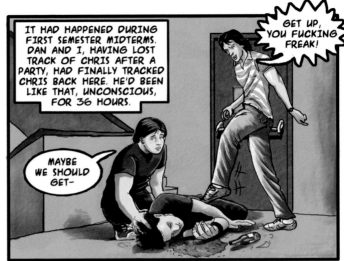

IT HAD HAPPENED DURING FIRST SEMESTER MIDTERMS. DAN AND I, HAVING LOST TRACK OF CHRIS AFTER A PARTY, HAD FINALLY TRACKED CHRIS BACK HERE. HE'D BEEN LIKE THAT, UNCONSCIOUS, FOR 36 HOURS.

MAYBE WE SHOULD GET—

GET UP, YOU FUCKING FREAK!

ONE FLIGHT UP AND I WAS ON THE ROOF. ...HOT WIND HIT ME FROM THE WEST. STEAM WHINED OUT ...F AN ALUMINUM VENT. I WALKED TO THE EDGE OF THE ROOF. I CLIMBED ONTO THE WALL. IT WASN'T HIGH.

WHICH IS BETTER? ...IOULD I JUMP? OR JUST STEP FORWARD?

WHICH IS EASIER?

WHICH WILL HURT THE LEAST?

21

THE PHYSICS WERE EASY TO CALCULATE.

THE RELEVANT EQUATION IS $S = 1/2 \times AT^2$, WHERE S=DISTANCE, A=THE RATE OF ACCELERATION OF GRAVITY AND T=TIME ELAPSED.

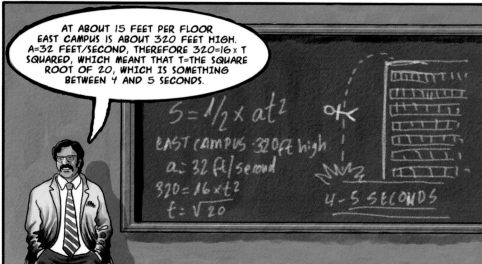

AT ABOUT 15 FEET PER FLOOR EAST CAMPUS IS ABOUT 320 FEET HIGH. A=32 FEET/SECOND, THEREFORE 320=16 × T SQUARED, WHICH MEANT THAT T=THE SQUARE ROOT OF 20, WHICH IS SOMETHING BETWEEN 4 AND 5 SECONDS.

$$S = 1/2 \times at^2$$
EAST CAMPUS 320ft high
$$a = 32 \, ft/second$$
$$320 = 16 \times t^2$$
$$t = \sqrt{20}$$

4-5 SECONDS

FOUR SECONDS PLUS IS ONE FUCK OF A LONG TIME TO KNOW YOUR BODY IS ABOUT TO SLAM INTO A HARD SIDEWALK...

... TO KNOW THA THERE'S NOTHIN YOU CAN DO TC TAKE IT BACK.

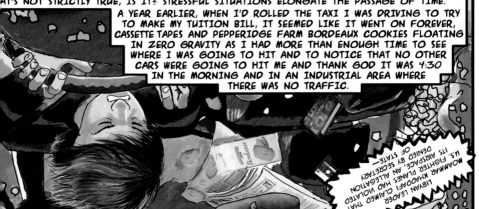

...TH, PEOPLE WOULD SAY AFTER THEY'D HEARD OF MY SUICIDE, WOULD COME INSTANTLY, BUT ...AT'S NOT STRICTLY TRUE, IS IT? STRESSFUL SITUATIONS ELONGATE THE PASSAGE OF TIME.

A YEAR EARLIER, WHEN I'D ROLLED THE TAXI I WAS DRIVING TO TRY TO MAKE MY TUITION BILL, IT SEEMED LIKE IT WENT ON FOREVER, CASSETTE TAPES AND PEPPERIDGE FARM BORDEAUX COOKIES FLOATING IN ZERO GRAVITY AS I HAD MORE THAN ENOUGH TIME TO SEE WHERE I WAS GOING TO HIT AND TO NOTICE THAT NO OTHER CARS WERE GOING TO HIT ME AND THANK GOD IT WAS 4:30 IN THE MORNING AND IN AN INDUSTRIAL AREA WHERE THERE WAS NO TRAFFIC.

—LIBYAN LEADER MOAMMAR KHADAFI CLAIMED THAT U.S. FIGHTER PLANES HAD VIOLATED ITS AIRSPACE; AN ALLEGATION DENIED BY SECRETARY OF STATE—

...A MERE CAR ACCIDENT EXPANDS TIME, ...'ANDS TO REASON THAT THE ULTIMATE ...SS TO WHICH THE HUMAN MIND CAN ...SUBJECTED FEELS LIKE AN ETERNITY. ... FRACTION OF A SECOND DURING ...CH MY BODY IMPACTS THE SIDEWALK, ...'DS EXPLODING LIKE A WATER BALLOON, ...ANS RUPTURING AND WHATEVER'S LEFT ...MY BRAIN FINALLY CEASING ACTIVITY ...WINKING OUT INTO BLACKNESS, MUST ...LIKE A HORRIBLE SERIES OF TRAUMAS.

OF COURSE, IT DOES.

IT MUST.

I LOOKED DOWN. IT WAS A LONG WAY.

JUMP, DAMN YOU.

23

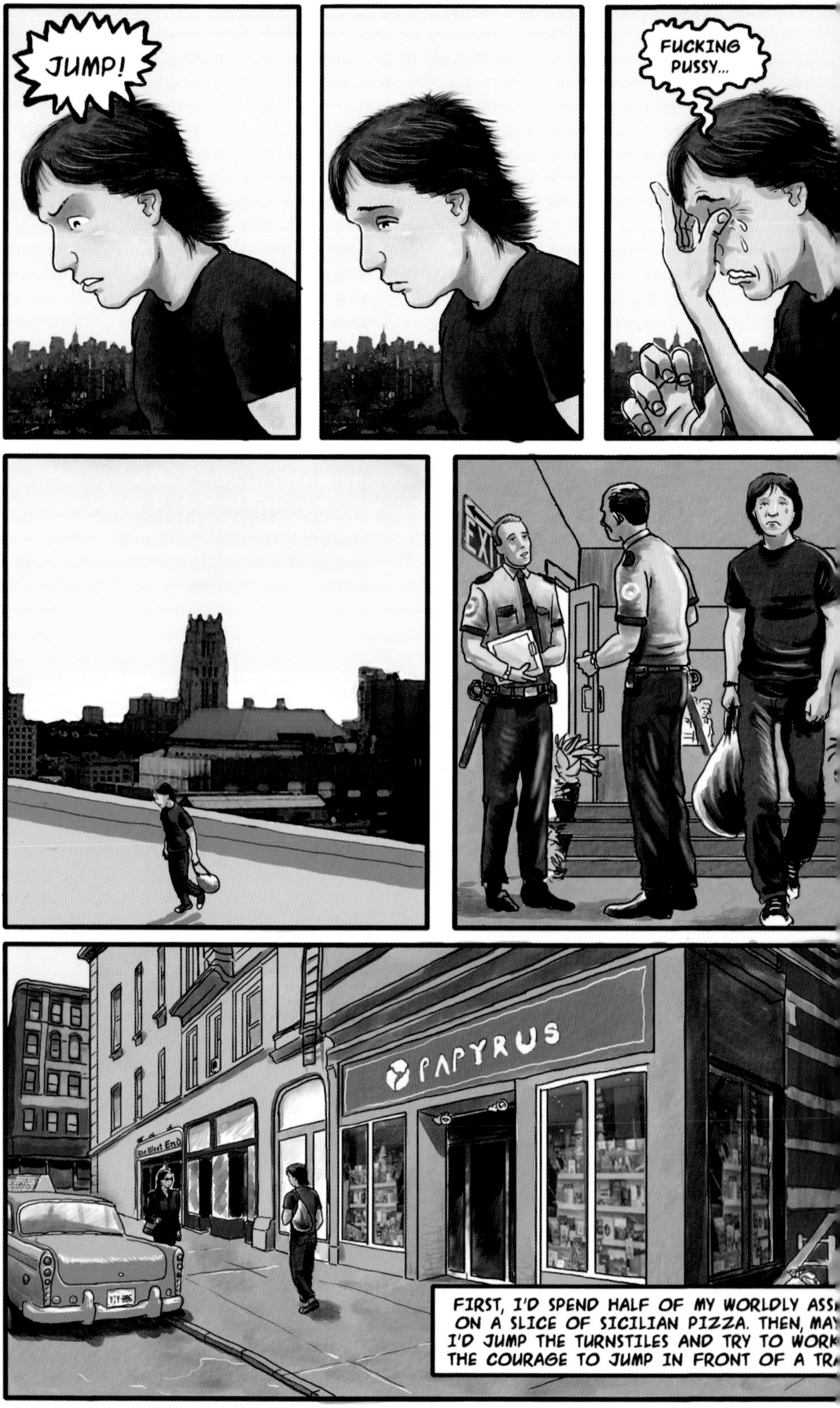
JUMP!
FUCKING PUSSY...
EXIT
PAPYRUS
The West End
FIRST, I'D SPEND HALF OF MY WORLDLY ASS
ON A SLICE OF SICILIAN PIZZA. THEN, MA
I'D JUMP THE TURNSTILES AND TRY TO WORK
THE COURAGE TO JUMP IN FRONT OF A TR

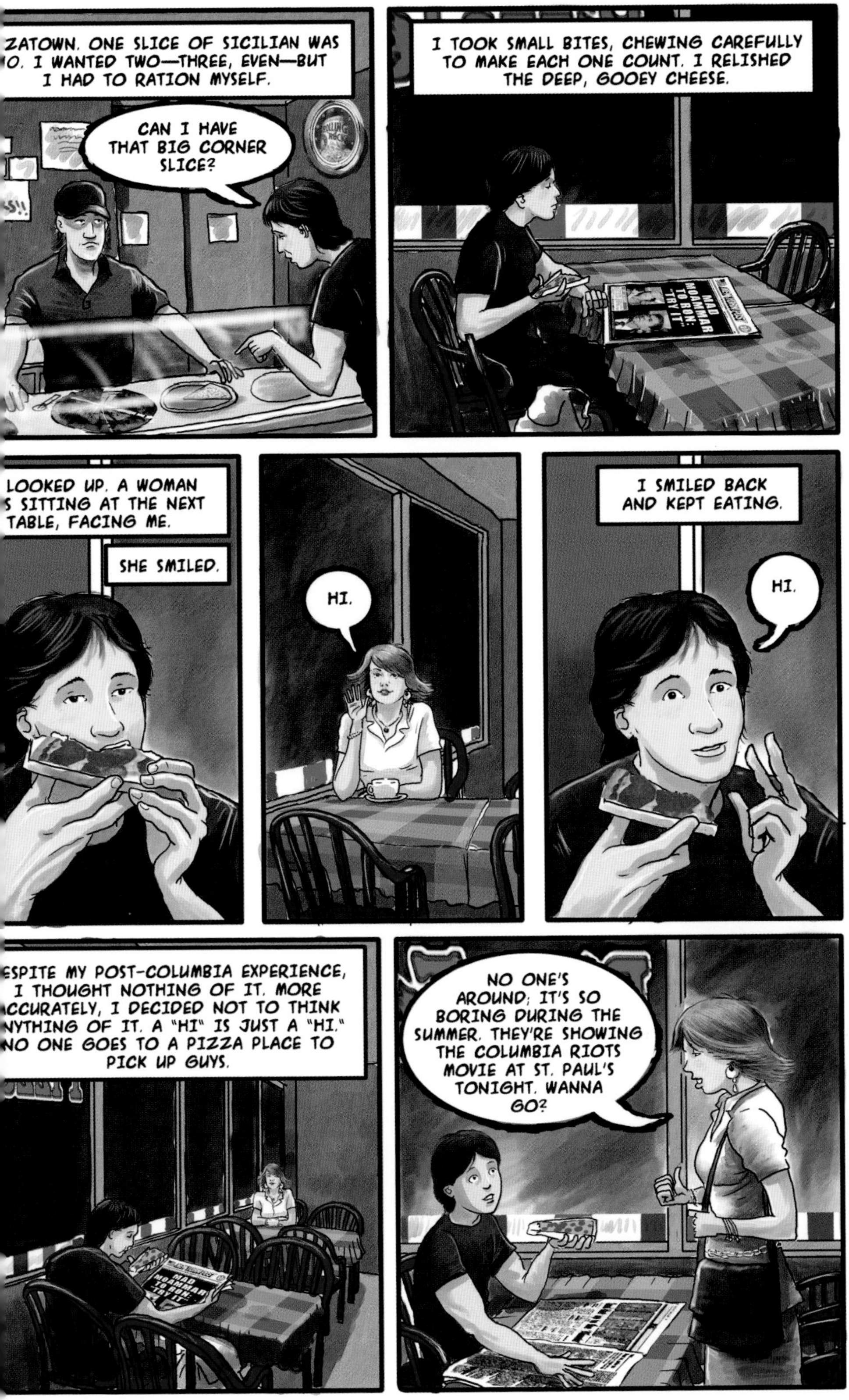
ZATOWN. ONE SLICE OF SICILIAN WAS
O. I WANTED TWO—THREE, EVEN—BUT I HAD TO RATION MYSELF.
CAN I HAVE THAT BIG CORNER SLICE?
I TOOK SMALL BITES, CHEWING CAREFULLY TO MAKE EACH ONE COUNT. I RELISHED THE DEEP, GOOEY CHEESE.
MAD MOAMMAR TO RON: "TRY IT"
LOOKED UP. A WOMAN
S SITTING AT THE NEXT TABLE, FACING ME.
SHE SMILED.
HI.
I SMILED BACK AND KEPT EATING.
HI.
ESPITE MY POST-COLUMBIA EXPERIENCE, I THOUGHT NOTHING OF IT. MORE
CCURATELY, I DECIDED NOT TO THINK
NYTHING OF IT. A "HI" IS JUST A "HI."
NO ONE GOES TO A PIZZA PLACE TO PICK UP GUYS.
NO ONE'S AROUND; IT'S SO BORING DURING THE SUMMER. THEY'RE SHOWING THE COLUMBIA RIOTS MOVIE AT ST. PAUL'S TONIGHT. WANNA GO?

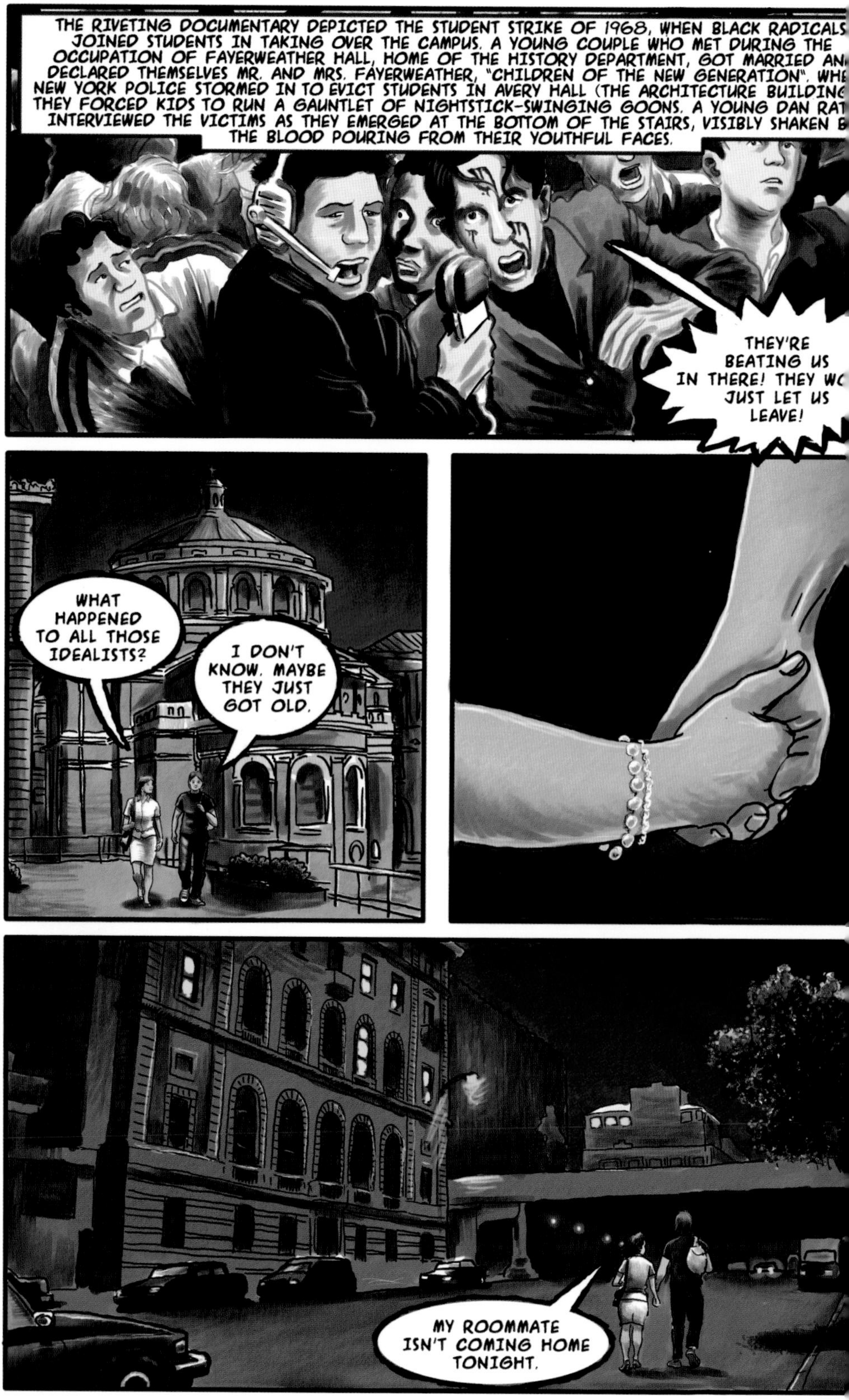
THE RIVETING DOCUMENTARY DEPICTED THE STUDENT STRIKE OF 1968, WHEN BLACK RADICALS JOINED STUDENTS IN TAKING OVER THE CAMPUS. A YOUNG COUPLE WHO MET DURING THE OCCUPATION OF FAYERWEATHER HALL, HOME OF THE HISTORY DEPARTMENT, GOT MARRIED AN DECLARED THEMSELVES MR. AND MRS. FAYERWEATHER, "CHILDREN OF THE NEW GENERATION". WHE NEW YORK POLICE STORMED IN TO EVICT STUDENTS IN AVERY HALL (THE ARCHITECTURE BUILDING THEY FORCED KIDS TO RUN A GAUNTLET OF NIGHTSTICK-SWINGING GOONS. A YOUNG DAN RAT INTERVIEWED THE VICTIMS AS THEY EMERGED AT THE BOTTOM OF THE STAIRS, VISIBLY SHAKEN B THE BLOOD POURING FROM THEIR YOUTHFUL FACES.
THEY'RE BEATING US IN THERE! THEY WO JUST LET US LEAVE!
WHAT HAPPENED TO ALL THOSE IDEALISTS?
I DON'T KNOW. MAYBE THEY JUST GOT OLD.
MY ROOMMATE ISN'T COMING HOME TONIGHT.

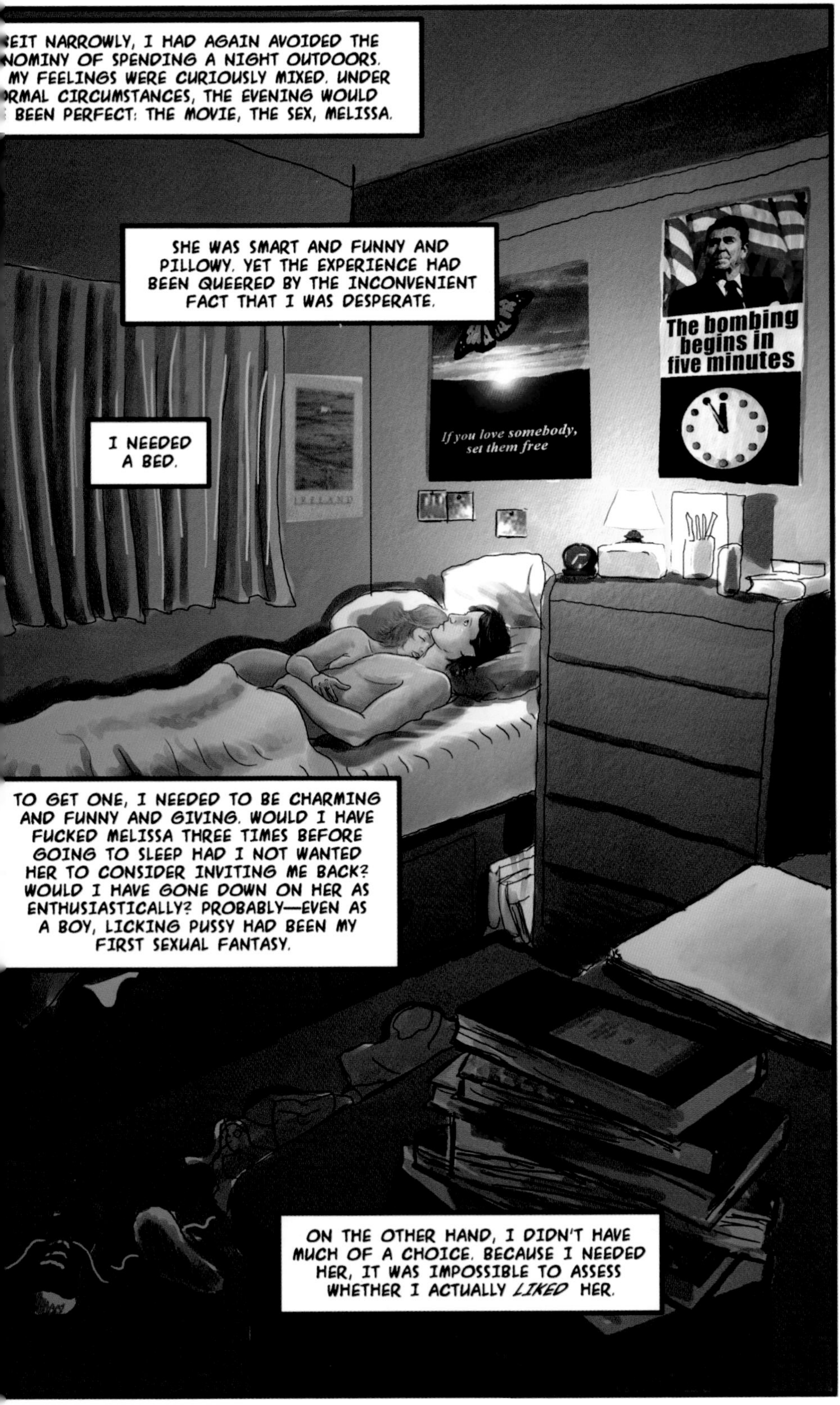
EIT NARROWLY, I HAD AGAIN AVOIDED THE NOMINY OF SPENDING A NIGHT OUTDOORS. MY FEELINGS WERE CURIOUSLY MIXED. UNDER RMAL CIRCUMSTANCES, THE EVENING WOULD BEEN PERFECT: THE MOVIE, THE SEX, MELISSA.
SHE WAS SMART AND FUNNY AND PILLOWY. YET THE EXPERIENCE HAD BEEN QUEERED BY THE INCONVENIENT FACT THAT I WAS DESPERATE.
The bombing begins in five minutes
If you love somebody, set them free
I NEEDED A BED.
TO GET ONE, I NEEDED TO BE CHARMING AND FUNNY AND GIVING. WOULD I HAVE FUCKED MELISSA THREE TIMES BEFORE GOING TO SLEEP HAD I NOT WANTED HER TO CONSIDER INVITING ME BACK? WOULD I HAVE GONE DOWN ON HER AS ENTHUSIASTICALLY? PROBABLY—EVEN AS A BOY, LICKING PUSSY HAD BEEN MY FIRST SEXUAL FANTASY.
ON THE OTHER HAND, I DIDN'T HAVE MUCH OF A CHOICE. BECAUSE I NEEDED HER, IT WAS IMPOSSIBLE TO ASSESS WHETHER I ACTUALLY *LIKED* HER.

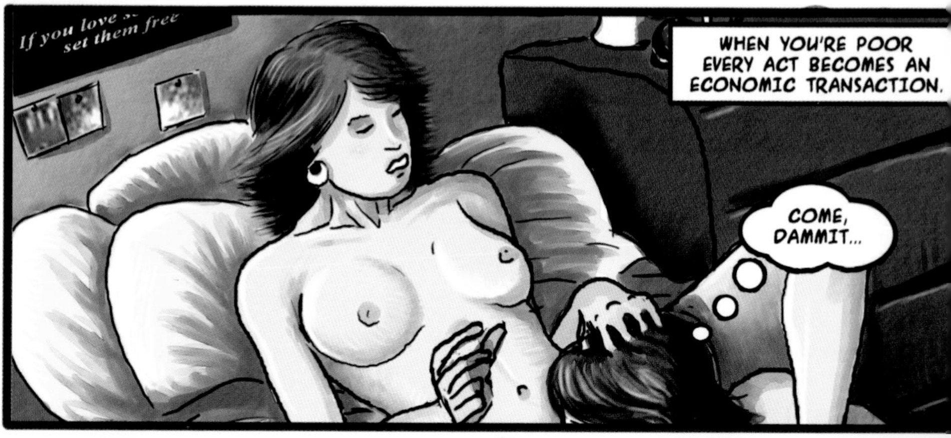
If you love
set them free
WHEN YOU'RE POOR EVERY ACT BECOMES AN ECONOMIC TRANSACTION.
COME, DAMMIT...

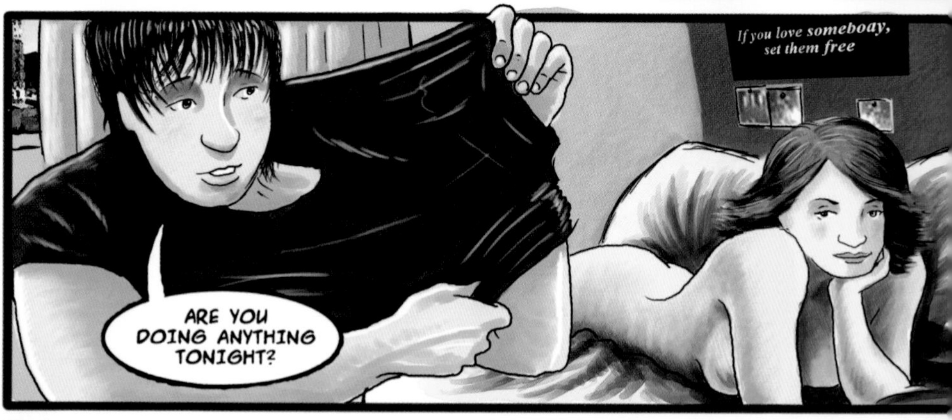
If you love someboay, set them free
ARE YOU DOING ANYTHING TONIGHT?

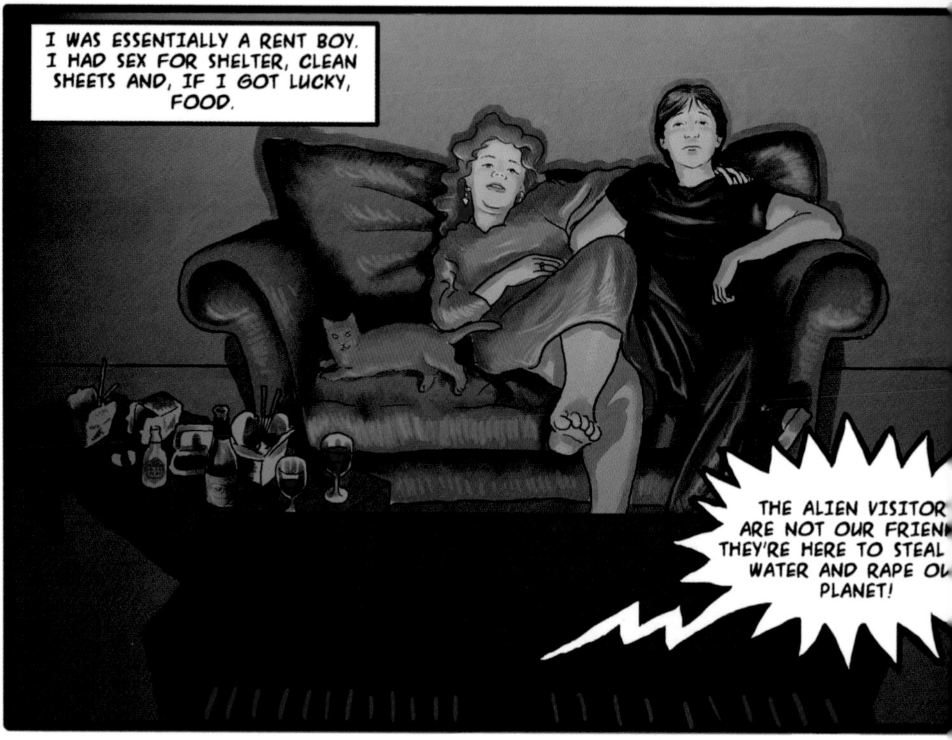
I WAS ESSENTIALLY A RENT BOY. I HAD SEX FOR SHELTER, CLEAN SHEETS AND, IF I GOT LUCKY, FOOD.
THE ALIEN VISITOR
ARE NOT OUR FRIEN
THEY'RE HERE TO STEAL
WATER AND RAPE O
PLANET!

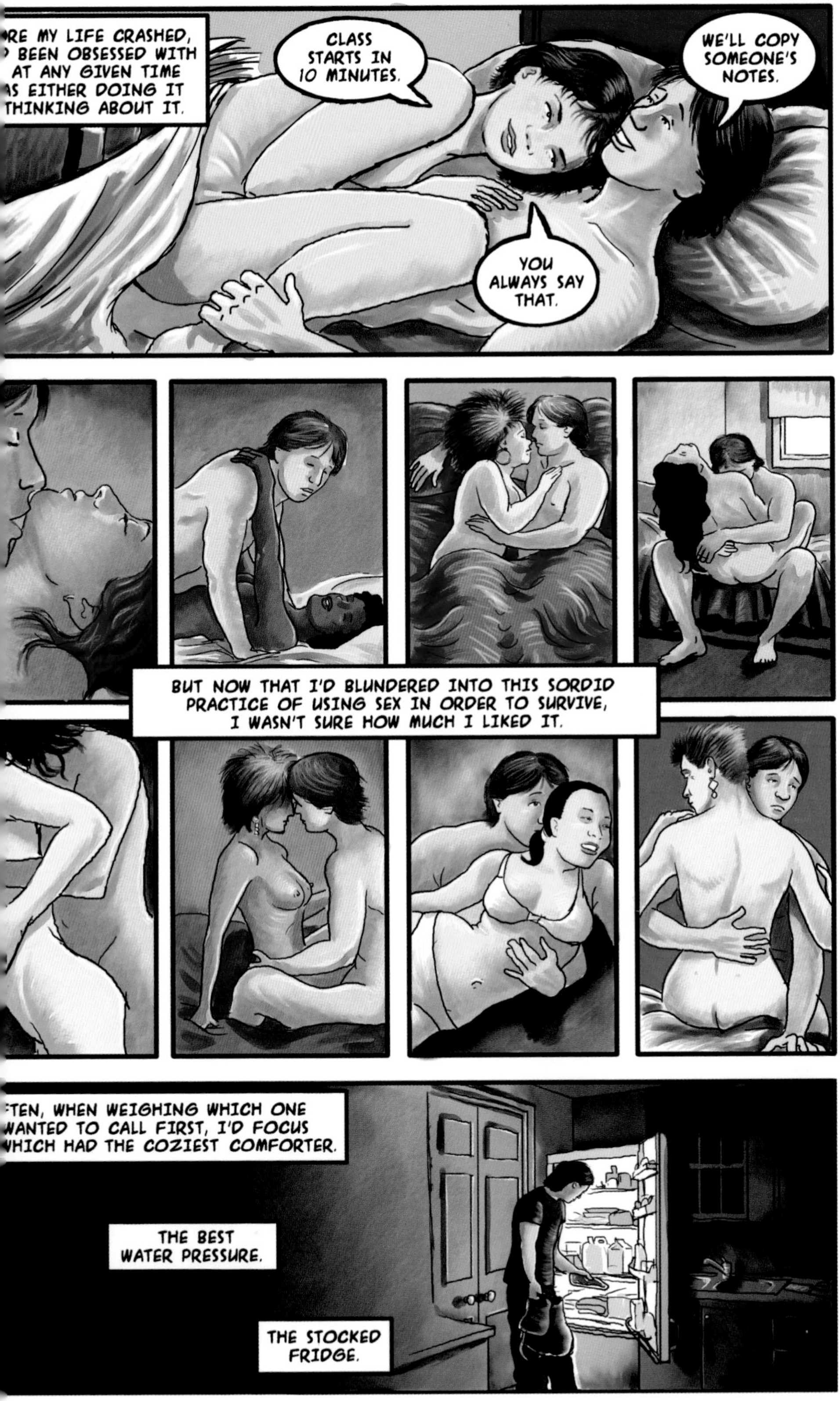
RE MY LIFE CRASHED,
BEEN OBSESSED WITH
AT ANY GIVEN TIME
S EITHER DOING IT
THINKING ABOUT IT.
CLASS STARTS IN 10 MINUTES.
WE'LL COPY SOMEONE'S NOTES.
YOU ALWAYS SAY THAT.
BUT NOW THAT I'D BLUNDERED INTO THIS SORDID PRACTICE OF USING SEX IN ORDER TO SURVIVE, I WASN'T SURE HOW MUCH I LIKED IT.
TEN, WHEN WEIGHING WHICH ONE
WANTED TO CALL FIRST, I'D FOCUS
HICH HAD THE COZIEST COMFORTER.
THE BEST WATER PRESSURE.
THE STOCKED FRIDGE.

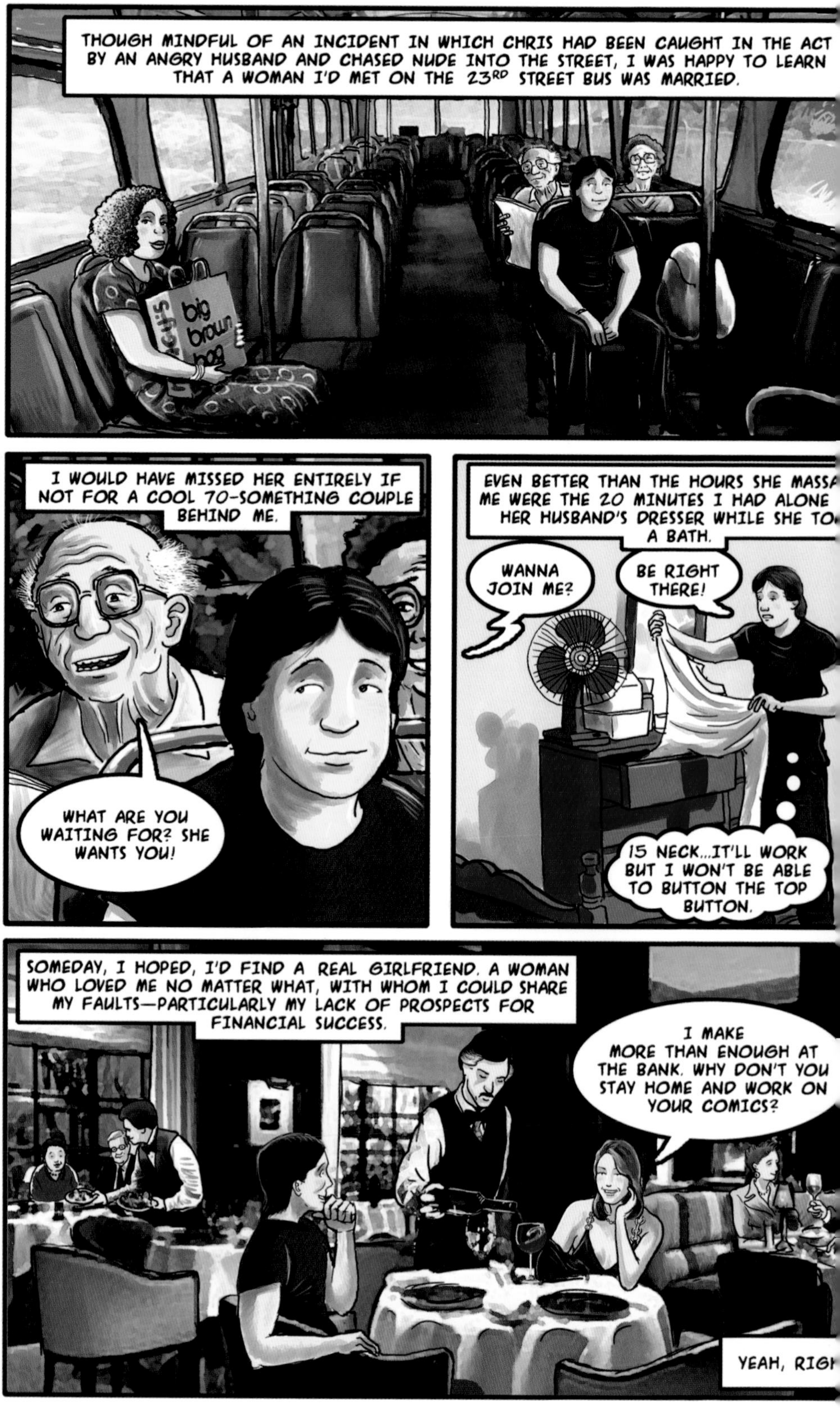
THOUGH MINDFUL OF AN INCIDENT IN WHICH CHRIS HAD BEEN CAUGHT IN THE ACT BY AN ANGRY HUSBAND AND CHASED NUDE INTO THE STREET, I WAS HAPPY TO LEARN THAT A WOMAN I'D MET ON THE 23RD STREET BUS WAS MARRIED.
big brown bag
I WOULD HAVE MISSED HER ENTIRELY IF NOT FOR A COOL 70-SOMETHING COUPLE BEHIND ME.
WHAT ARE YOU WAITING FOR? SHE WANTS YOU!
EVEN BETTER THAN THE HOURS SHE MASSA
ME WERE THE 20 MINUTES I HAD ALONE
HER HUSBAND'S DRESSER WHILE SHE TO
A BATH.
WANNA JOIN ME?
BE RIGHT THERE!
15 NECK...IT'LL WORK BUT I WON'T BE ABLE TO BUTTON THE TOP BUTTON.
SOMEDAY, I HOPED, I'D FIND A REAL GIRLFRIEND. A WOMAN WHO LOVED ME NO MATTER WHAT, WITH WHOM I COULD SHARE MY FAULTS—PARTICULARLY MY LACK OF PROSPECTS FOR FINANCIAL SUCCESS.
I MAKE MORE THAN ENOUGH AT THE BANK. WHY DON'T YOU STAY HOME AND WORK ON YOUR COMICS?
YEAH, RIG

YOU HAVE TO BELIEVE ME. THEY WEREN'T [JE]RKS OR SUCKERS. THEY WERE ALL—EVEN THOSE WHO ONLY TOOK ME IN FOR A SINGLE NIGHT—MY GIRLFRIENDS.

THIS IS FUN, BUT I COULD NEVER MARRY A GUY WHO ISN'T JEWISH.

I KNOW I'M NOT THE PRETTIEST OR THE YOUNGEST WOMAN EVER, BUT I'M NOT THAT BAD. AM I?

I HATE MY BOSS, BUT I CAN'T QUIT. THEY NEED ME.

NEEDN'T BE ALONE [D]ON'T CARE WHAT YOU DO I'M COMING BACK [C]AN LOOK FORWARD TOO I'M COMING BACK*

I [D...] [...]ATI[...] WH[...] [...]E[...] YOU

TH[...] [...]ID THIS [D]OING [...]EN[I]S [...]LL[...]

SHE DRIVES ME CRAZY, BUT I LOVE HER.

*["...ing back", by the Human League (1984)]

31

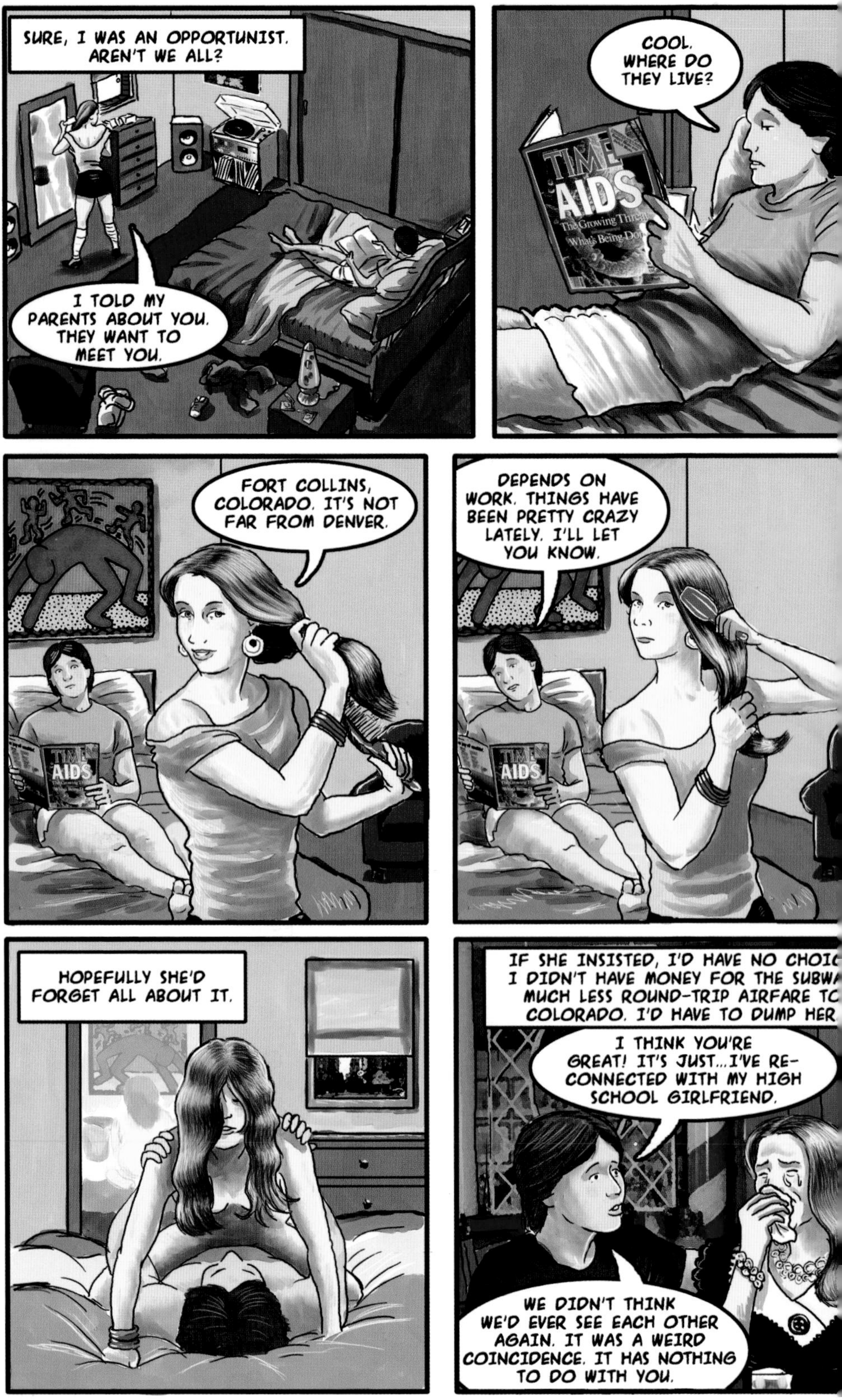
SURE, I WAS AN OPPORTUNIST. AREN'T WE ALL?
I TOLD MY PARENTS ABOUT YOU. THEY WANT TO MEET YOU.
COOL. WHERE DO THEY LIVE?
TIME
AIDS
The Growing Threat
What's Being Done
FORT COLLINS, COLORADO. IT'S NOT FAR FROM DENVER.
DEPENDS ON WORK. THINGS HAVE BEEN PRETTY CRAZY LATELY. I'LL LET YOU KNOW.
HOPEFULLY SHE'D FORGET ALL ABOUT IT.
IF SHE INSISTED, I'D HAVE NO CHOIC I DIDN'T HAVE MONEY FOR THE SUBWA MUCH LESS ROUND-TRIP AIRFARE TO COLORADO. I'D HAVE TO DUMP HER
I THINK YOU'RE GREAT! IT'S JUST...I'VE RE-CONNECTED WITH MY HIGH SCHOOL GIRLFRIEND.
WE DIDN'T THINK WE'D EVER SEE EACH OTHER AGAIN. IT WAS A WEIRD COINCIDENCE. IT HAS NOTHING TO DO WITH YOU.

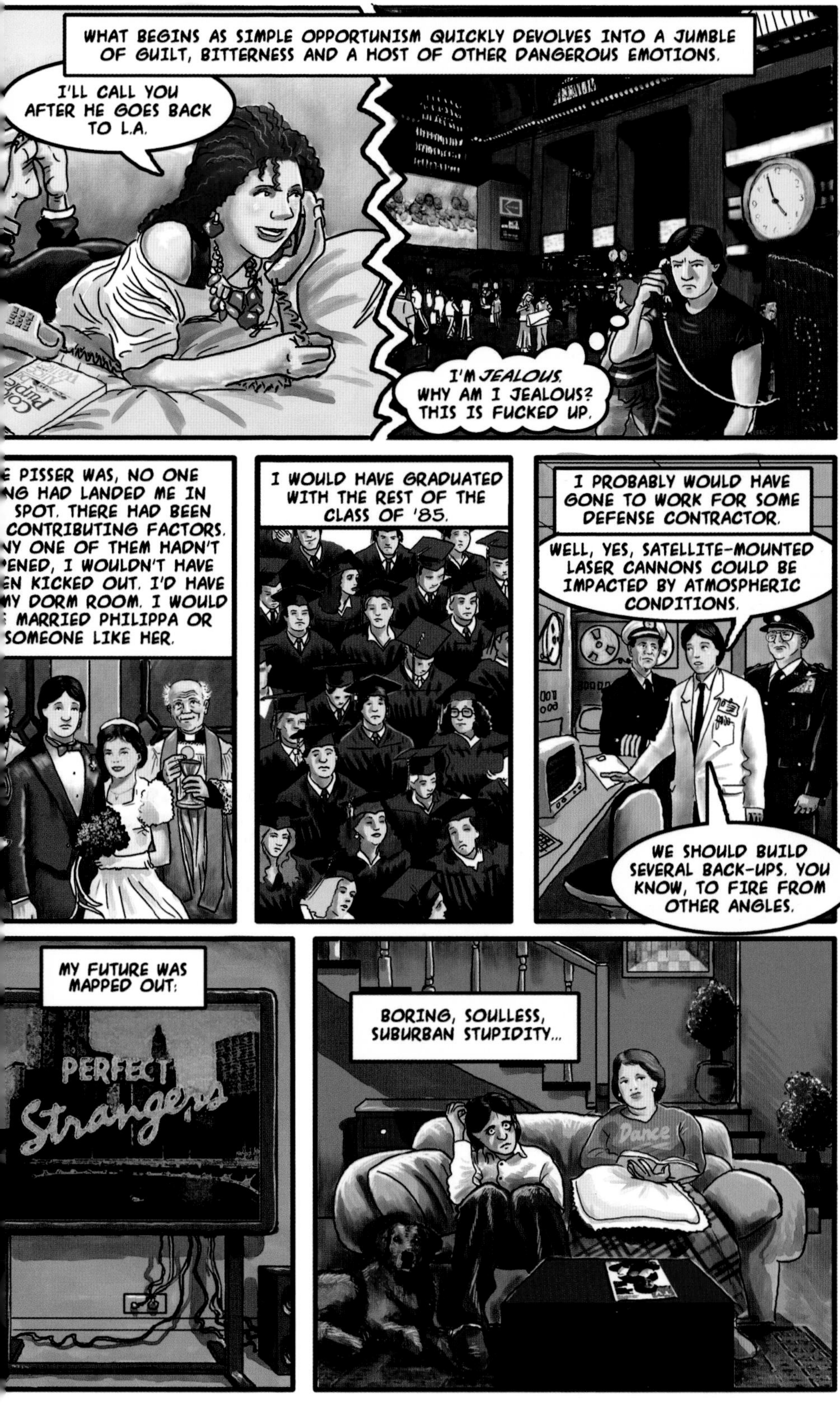
WHAT BEGINS AS SIMPLE OPPORTUNISM QUICKLY DEVOLVES INTO A JUMBLE OF GUILT, BITTERNESS AND A HOST OF OTHER DANGEROUS EMOTIONS.
I'LL CALL YOU AFTER HE GOES BACK TO L.A.
I'M JEALOUS. WHY AM I JEALOUS? THIS IS FUCKED UP.
E PISSER WAS, NO ONE
NG HAD LANDED ME IN
SPOT. THERE HAD BEEN
CONTRIBUTING FACTORS.
NY ONE OF THEM HADN'T
PENED, I WOULDN'T HAVE
EN KICKED OUT. I'D HAVE
MY DORM ROOM. I WOULD
MARRIED PHILIPPA OR
SOMEONE LIKE HER.
I WOULD HAVE GRADUATED WITH THE REST OF THE CLASS OF '85.
I PROBABLY WOULD HAVE GONE TO WORK FOR SOME DEFENSE CONTRACTOR.
WELL, YES, SATELLITE-MOUNTED LASER CANNONS COULD BE IMPACTED BY ATMOSPHERIC CONDITIONS.
WE SHOULD BUILD SEVERAL BACK-UPS. YOU KNOW, TO FIRE FROM OTHER ANGLES.
MY FUTURE WAS MAPPED OUT:
PERFECT Strangers
BORING, SOULLESS, SUBURBAN STUPIDITY...
Dance

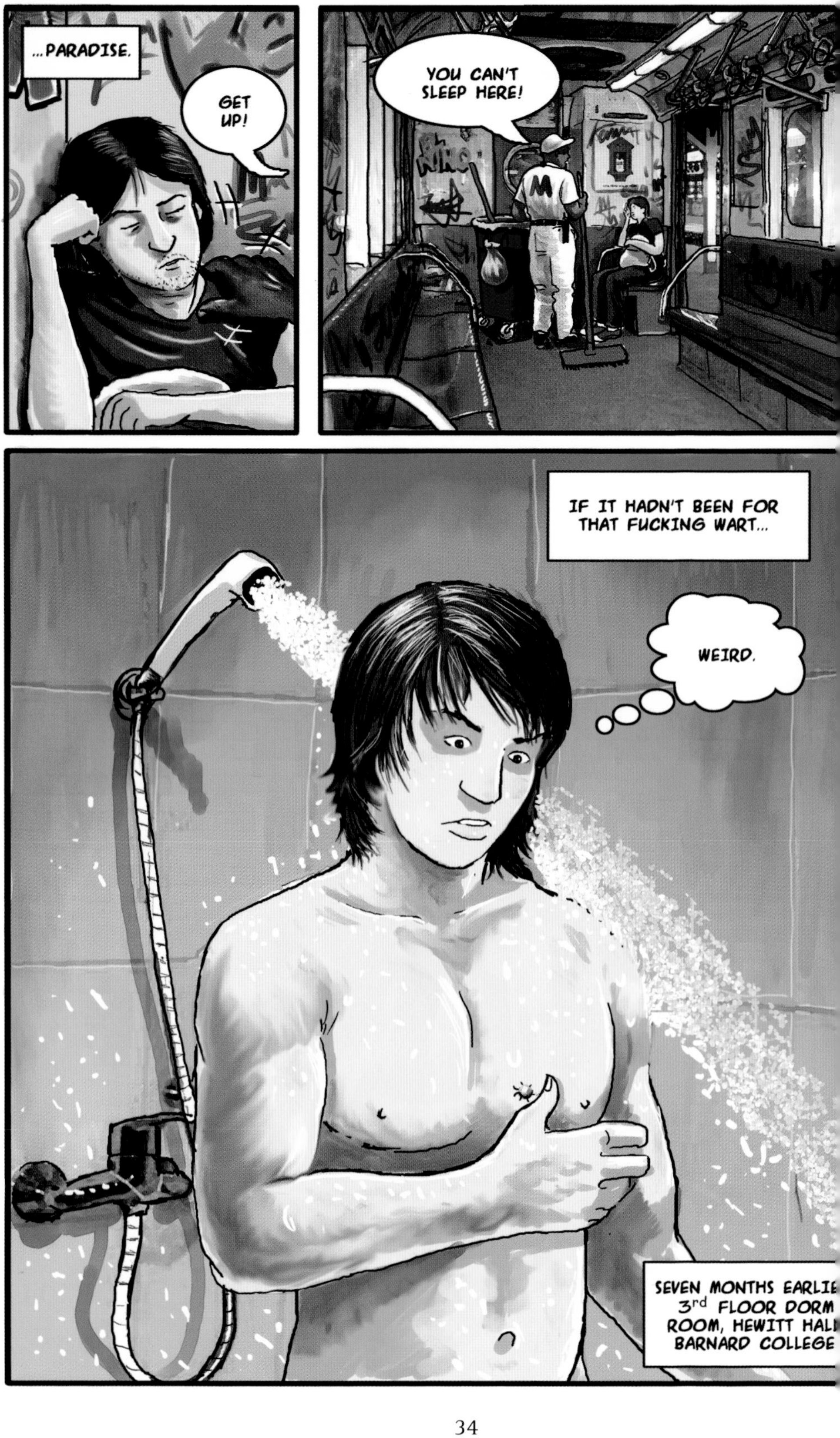

...PARADISE.
GET UP!
YOU CAN'T SLEEP HERE!
IF IT HADN'T BEEN FOR THAT FUCKING WART...
WEIRD.
SEVEN MONTHS EARLIE
3rd FLOOR DORM
ROOM, HEWITT HALL
BARNARD COLLEGE

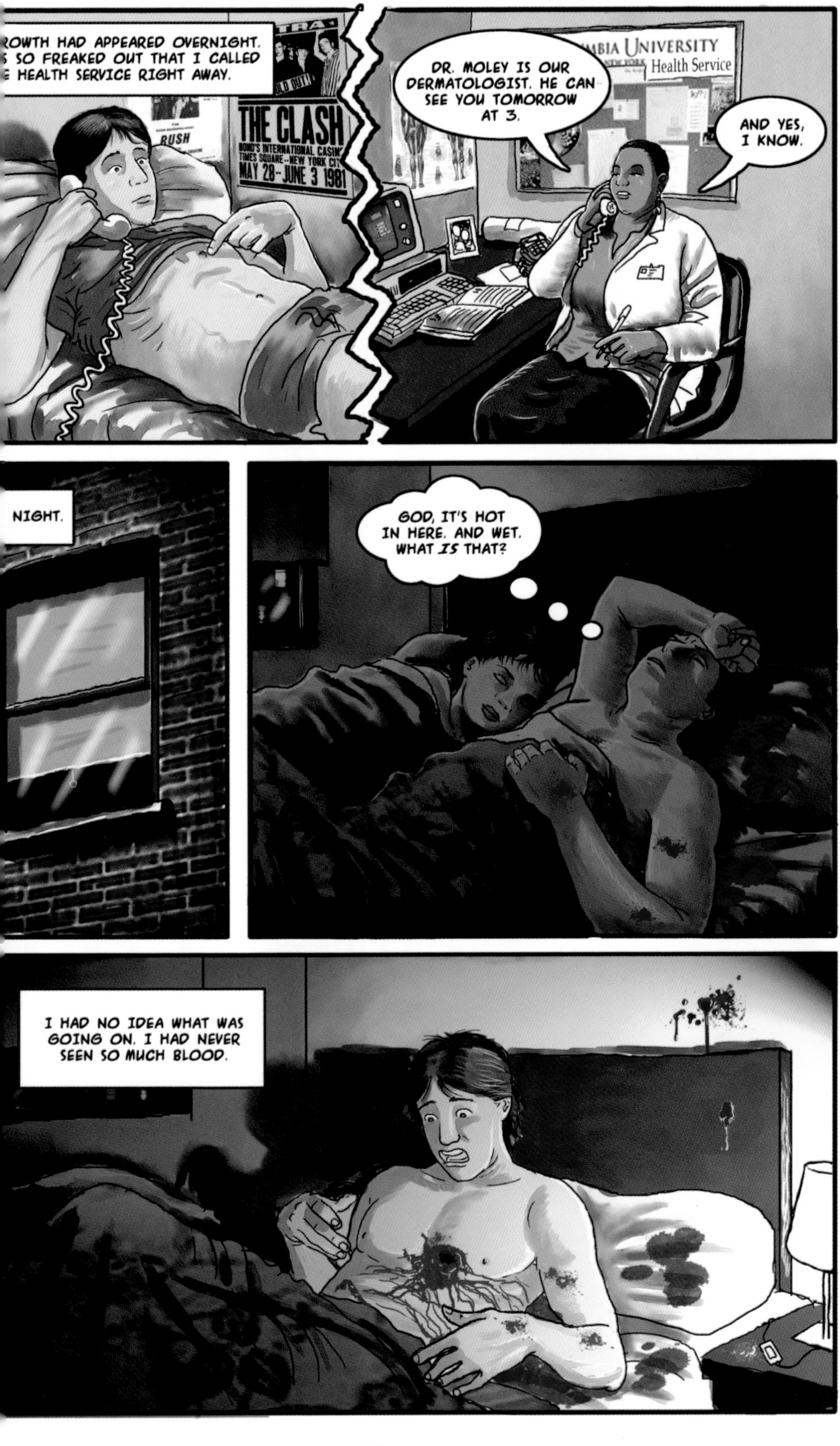
ROWTH HAD APPEARED OVERNIGHT.
S SO FREAKED OUT THAT I CALLED
E HEALTH SERVICE RIGHT AWAY.
THE CLASH
BOND'S INTERNATIONAL CASINO
TIMES SQUARE—NEW YORK CITY
MAY 28–JUNE 3 1981
RUSH
MBIA UNIVERSITY
Health Service
DR. MOLEY IS OUR DERMATOLOGIST. HE CAN SEE YOU TOMORROW AT 3.
AND YES, I KNOW.
NIGHT.
GOD, IT'S HOT IN HERE. AND WET. WHAT IS THAT?
I HAD NO IDEA WHAT WAS GOING ON. I HAD NEVER SEEN SO MUCH BLOOD.

THE E.R. DOCTORS HAD FUN WITH ME.

GUNSHOT WOUND COMING THROUGH!

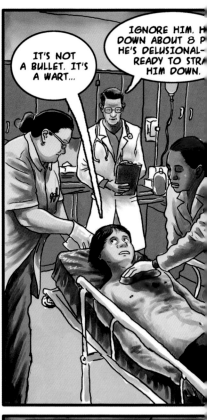

IT'S NOT A BULLET, IT'S A WART...

IGNORE HIM. H[...] DOWN ABOUT 8 P[...] HE'S DELUSIONAL— READY TO STR[...] HIM DOWN.

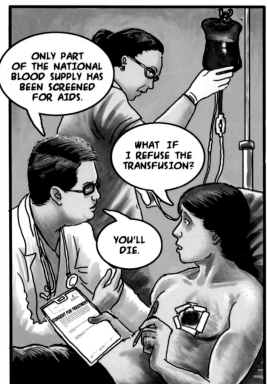

ONLY PART OF THE NATIONAL BLOOD SUPPLY HAS BEEN SCREENED FOR AIDS.

WHAT IF I REFUSE THE TRANSFUSION?

YOU'LL DIE.

I SPENT A WEEK—FINALS WEEK—I[...] THE HOSPITAL.

THE ROOT GREW INTO THE AORTA, THEN POPPED LIKE A CORK.

WHY DIDN'T THEY TAKE IT OUT?

THEY SAID IT WOULD CAUSE MORE BLEEDING. THIS WAY THEY CAN LOOK AT IT AND SEE WHAT'S GOING ON.

KIL[...] WAR[...]

SEVERAL YEARS LATER MY CASE W[...] WRITTEN UP IN A MEDICAL JOUR[...] AS A RARE EXAMPLE OF A (POTENTI[...] FATAL DERMATOLOGICAL CONDITI[...]

36

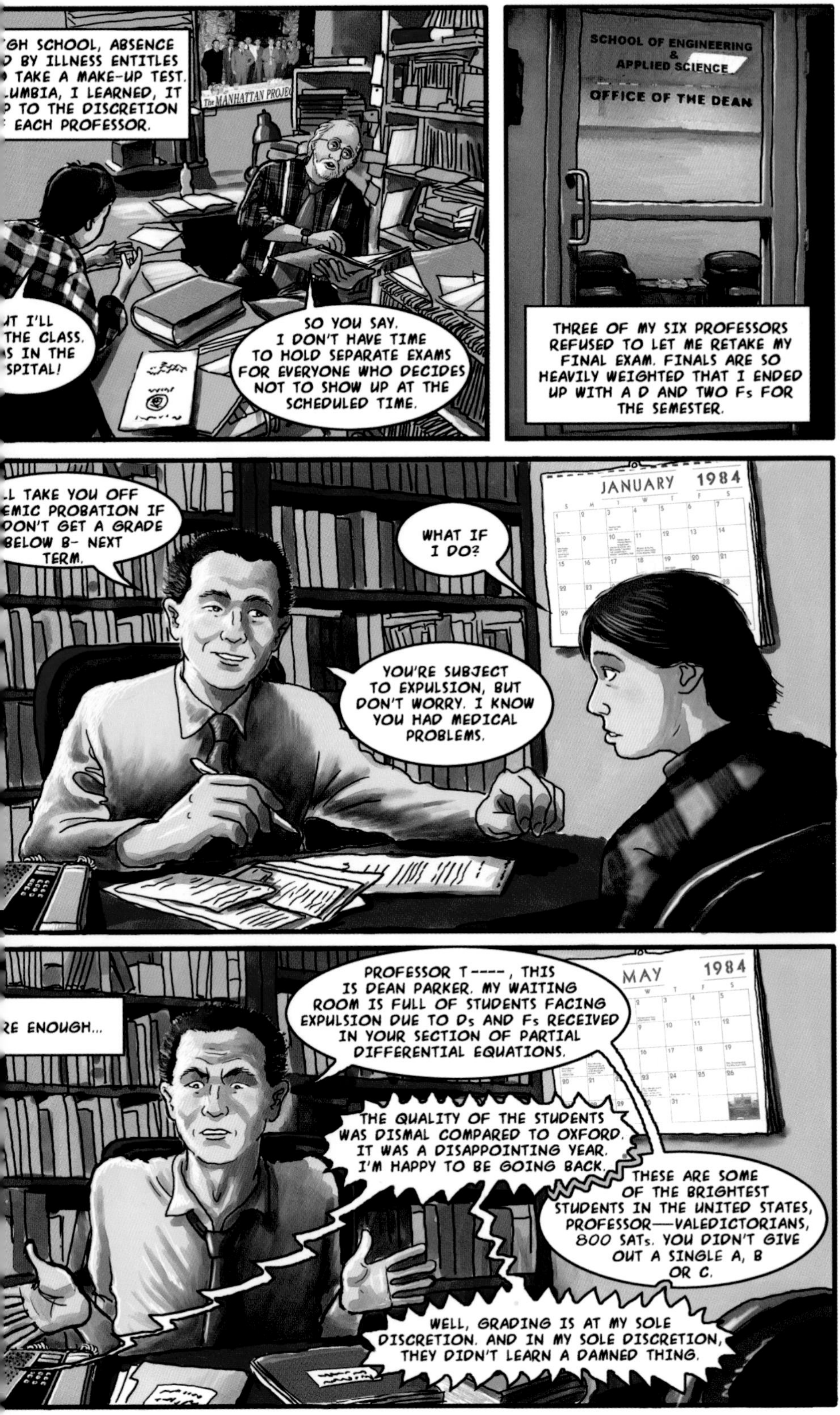

GH SCHOOL, ABSENCE
D BY ILLNESS ENTITLES
TAKE A MAKE-UP TEST.
LUMBIA, I LEARNED, IT
P TO THE DISCRETION
EACH PROFESSOR.
The MANHATTAN PROJEC
UT I'LL
THE CLASS.
S IN THE
SPITAL!
SO YOU SAY. I DON'T HAVE TIME TO HOLD SEPARATE EXAMS FOR EVERYONE WHO DECIDES NOT TO SHOW UP AT THE SCHEDULED TIME.
SCHOOL OF ENGINEERING & APPLIED SCIENCE
OFFICE OF THE DEAN
THREE OF MY SIX PROFESSORS REFUSED TO LET ME RETAKE MY FINAL EXAM. FINALS ARE SO HEAVILY WEIGHTED THAT I ENDED UP WITH A D AND TWO Fs FOR THE SEMESTER.
L TAKE YOU OFF
EMIC PROBATION IF
DON'T GET A GRADE
BELOW B- NEXT
TERM.
JANUARY 1984
WHAT IF I DO?
YOU'RE SUBJECT TO EXPULSION, BUT DON'T WORRY. I KNOW YOU HAD MEDICAL PROBLEMS.
RE ENOUGH...
PROFESSOR T----, THIS IS DEAN PARKER. MY WAITING ROOM IS FULL OF STUDENTS FACING EXPULSION DUE TO Ds AND Fs RECEIVED IN YOUR SECTION OF PARTIAL DIFFERENTIAL EQUATIONS.
MAY 1984
THE QUALITY OF THE STUDENTS WAS DISMAL COMPARED TO OXFORD. IT WAS A DISAPPOINTING YEAR. I'M HAPPY TO BE GOING BACK.
THESE ARE SOME OF THE BRIGHTEST STUDENTS IN THE UNITED STATES, PROFESSOR—VALEDICTORIANS, 800 SATs. YOU DIDN'T GIVE OUT A SINGLE A, B OR C.
WELL, GRADING IS AT MY SOLE DISCRETION. AND IN MY SOLE DISCRETION, THEY DIDN'T LEARN A DAMNED THING.

TWO WEEKS LATER, THEY EXPELLED ME.

THEY SHOULDN'T HAVE GENERATED THAT EXPULSION LETTER—YOUR CASE IS DIFFERENT BECAUSE OF THE MEDICAL ISSUES AND WHAT HAPPENED WITH PDE. LISTEN—I HATE TO DO THIS TO YOU, BUT I'M FLYING TO PARIS TONIGHT TO TAKE A NEW JOB.

WHAT HAPPENS TO *ME*?

EVERYTHING'S IN THE FILE. MY REPLACEMENT WILL KNOW RIGHT AWAY THAT IT'S A MISTAKE. DON'T WORRY.

DEAN PARKER'S REPLACEMENT WOULDN'T ARRIVE UNTIL SEPTEMBER, AFTER THE START OF THE NEW SEMESTER THAT WAS SUPPOSED TO MARK THE START OF MY SENIOR YEAR. BY THEN I'D BEEN EVICTED FROM MY DORM ROOM, FIRED FROM MY JOB, DUMPED BY MY GIRLFRIEND AND FORCED INTO HOMELESSNESS.

CONTRARY TO DEAN PARKER'S GLIB ASSURA MY SALVATION DID NOT RESIDE IN MY FI

I STAND BY MY PREDECESSOR'S DECISION. YOUR FALL '8 GRADES TELL THE STORY PERHAPS YOU SHOULD CONS BROOKLYN POLYTECHNI SOME OF OUR FORMER STUDENTS HAVE...

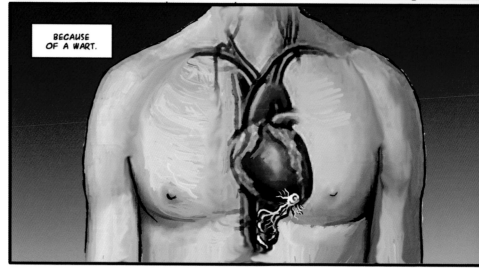

BECAUSE OF A WART.

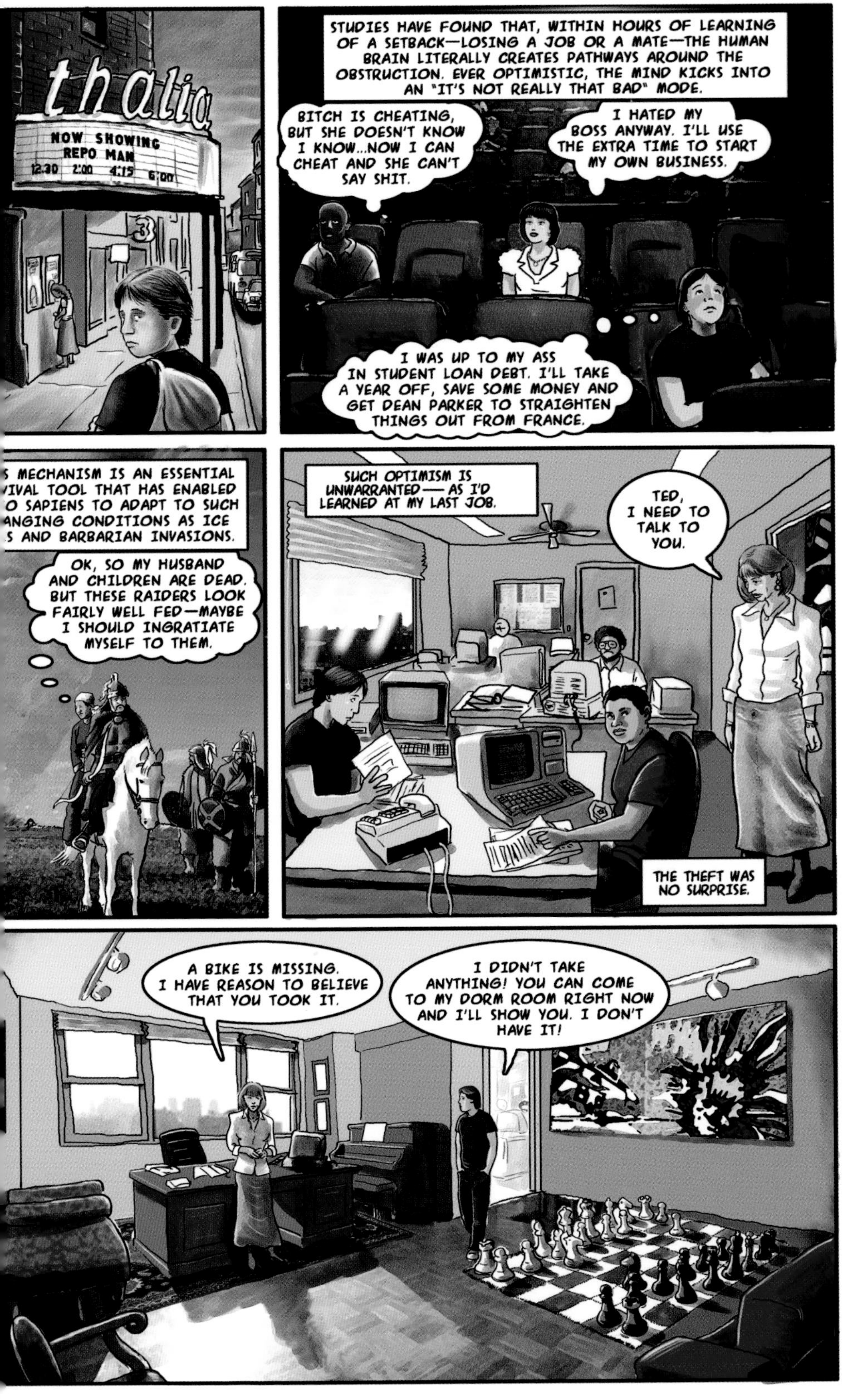
thalia
NOW SHOWING
REPO MAN
12:30 2:00 4:15 6:00
3
STUDIES HAVE FOUND THAT, WITHIN HOURS OF LEARNING OF A SETBACK—LOSING A JOB OR A MATE—THE HUMAN BRAIN LITERALLY CREATES PATHWAYS AROUND THE OBSTRUCTION. EVER OPTIMISTIC, THE MIND KICKS INTO AN "IT'S NOT REALLY THAT BAD" MODE.
BITCH IS CHEATING, BUT SHE DOESN'T KNOW I KNOW...NOW I CAN CHEAT AND SHE CAN'T SAY SHIT.
I HATED MY BOSS ANYWAY. I'LL USE THE EXTRA TIME TO START MY OWN BUSINESS.
I WAS UP TO MY ASS IN STUDENT LOAN DEBT. I'LL TAKE A YEAR OFF, SAVE SOME MONEY AND GET DEAN PARKER TO STRAIGHTEN THINGS OUT FROM FRANCE.
S MECHANISM IS AN ESSENTIAL VIVAL TOOL THAT HAS ENABLED O SAPIENS TO ADAPT TO SUCH ANGING CONDITIONS AS ICE S AND BARBARIAN INVASIONS.
OK, SO MY HUSBAND AND CHILDREN ARE DEAD. BUT THESE RAIDERS LOOK FAIRLY WELL FED—MAYBE I SHOULD INGRATIATE MYSELF TO THEM.
SUCH OPTIMISM IS UNWARRANTED— AS I'D LEARNED AT MY LAST JOB.
TED, I NEED TO TALK TO YOU.
THE THEFT WAS NO SURPRISE.
A BIKE IS MISSING. I HAVE REASON TO BELIEVE THAT YOU TOOK IT.
I DIDN'T TAKE ANYTHING! YOU CAN COME TO MY DORM ROOM RIGHT NOW AND I'LL SHOW YOU. I DON'T HAVE IT!

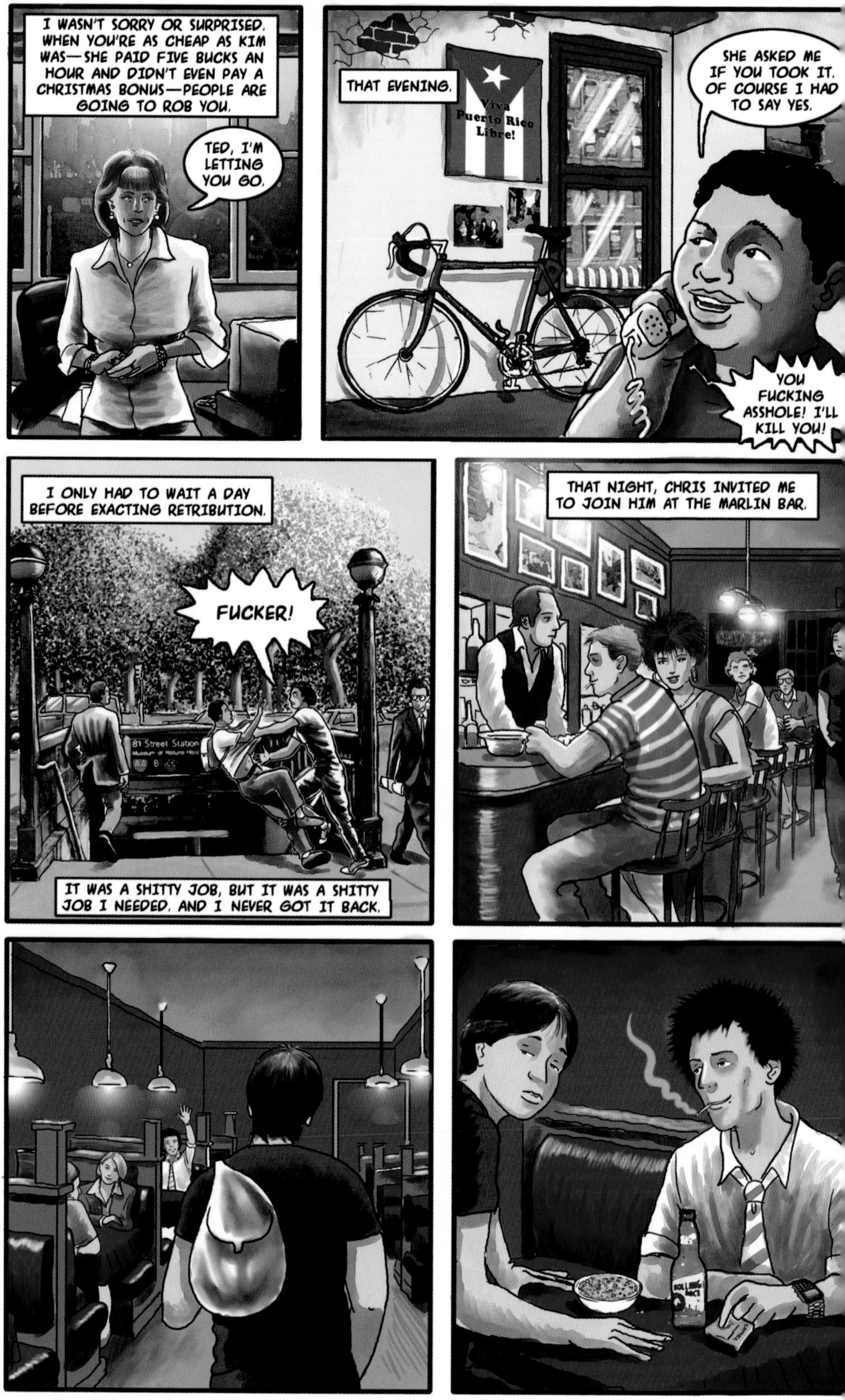
I WASN'T SORRY OR SURPRISED. WHEN YOU'RE AS CHEAP AS KIM WAS—SHE PAID FIVE BUCKS AN HOUR AND DIDN'T EVEN PAY A CHRISTMAS BONUS—PEOPLE ARE GOING TO ROB YOU.
TED, I'M LETTING YOU GO.
THAT EVENING.
Viva Puerto Rico Libre!
SHE ASKED ME IF YOU TOOK IT. OF COURSE I HAD TO SAY YES.
YOU FUCKING ASSHOLE! I'LL KILL YOU!
I ONLY HAD TO WAIT A DAY BEFORE EXACTING RETRIBUTION.
FUCKER!
81 Street Station
IT WAS A SHITTY JOB, BUT IT WAS A SHITTY JOB I NEEDED. AND I NEVER GOT IT BACK.
THAT NIGHT, CHRIS INVITED ME TO JOIN HIM AT THE MARLIN BAR.

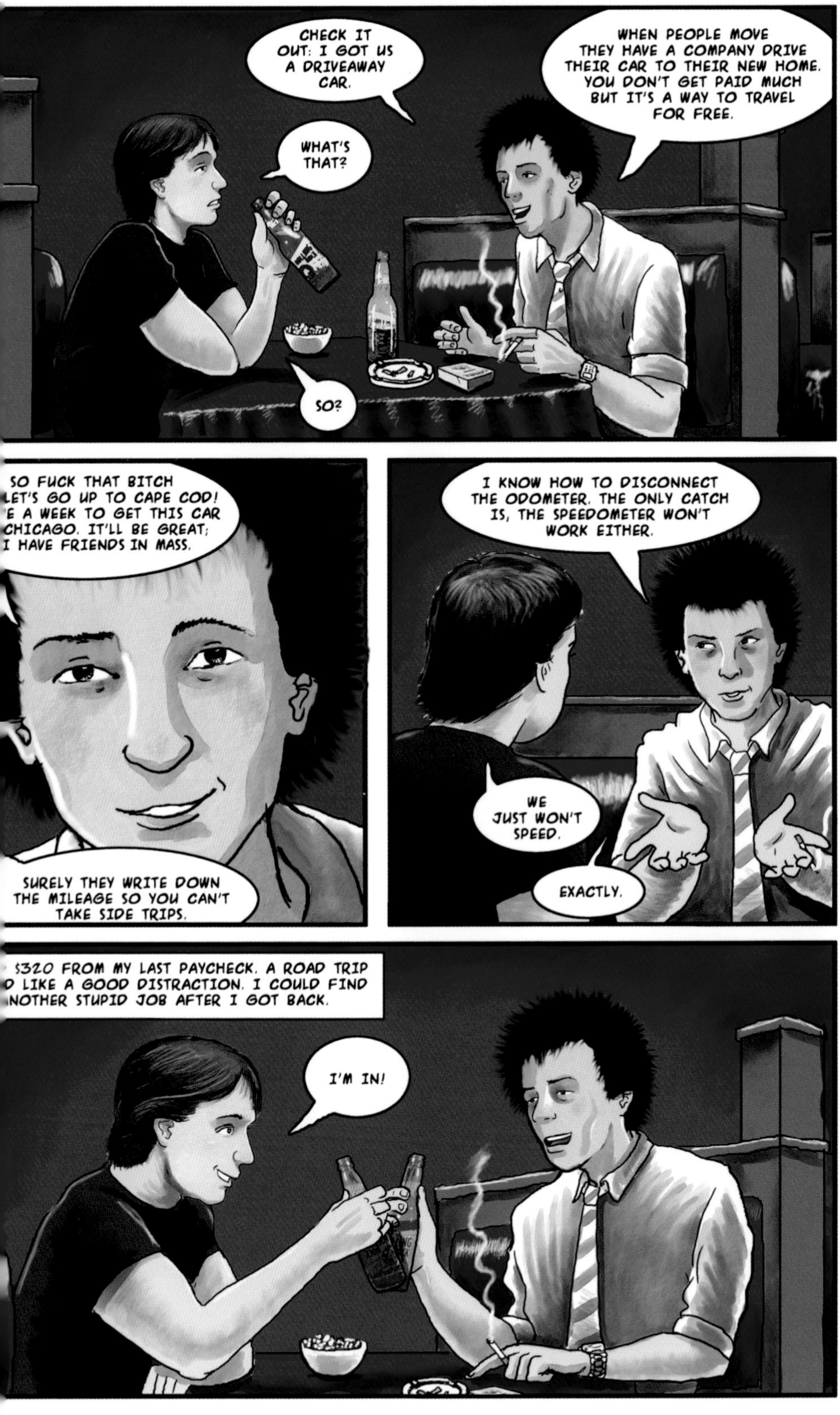
CHECK IT OUT: I GOT US A DRIVEAWAY CAR.
WHAT'S THAT?
WHEN PEOPLE MOVE THEY HAVE A COMPANY DRIVE THEIR CAR TO THEIR NEW HOME. YOU DON'T GET PAID MUCH BUT IT'S A WAY TO TRAVEL FOR FREE.
SO?
SO FUCK THAT BITCH
LET'S GO UP TO CAPE COD!
'E A WEEK TO GET THIS CAR
CHICAGO. IT'LL BE GREAT;
I HAVE FRIENDS IN MASS.
SURELY THEY WRITE DOWN THE MILEAGE SO YOU CAN'T TAKE SIDE TRIPS.
I KNOW HOW TO DISCONNECT THE ODOMETER. THE ONLY CATCH IS, THE SPEEDOMETER WON'T WORK EITHER.
WE JUST WON'T SPEED.
EXACTLY.
$320 FROM MY LAST PAYCHECK. A ROAD TRIP
D LIKE A GOOD DISTRACTION. I COULD FIND
NOTHER STUPID JOB AFTER I GOT BACK.
I'M IN!

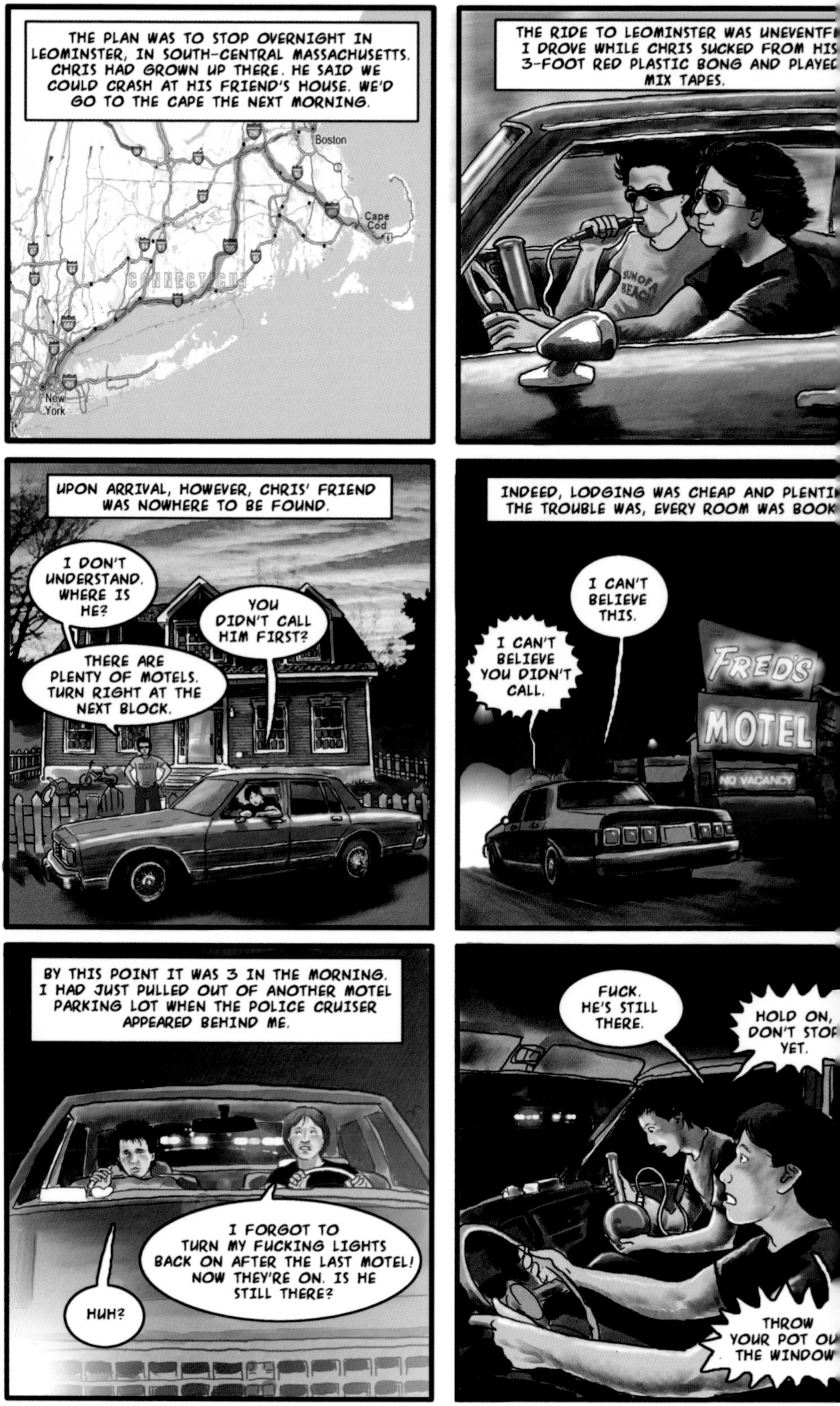
THE PLAN WAS TO STOP OVERNIGHT IN LEOMINSTER, IN SOUTH-CENTRAL MASSACHUSETTS. CHRIS HAD GROWN UP THERE. HE SAID WE COULD CRASH AT HIS FRIEND'S HOUSE. WE'D GO TO THE CAPE THE NEXT MORNING.
Boston
Cape Cod
CONNECTICUT
New York
THE RIDE TO LEOMINSTER WAS UNEVENTF
I DROVE WHILE CHRIS SUCKED FROM HIS
3-FOOT RED PLASTIC BONG AND PLAYED
MIX TAPES.
SUNOFA BEACH
UPON ARRIVAL, HOWEVER, CHRIS' FRIEND WAS NOWHERE TO BE FOUND.
I DON'T UNDERSTAND. WHERE IS HE?
YOU DIDN'T CALL HIM FIRST?
THERE ARE PLENTY OF MOTELS. TURN RIGHT AT THE NEXT BLOCK.
INDEED, LODGING WAS CHEAP AND PLENTI
THE TROUBLE WAS, EVERY ROOM WAS BOOK
I CAN'T BELIEVE THIS.
I CAN'T BELIEVE YOU DIDN'T CALL.
FRED'S
MOTEL
NO VACANCY
BY THIS POINT IT WAS 3 IN THE MORNING. I HAD JUST PULLED OUT OF ANOTHER MOTEL PARKING LOT WHEN THE POLICE CRUISER APPEARED BEHIND ME.
I FORGOT TO TURN MY FUCKING LIGHTS BACK ON AFTER THE LAST MOTEL! NOW THEY'RE ON. IS HE STILL THERE?
HUH?
FUCK. HE'S STILL THERE.
HOLD ON, DON'T STOP YET.
THROW YOUR POT OU THE WINDOW

YOU KNOW YOU'RE IN A SMALL TOWN WHEN YOUR COP'S BADGE NUMBER IS TWO DIGITS.

LICENSE AND REGISTRATION.

OK, HOLD ON.

I THINK THE DRIVEAWAY PAPERS ARE IN THE TRUNK.

I'M GOING TO HAVE TO ASK YOU BOYS TO STEP OUT OF THE CAR.

WE FOUND THE DOCUMENTS LATER. THEY WERE IN THE GLOVE COMPARTMENT, RIGHT WHERE THEY WERE SUPPOSED TO BE.

THE BONG FELL OUT WHEN THE COP OPENED THE PASSENGER DOOR. HE TORE THE CAR APART EVEN RIPPED THE CARPET FROM THE FLOOR—BUT HE DIDN'T FIND ANYTHING ELSE. WELL, THERE *WERE* FIREWORKS. BUT THE ARREST WAS ALL ABOUT THE BONG.

I CAN'T BELIEVE THIS.

IT'S YOUR FAULT.

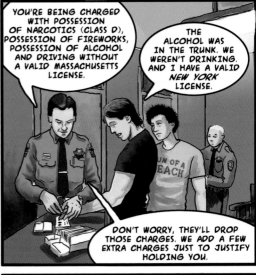

YOU'RE BEING CHARGED WITH POSSESSION OF NARCOTICS (CLASS D), POSSESSION OF FIREWORKS, POSSESSION OF ALCOHOL AND DRIVING WITHOUT A VALID MASSACHUSETTS LICENSE.

THE ALCOHOL WAS IN THE TRUNK. WE WEREN'T DRINKING. AND I HAVE A VALID *NEW YORK* LICENSE.

DON'T WORRY, THEY'LL DROP THOSE CHARGES. WE ADD A FEW EXTRA CHARGES JUST TO JUSTIFY HOLDING YOU.

THEY ONLY KEPT US IN LOCKUP FOR A FEW HOURS.

NOBODY KNOWS...

THE TROUBLE I'VE SEEN...

SHUT THE FUCK UP, OTIS!

FINALLY...

WE'RE RELEASING YOU ON YOUR OWN RECOGNIZANCE. YOUR COURT DATE IS SEPTEMBER—

THERE'S ONLY $40 IN HERE! I HAD—

EVERYTHING'S HERE. THANKS.

LET'S GO.

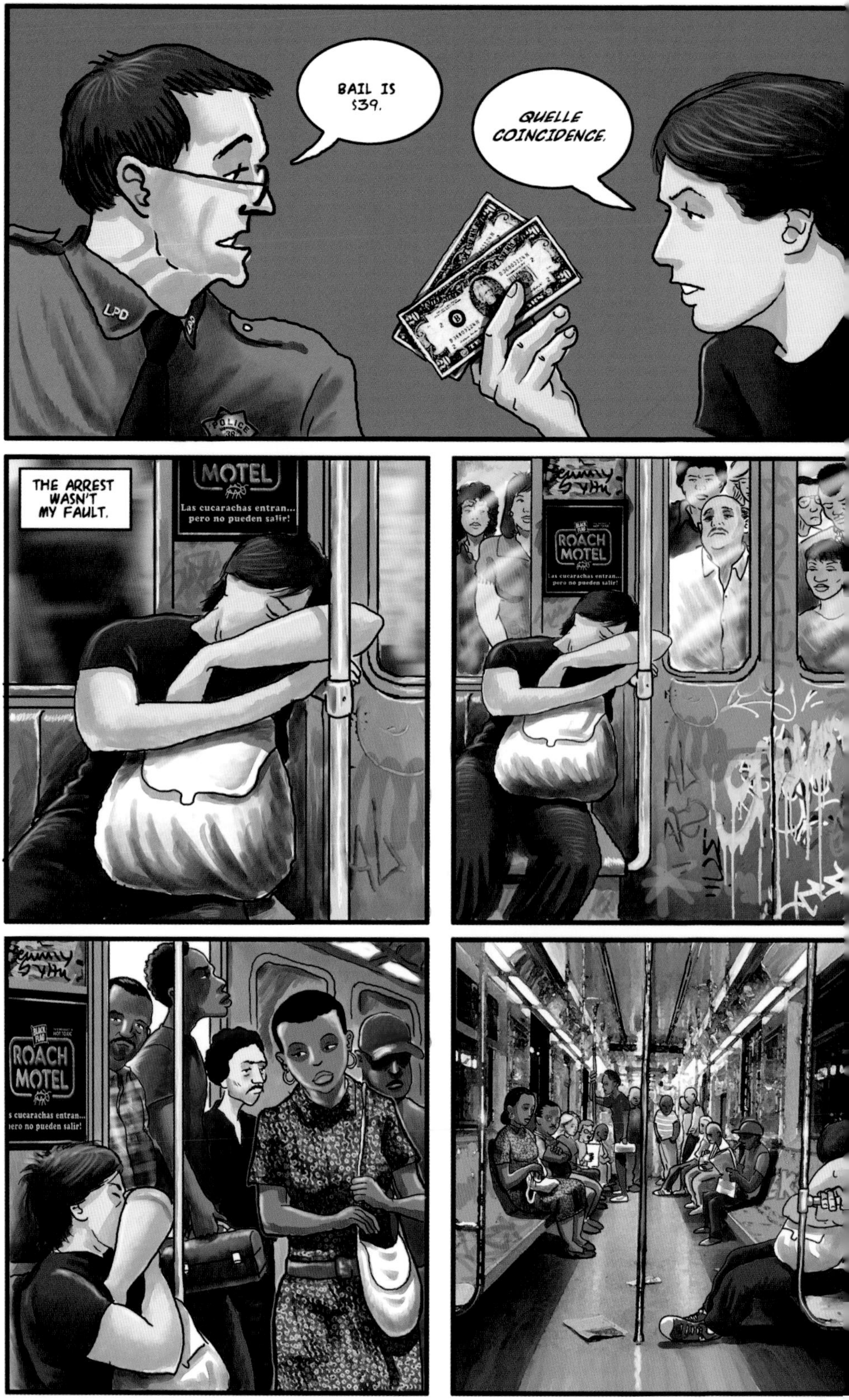
BAIL IS $39.
QUELLE COINCIDENCE.
LPD
POLICE
THE ARREST WASN'T MY FAULT.
MOTEL
Las cucarachas entran... pero no pueden salir!
ROACH MOTEL
Las cucarachas entran... pero no pueden salir!
ROACH MOTEL
s cucarachas entran...
ero no pueden salir!

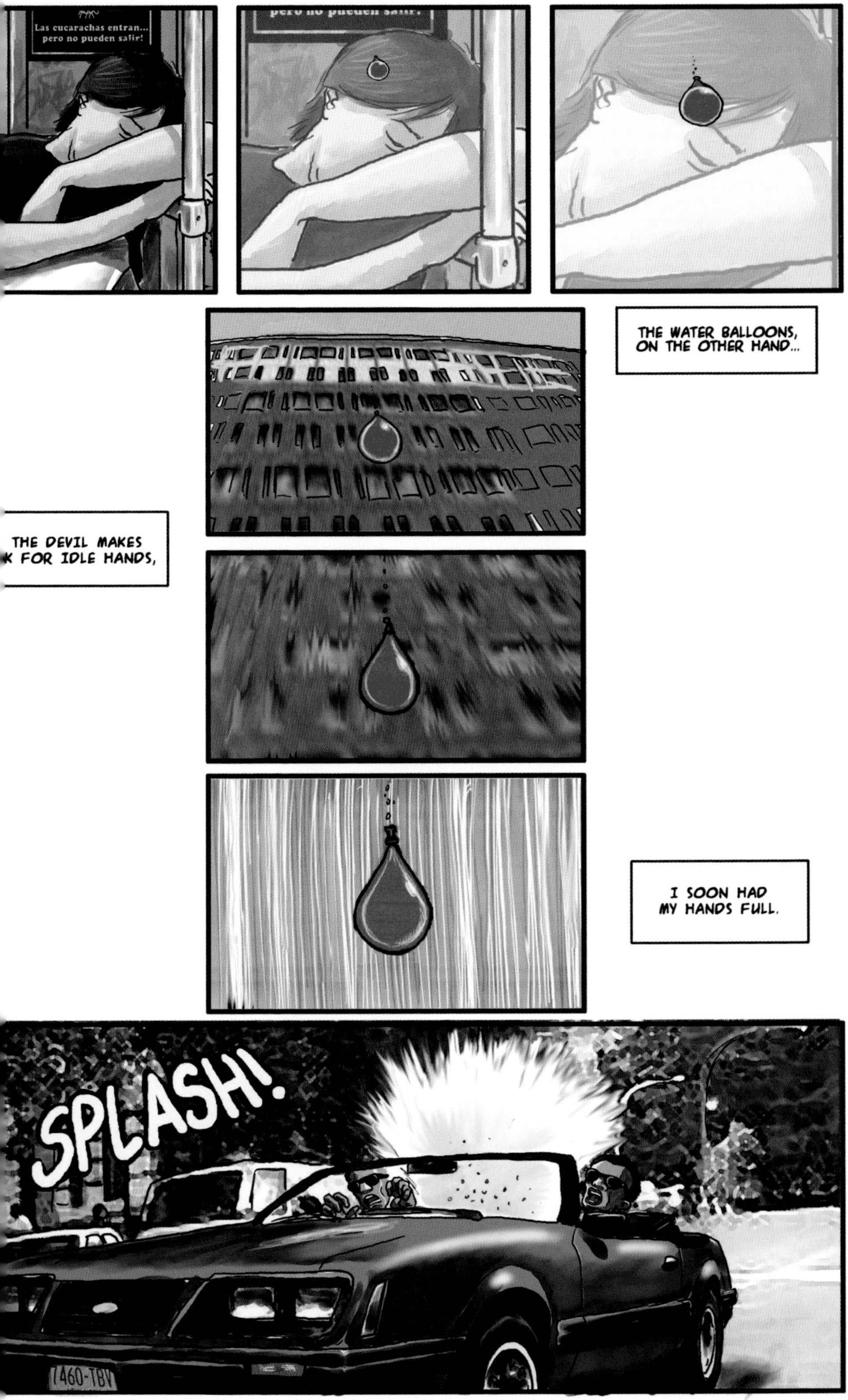
Las cucarachas entran...
pero no pueden salir!
pero no pueden salir!
THE DEVIL MAKES
K FOR IDLE HANDS,
THE WATER BALLOONS, ON THE OTHER HAND...
I SOON HAD MY HANDS FULL.
SPLASH!
1460-TBV

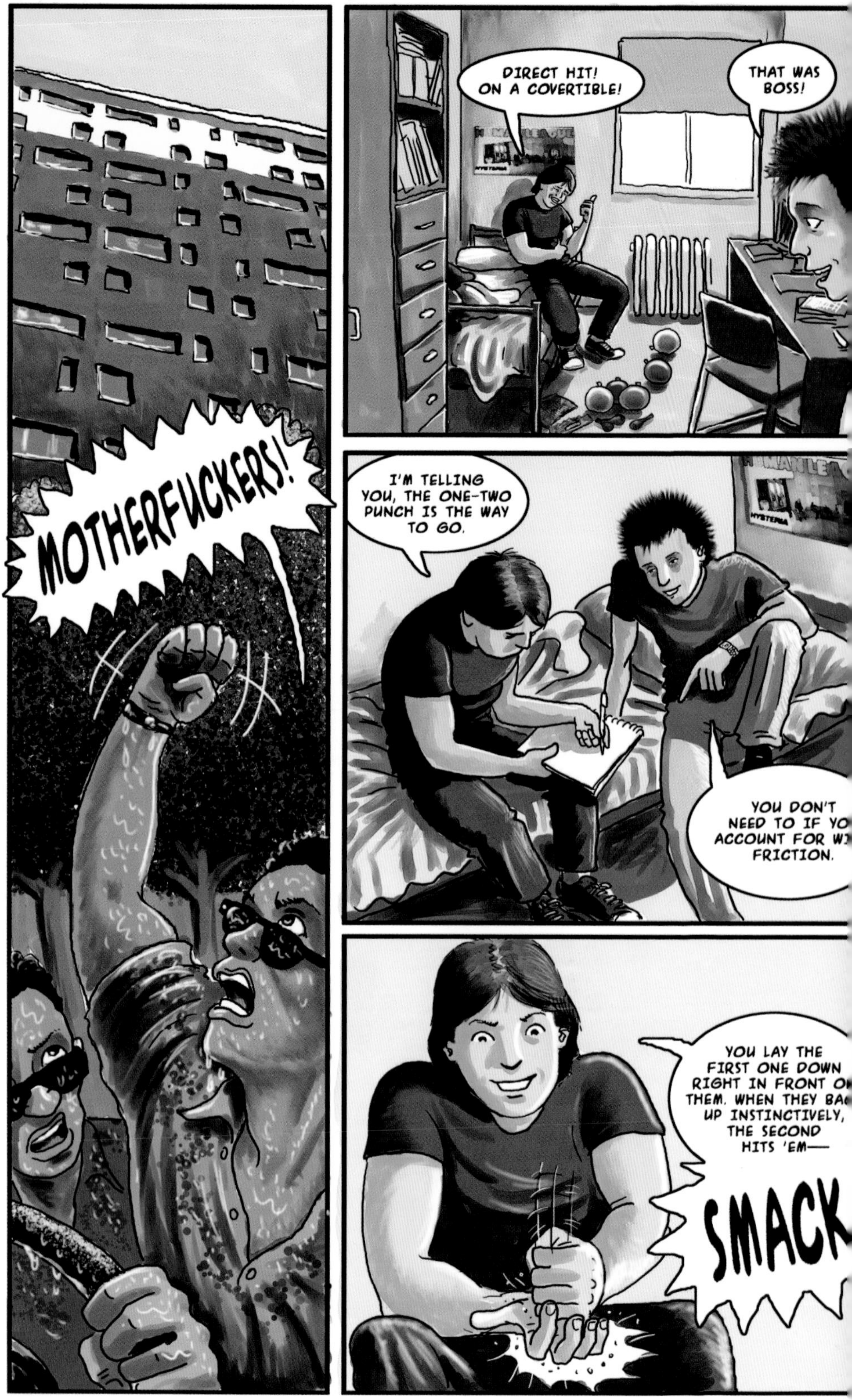
MOTHERFUCKERS!
DIRECT HIT! ON A COVERTIBLE!
THAT WAS BOSS!
HYSTERIA
I'M TELLING YOU, THE ONE-TWO PUNCH IS THE WAY TO GO.
YOU DON'T NEED TO IF YO ACCOUNT FOR W FRICTION.
HYSTERIA
YOU LAY THE FIRST ONE DOWN RIGHT IN FRONT O THEM. WHEN THEY BA UP INSTINCTIVELY, THE SECOND HITS 'EM—
SMACK

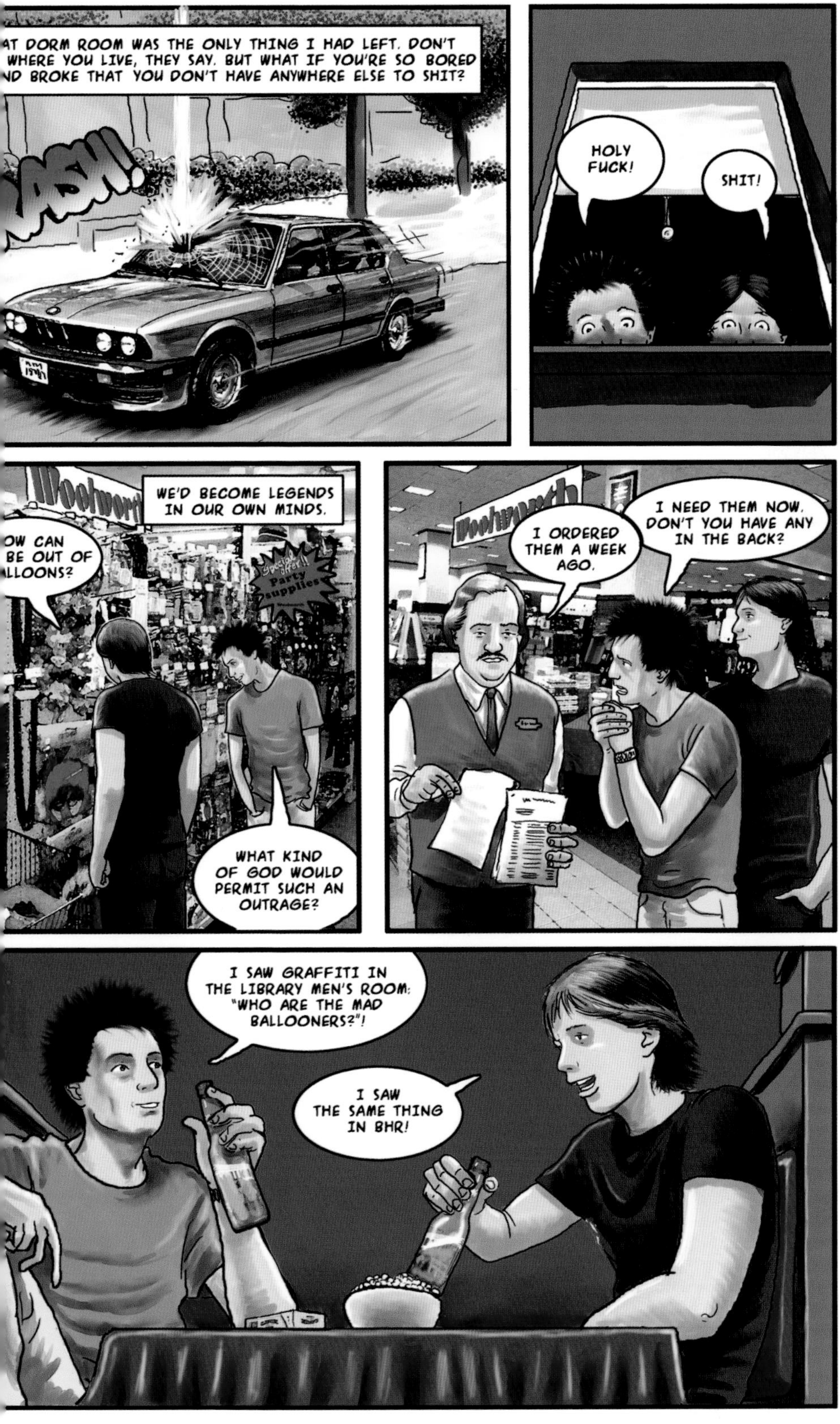
AT DORM ROOM WAS THE ONLY THING I HAD LEFT. DON'T
WHERE YOU LIVE, THEY SAY. BUT WHAT IF YOU'RE SO BORED
ND BROKE THAT YOU DON'T HAVE ANYWHERE ELSE TO SHIT?
ASH!
HOLY FUCK!
SHIT!
WE'D BECOME LEGENDS IN OUR OWN MINDS.
OW CAN BE OUT OF LLOONS?
Special offer!! Party supplies
WHAT KIND OF GOD WOULD PERMIT SUCH AN OUTRAGE?
I ORDERED THEM A WEEK AGO.
I NEED THEM NOW. DON'T YOU HAVE ANY IN THE BACK?
I SAW GRAFFITI IN THE LIBRARY MEN'S ROOM: "WHO ARE THE MAD BALLOONERS?"!
I SAW THE SAME THING IN BHR!

THAT WASN'T THE ONLY KIND OF ATTENTION WE WERE ATTRACTING.

ARE YOU TED RALL?

WHO ARE YOU?

CAMPUS SECURITY. YOU'VE BEEN THROWING OBJECTS OUT THE WINDOW.

WHAT ARE YOU TALKING ABOUT?

WHAT A LAME LINE. BUT WHAT ELSE WOULD YOU SAY? EVEN IF YOU WERE INNOCENT?

I'M THE ASSISTANT CHIEF OF CU SECURITY AND, WITH GOD AS MY WITNESS I'M GOING TO MAKE SURE YOU'RE *OUT* OF HERE! THAT YOU *NEVER* LIVE IN UNIVERSITY HOUSING FOR THE REST OF YOUR *LIFE*!

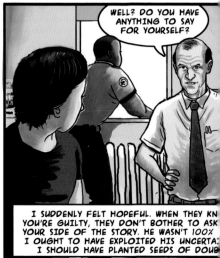

WELL? DO YOU HAVE ANYTHING TO SAY FOR YOURSELF?

I SUDDENLY FELT HOPEFUL. WHEN THEY KN YOU'RE GUILTY, THEY DON'T BOTHER TO ASK YOUR SIDE OF THE STORY. HE WASN'T 100% I OUGHT TO HAVE EXPLOITED HIS UNCERTA I SHOULD HAVE PLANTED SEEDS OF DOUB

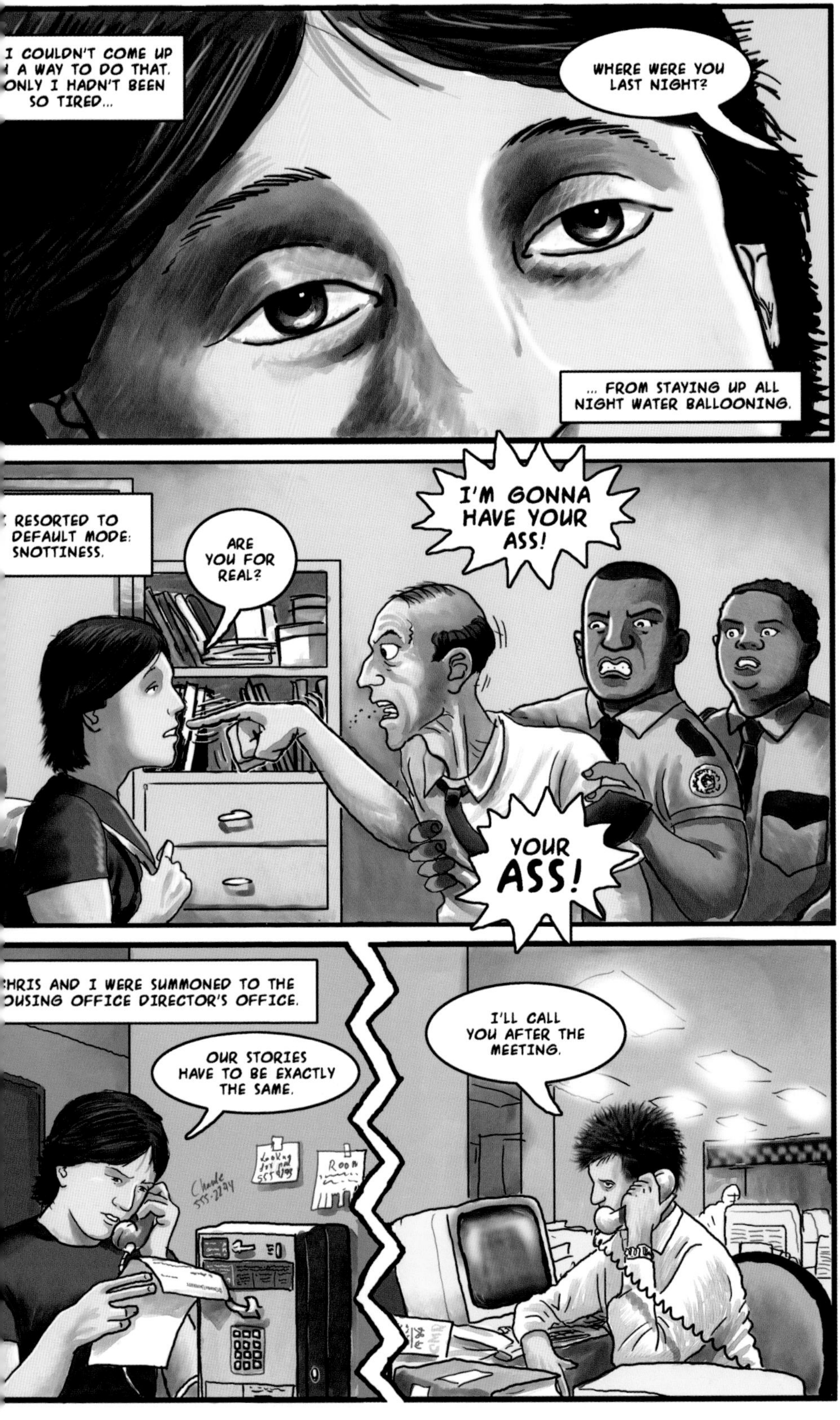
I COULDN'T COME UP
A WAY TO DO THAT.
ONLY I HADN'T BEEN
SO TIRED...
WHERE WERE YOU
LAST NIGHT?
... FROM STAYING UP ALL
NIGHT WATER BALLOONING.
RESORTED TO
DEFAULT MODE:
SNOTTINESS.
ARE
YOU FOR
REAL?
I'M GONNA
HAVE YOUR
ASS!
YOUR
ASS!
HRIS AND I WERE SUMMONED TO THE
OUSING OFFICE DIRECTOR'S OFFICE.
OUR STORIES
HAVE TO BE EXACTLY
THE SAME.
I'LL CALL
YOU AFTER THE
MEETING.

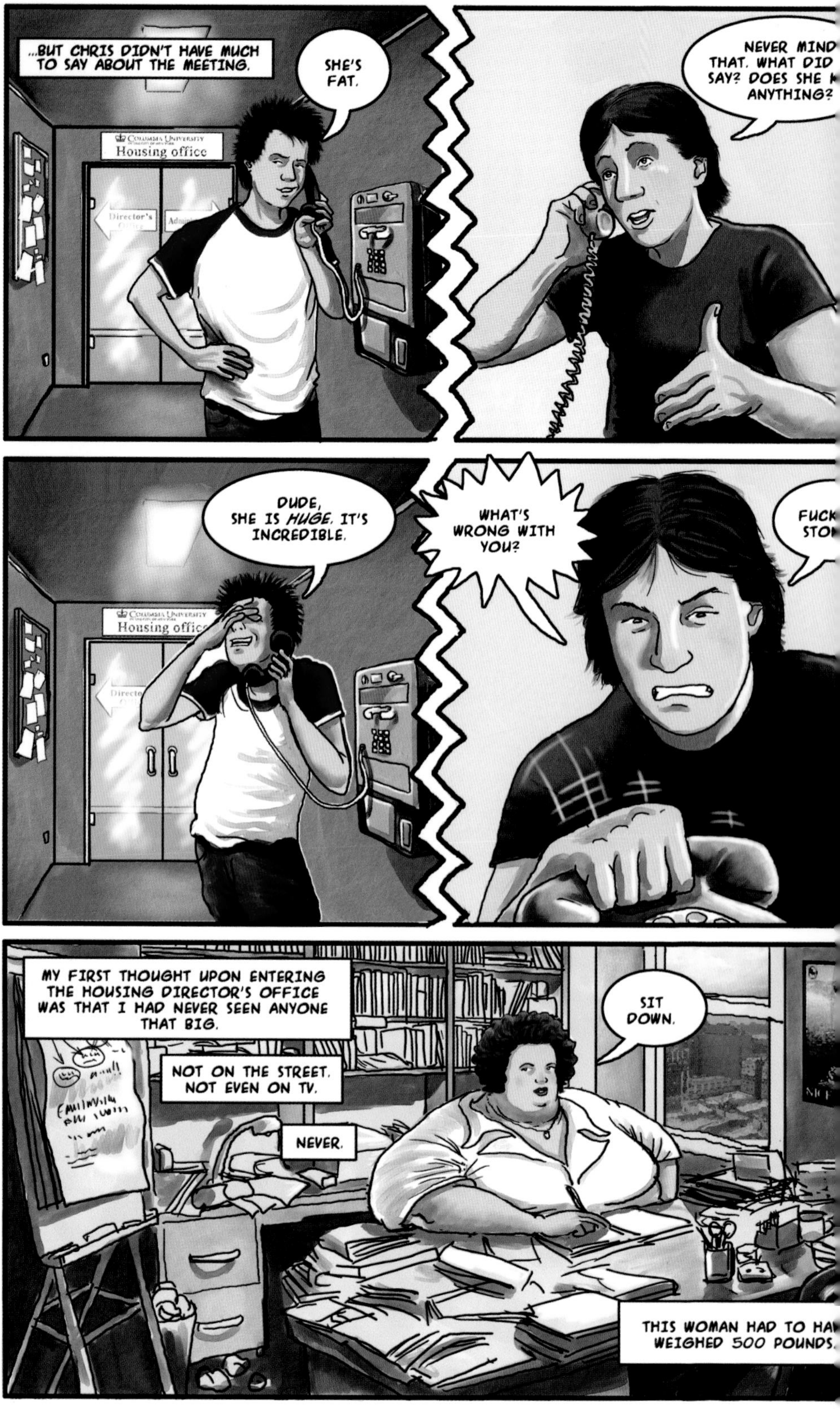
...BUT CHRIS DIDN'T HAVE MUCH TO SAY ABOUT THE MEETING.
Columbia University
Housing office
Director's Office
SHE'S FAT.
NEVER MIND THAT. WHAT DID SAY? DOES SHE ANYTHING?
DUDE, SHE IS *HUGE*. IT'S INCREDIBLE.
WHAT'S WRONG WITH YOU?
FUCK
MY FIRST THOUGHT UPON ENTERING THE HOUSING DIRECTOR'S OFFICE WAS THAT I HAD NEVER SEEN ANYONE THAT BIG.
NOT ON THE STREET. NOT EVEN ON TV.
NEVER.
SIT DOWN.
THIS WOMAN HAD TO HA WEIGHED 500 POUNDS.

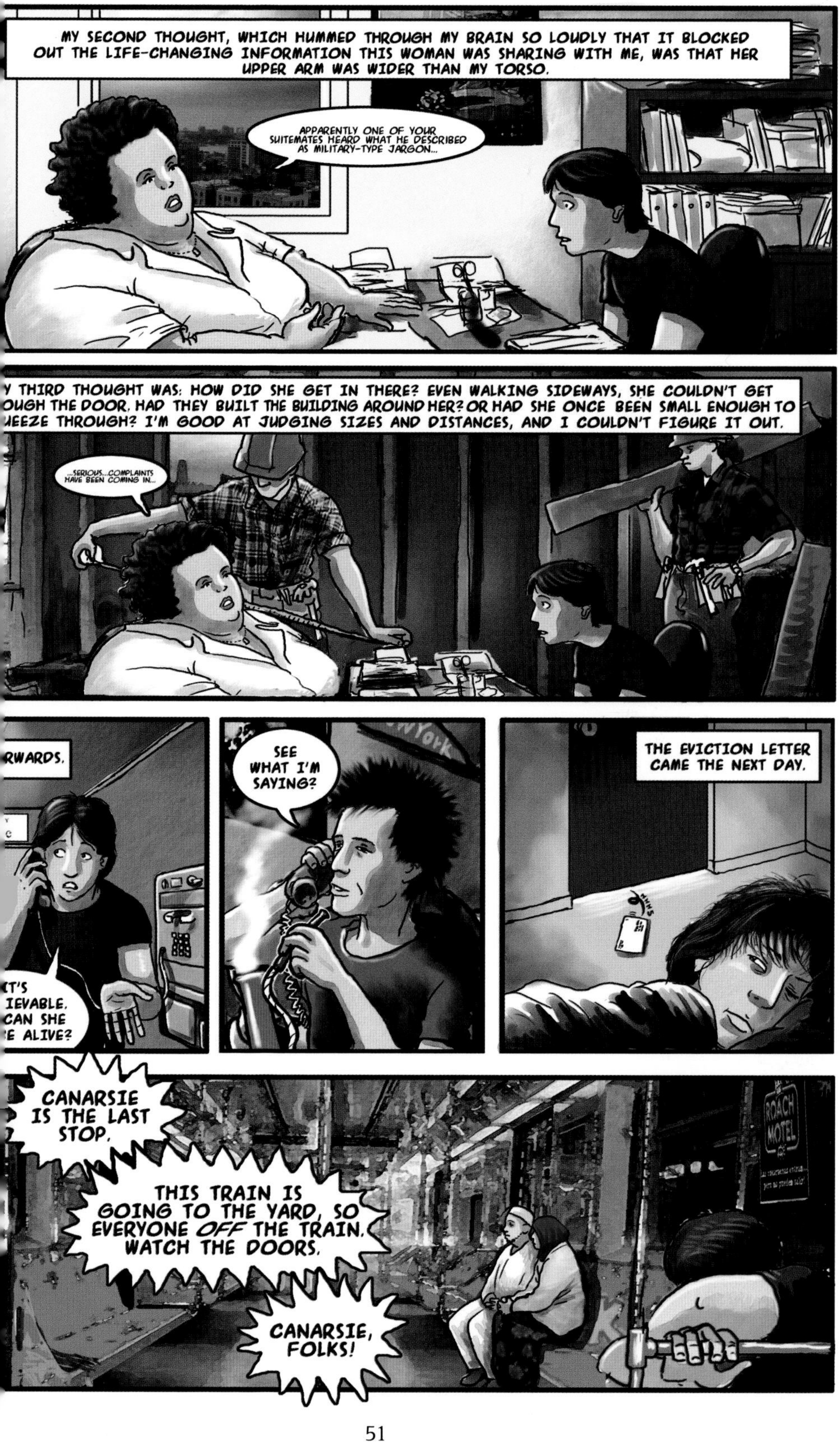
MY SECOND THOUGHT, WHICH HUMMED THROUGH MY BRAIN SO LOUDLY THAT IT BLOCKED OUT THE LIFE-CHANGING INFORMATION THIS WOMAN WAS SHARING WITH ME, WAS THAT HER UPPER ARM WAS WIDER THAN MY TORSO.
APPARENTLY ONE OF YOUR SUITEMATES HEARD WHAT HE DESCRIBED AS MILITARY-TYPE JARGON...
Y THIRD THOUGHT WAS: HOW DID SHE GET IN THERE? EVEN WALKING SIDEWAYS, SHE COULDN'T GET OUGH THE DOOR. HAD THEY BUILT THE BUILDING AROUND HER? OR HAD SHE ONCE BEEN SMALL ENOUGH TO UEEZE THROUGH? I'M GOOD AT JUDGING SIZES AND DISTANCES, AND I COULDN'T FIGURE IT OUT.
...SERIOUS...COMPLAINTS HAVE BEEN COMING IN...
RWARDS.
T'S IEVABLE. CAN SHE E ALIVE?
SEE WHAT I'M SAYING?
THE EVICTION LETTER CAME THE NEXT DAY.
CANARSIE IS THE LAST STOP.
THIS TRAIN IS GOING TO THE YARD, SO EVERYONE OFF THE TRAIN. WATCH THE DOORS.
CANARSIE, FOLKS!
ROACH MOTEL

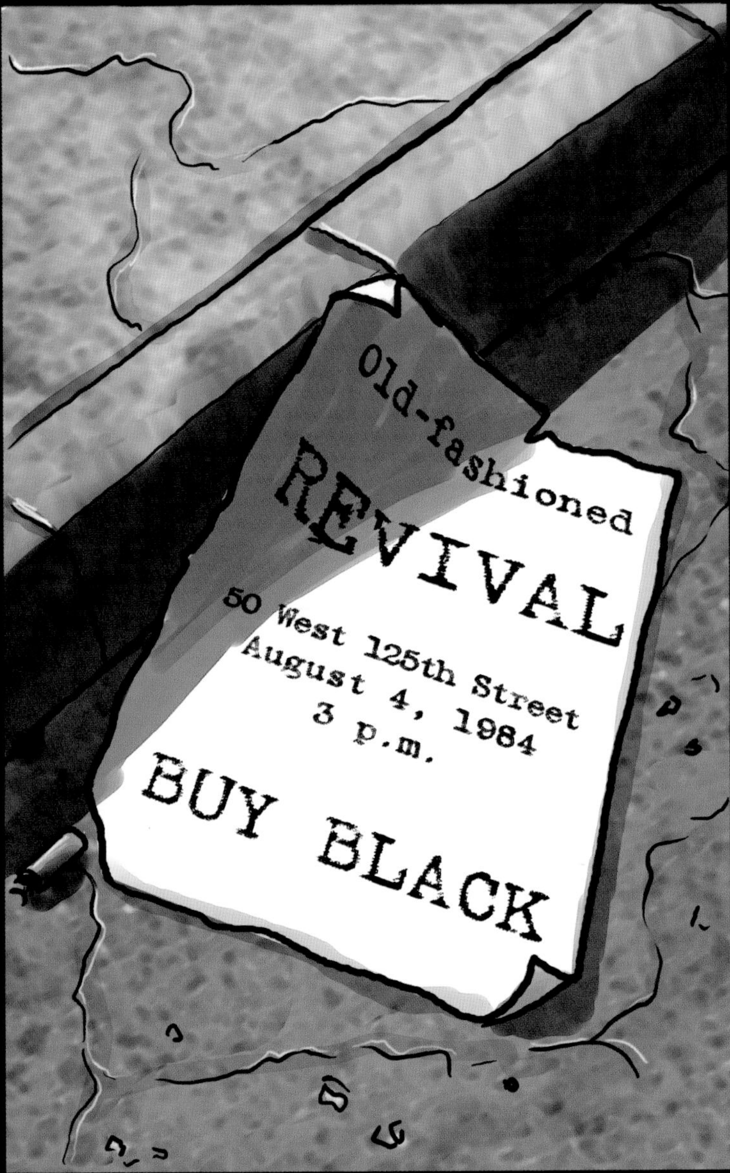
Old-fashioned
REVIVAL
50 West 125th Street
August 4, 1984
3 p.m.
BUY BLACK

II

A School You Couldn't Get Into

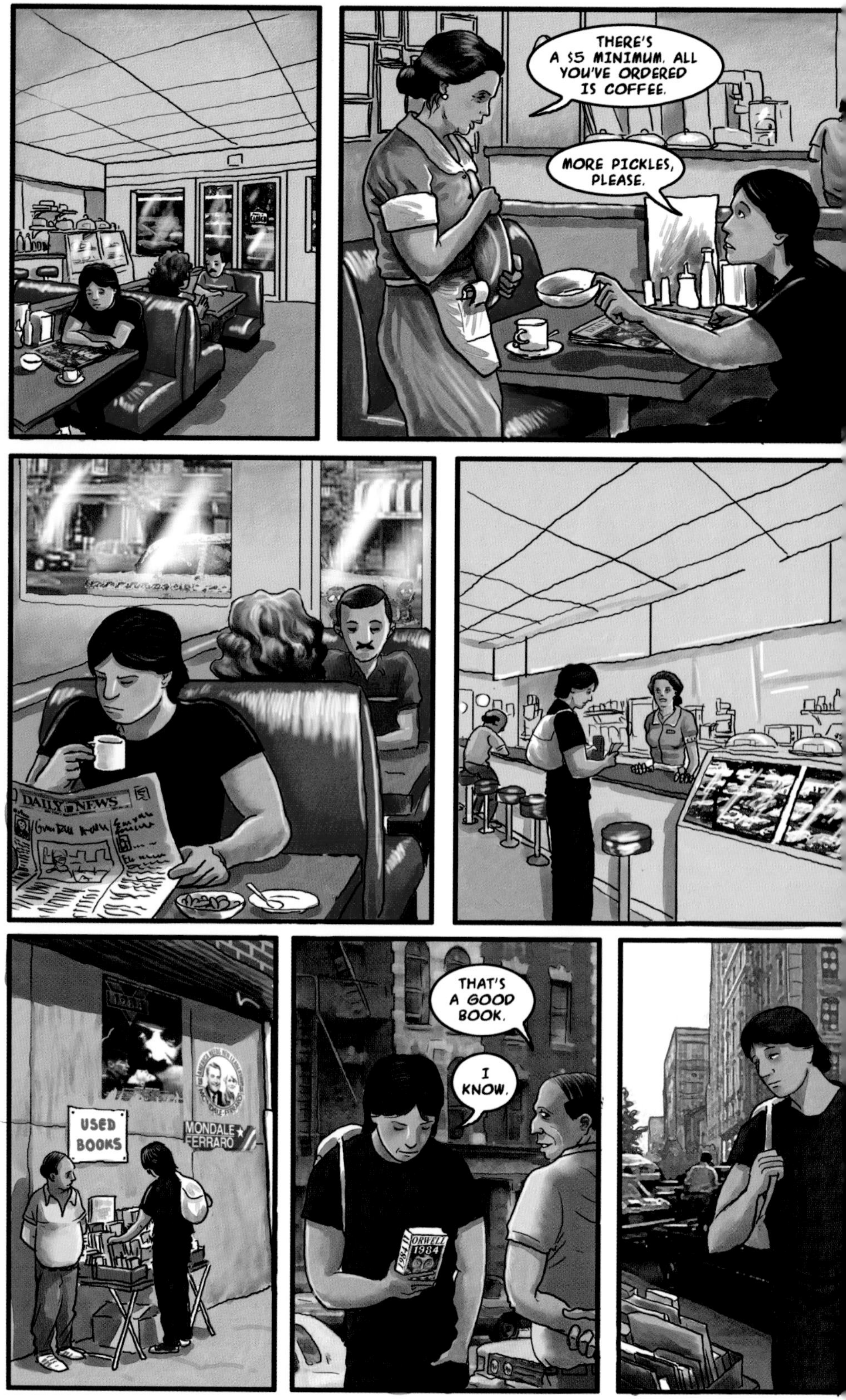
THERE'S A $5 MINIMUM. ALL YOU'VE ORDERED IS COFFEE.
MORE PICKLES, PLEASE.
DAILY NEWS
USED BOOKS
MONDALE FERRARO
THAT'S A GOOD BOOK.
I KNOW.
ORWELL 1984

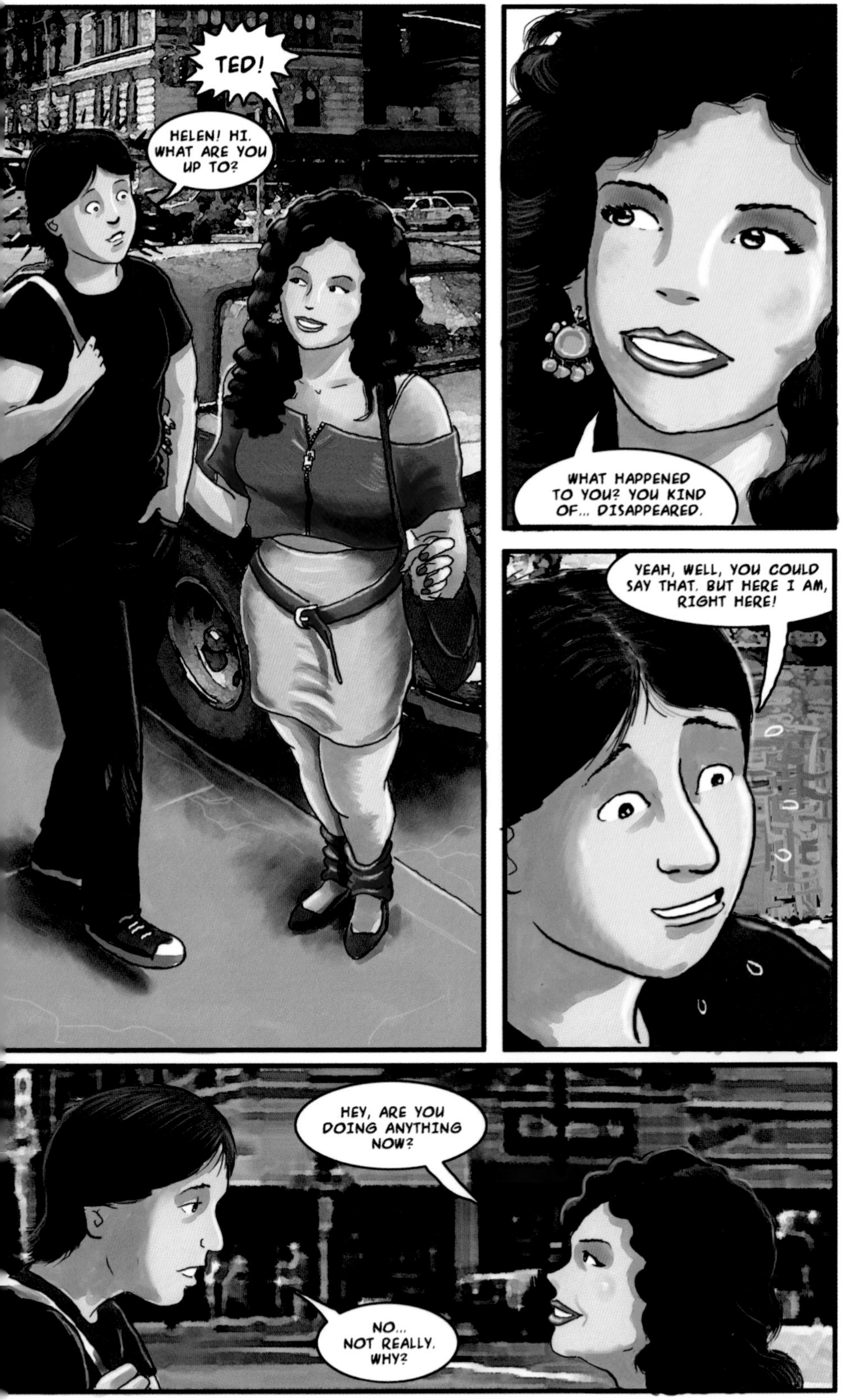
TED!
HELEN! HI. WHAT ARE YOU UP TO?
WHAT HAPPENED TO YOU? YOU KIND OF... DISAPPEARED.
YEAH, WELL, YOU COULD SAY THAT. BUT HERE I AM, RIGHT HERE!
HEY, ARE YOU DOING ANYTHING NOW?
NO... NOT REALLY. WHY?

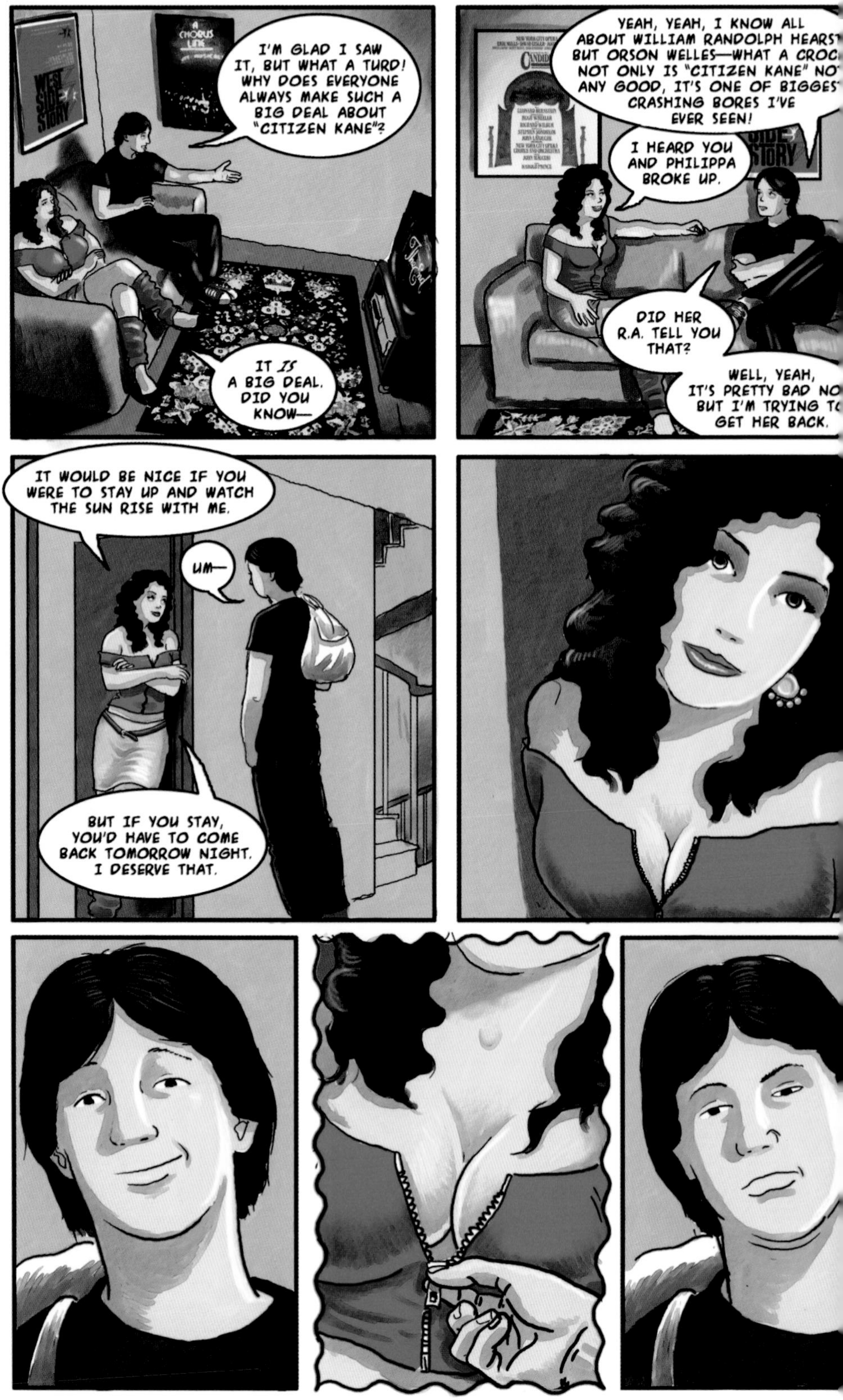
I'M GLAD I SAW IT, BUT WHAT A TURD! WHY DOES EVERYONE ALWAYS MAKE SUCH A BIG DEAL ABOUT "CITIZEN KANE"?
IT IS A BIG DEAL. DID YOU KNOW—
YEAH, YEAH, I KNOW ALL ABOUT WILLIAM RANDOLPH HEARST BUT ORSON WELLES—WHAT A CROC NOT ONLY IS "CITIZEN KANE" NO ANY GOOD, IT'S ONE OF BIGGES CRASHING BORES I'VE EVER SEEN!
I HEARD YOU AND PHILIPPA BROKE UP.
DID HER R.A. TELL YOU THAT?
WELL, YEAH, IT'S PRETTY BAD NO BUT I'M TRYING T GET HER BACK.
IT WOULD BE NICE IF YOU WERE TO STAY UP AND WATCH THE SUN RISE WITH ME.
UM—
BUT IF YOU STAY, YOU'D HAVE TO COME BACK TOMORROW NIGHT. I DESERVE THAT.

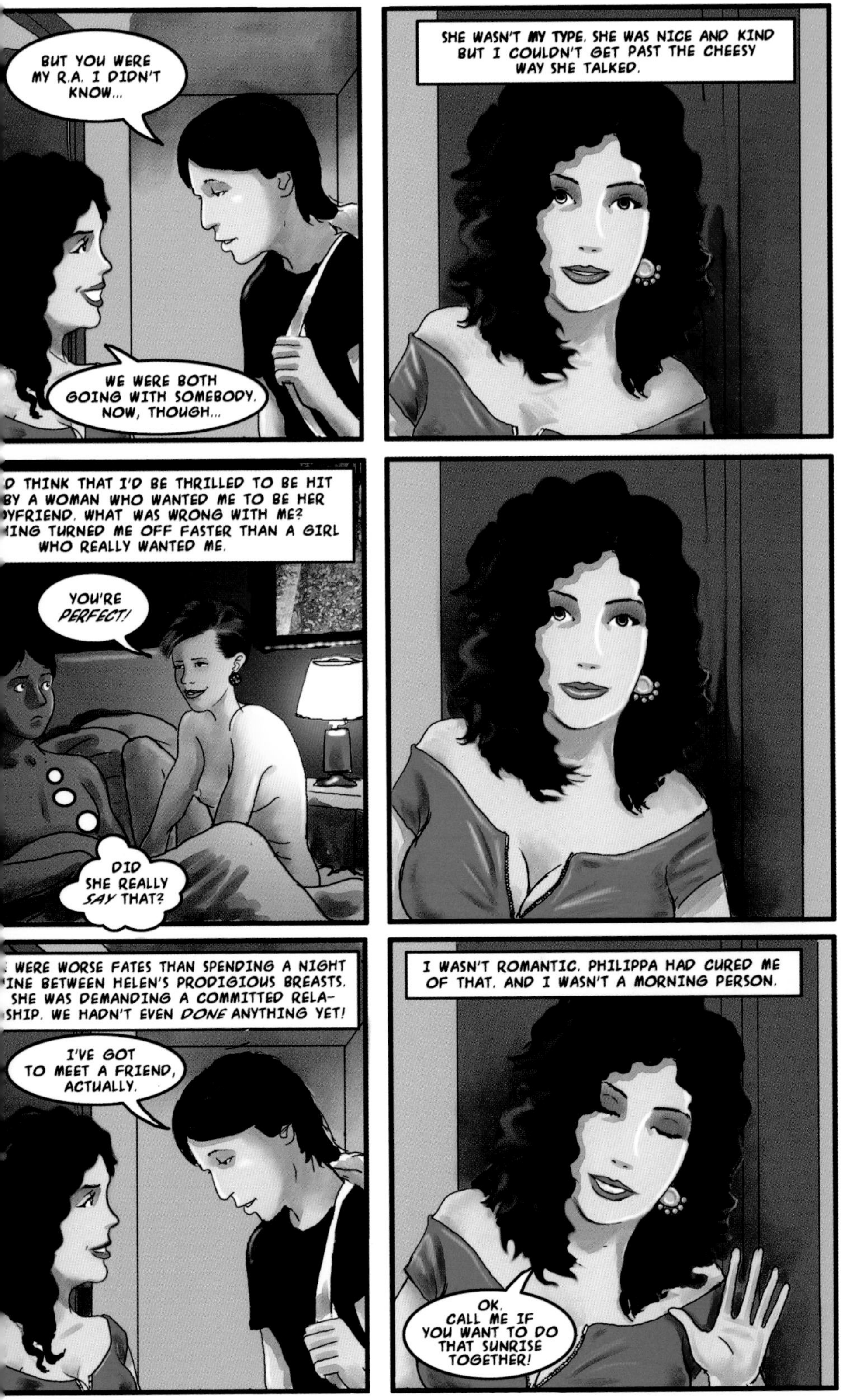

BUT YOU WERE MY R.A. I DIDN'T KNOW...
WE WERE BOTH GOING WITH SOMEBODY. NOW, THOUGH...
SHE WASN'T MY TYPE. SHE WAS NICE AND KIND BUT I COULDN'T GET PAST THE CHEESY WAY SHE TALKED.
D THINK THAT I'D BE THRILLED TO BE HIT BY A WOMAN WHO WANTED ME TO BE HER YFRIEND. WHAT WAS WRONG WITH ME? IING TURNED ME OFF FASTER THAN A GIRL WHO REALLY WANTED ME.
YOU'RE PERFECT!
DID SHE REALLY SAY THAT?
WERE WORSE FATES THAN SPENDING A NIGHT INE BETWEEN HELEN'S PRODIGIOUS BREASTS. SHE WAS DEMANDING A COMMITTED RELA-SHIP. WE HADN'T EVEN DONE ANYTHING YET!
I'VE GOT TO MEET A FRIEND, ACTUALLY.
I WASN'T ROMANTIC. PHILIPPA HAD CURED ME OF THAT. AND I WASN'T A MORNING PERSON.
OK. CALL ME IF YOU WANT TO DO THAT SUNRISE TOGETHER!

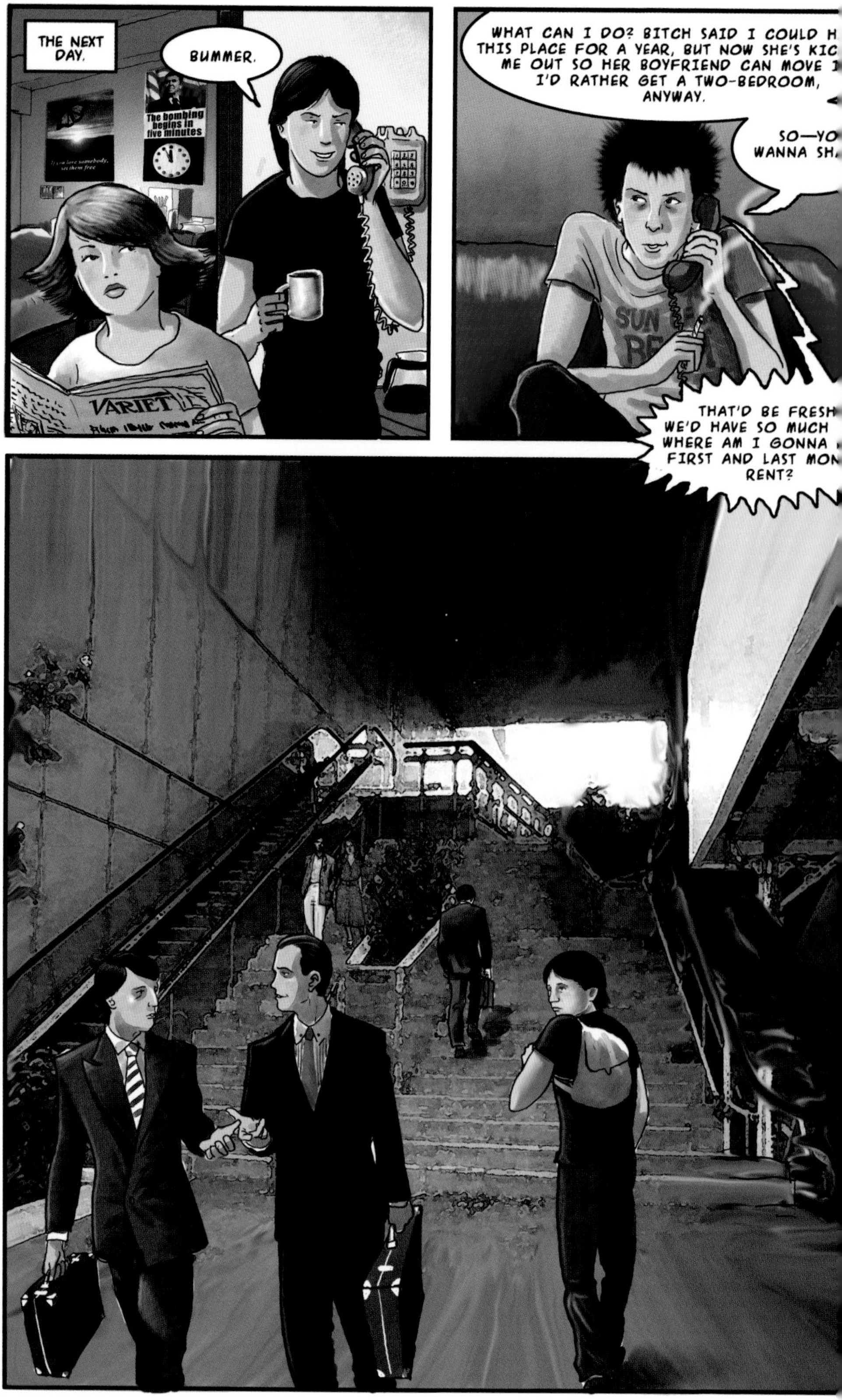
THE NEXT DAY.
BUMMER.
The bombing begins in five minutes
If you love somebody, set them free
VARIET
WHAT CAN I DO? BITCH SAID I COULD H
THIS PLACE FOR A YEAR, BUT NOW SHE'S KIC
ME OUT SO HER BOYFRIEND CAN MOVE I
I'D RATHER GET A TWO-BEDROOM,
ANYWAY.
SO—YO
WANNA SH
THAT'D BE FRESH
WE'D HAVE SO MUCH
WHERE AM I GONNA
FIRST AND LAST MON
RENT?

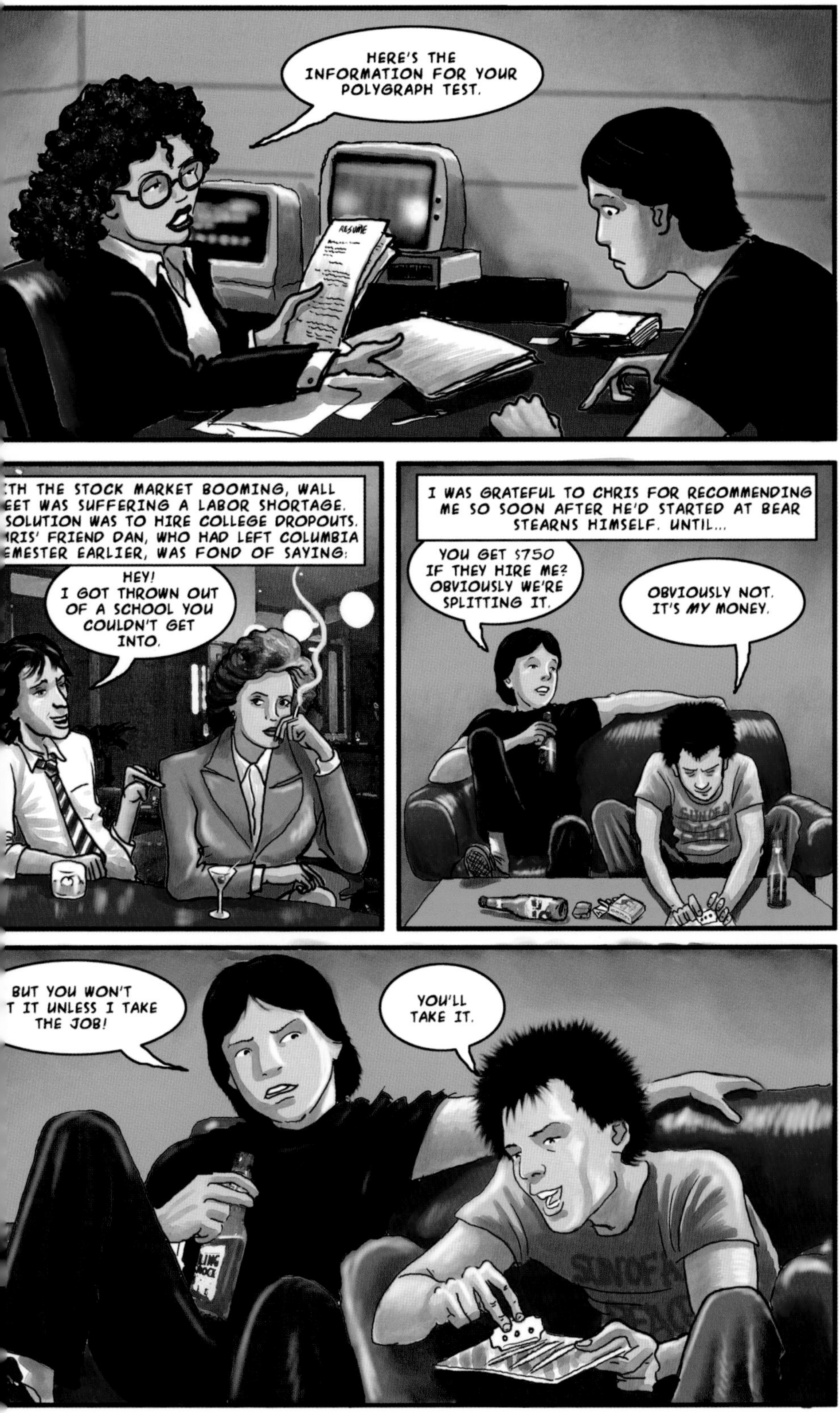
HERE'S THE INFORMATION FOR YOUR POLYGRAPH TEST.
RESUME
ITH THE STOCK MARKET BOOMING, WALL EET WAS SUFFERING A LABOR SHORTAGE. SOLUTION WAS TO HIRE COLLEGE DROPOUTS. IRIS' FRIEND DAN, WHO HAD LEFT COLUMBIA EMESTER EARLIER, WAS FOND OF SAYING:
HEY! I GOT THROWN OUT OF A SCHOOL YOU COULDN'T GET INTO.
I WAS GRATEFUL TO CHRIS FOR RECOMMENDING ME SO SOON AFTER HE'D STARTED AT BEAR STEARNS HIMSELF. UNTIL...
YOU GET $750 IF THEY HIRE ME? OBVIOUSLY WE'RE SPLITTING IT.
OBVIOUSLY NOT. IT'S MY MONEY.
BUT YOU WON'T T IT UNLESS I TAKE THE JOB!
YOU'LL TAKE IT.

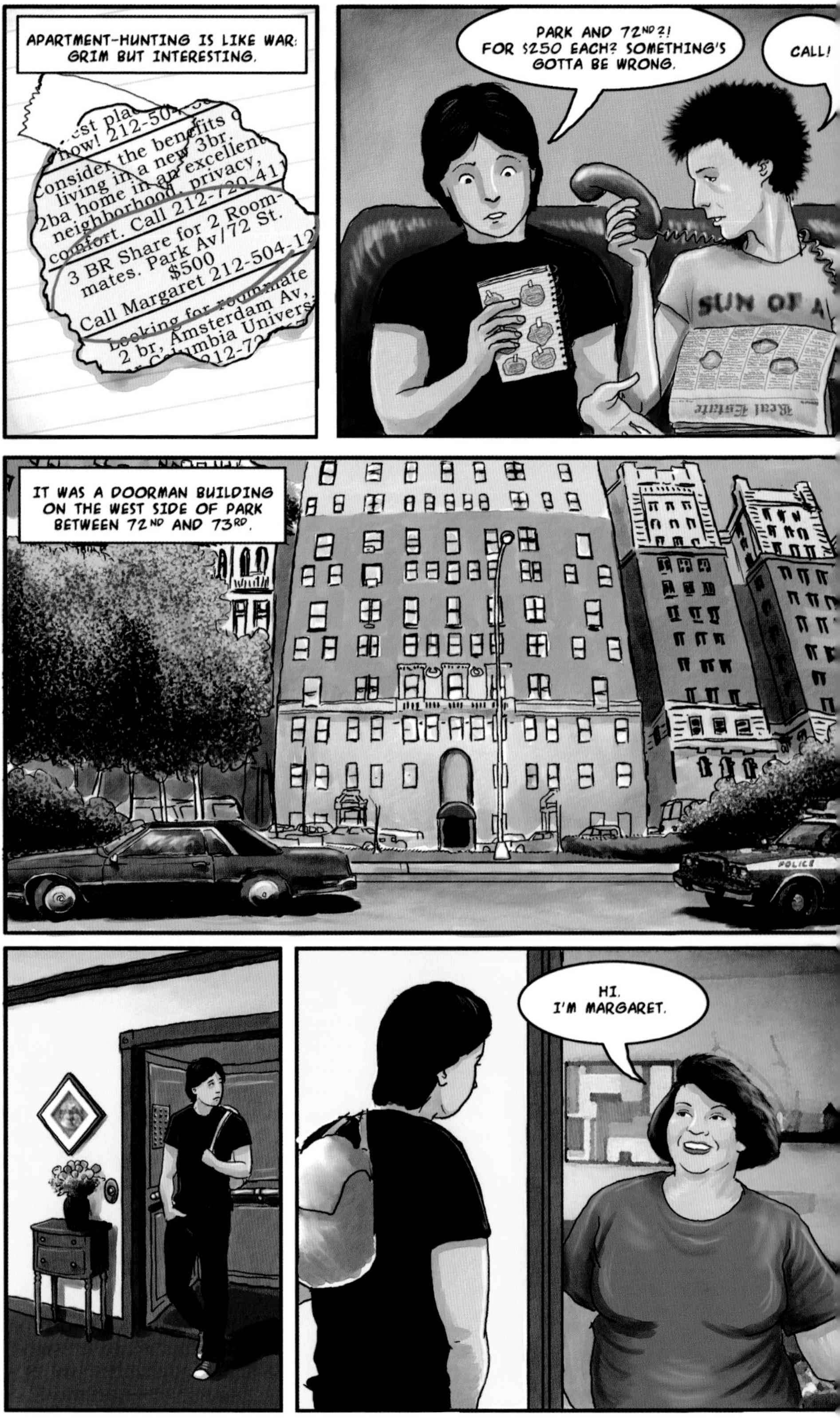
APARTMENT-HUNTING IS LIKE WAR: GRIM BUT INTERESTING.
3 BR Share for 2 Room-
mates. Park Av/72 St.
$500
PARK AND 72ND?! FOR $250 EACH? SOMETHING'S GOTTA BE WRONG.
CALL!
SUN OF A
Real Estate
IT WAS A DOORMAN BUILDING ON THE WEST SIDE OF PARK BETWEEN 72ND AND 73RD.
POLICE
HI. I'M MARGARET.

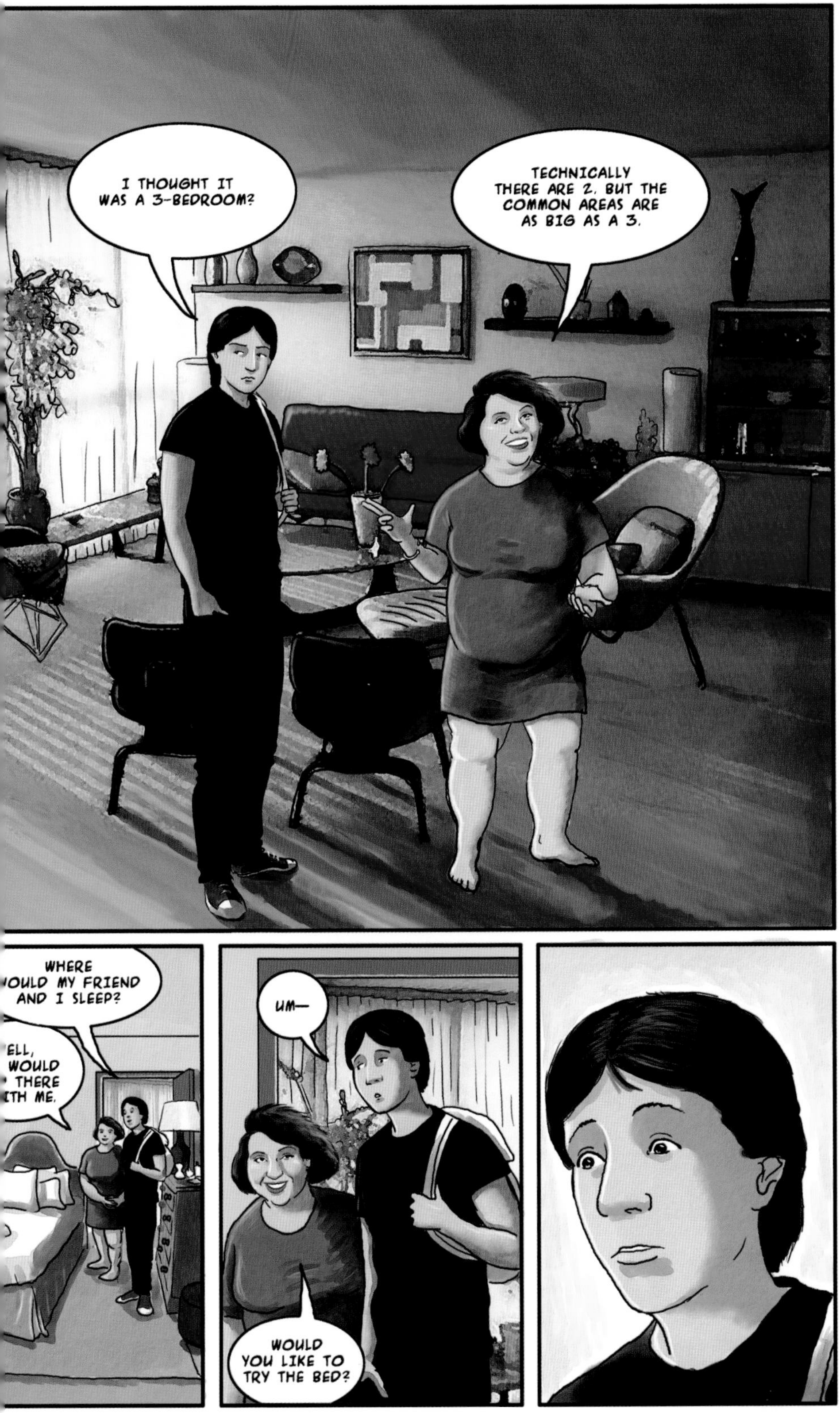
I THOUGHT IT WAS A 3-BEDROOM?
TECHNICALLY THERE ARE 2. BUT THE COMMON AREAS ARE AS BIG AS A 3.
WHERE OULD MY FRIEND AND I SLEEP?
ELL, WOULD THERE ITH ME.
UM—
WOULD YOU LIKE TO TRY THE BED?

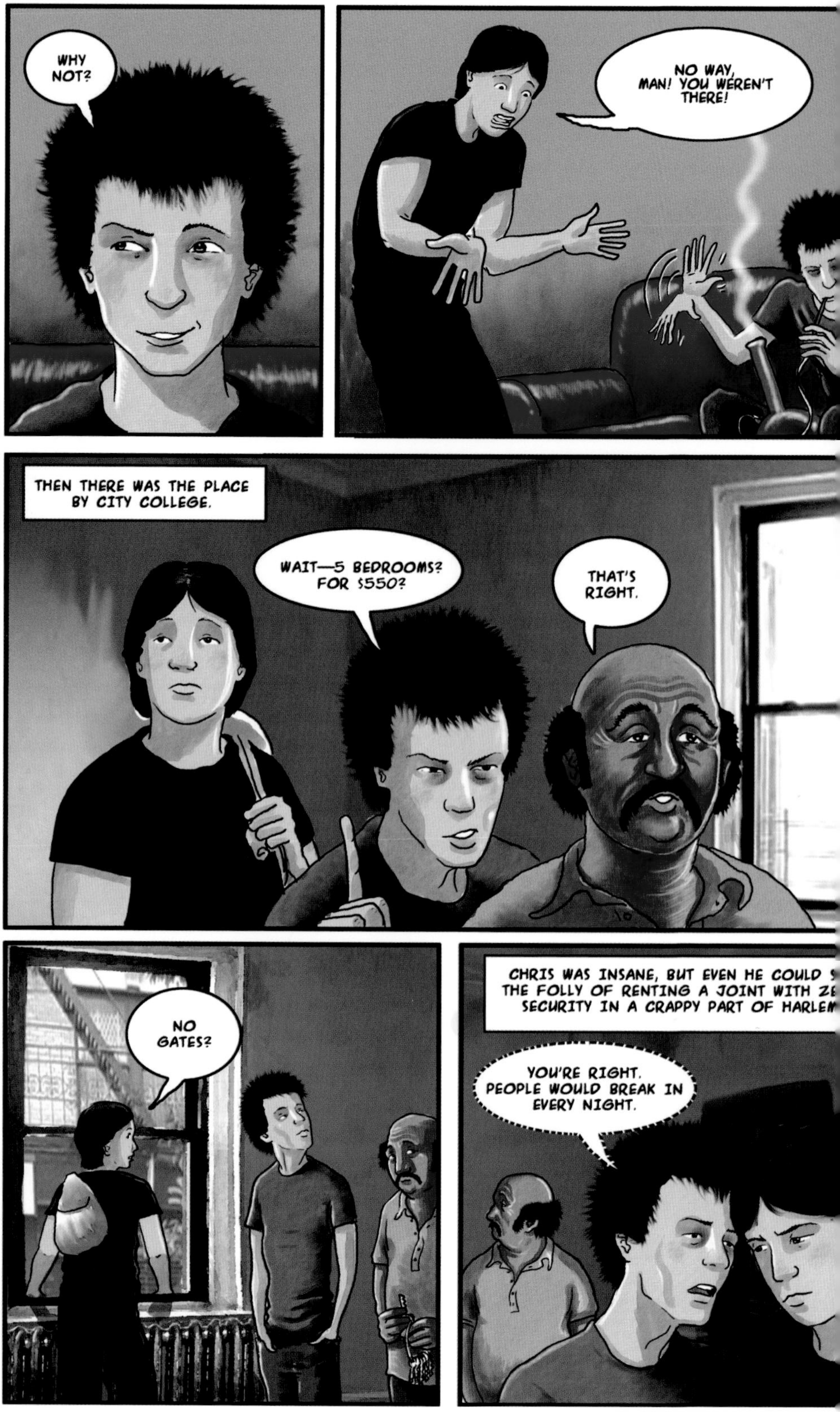
WHY NOT?
NO WAY, MAN! YOU WEREN'T THERE!
THEN THERE WAS THE PLACE BY CITY COLLEGE.
WAIT—5 BEDROOMS? FOR $550?
THAT'S RIGHT.
NO GATES?
CHRIS WAS INSANE, BUT EVEN HE COULD S
THE FOLLY OF RENTING A JOINT WITH ZE
SECURITY IN A CRAPPY PART OF HARLEM
YOU'RE RIGHT. PEOPLE WOULD BREAK IN EVERY NIGHT.

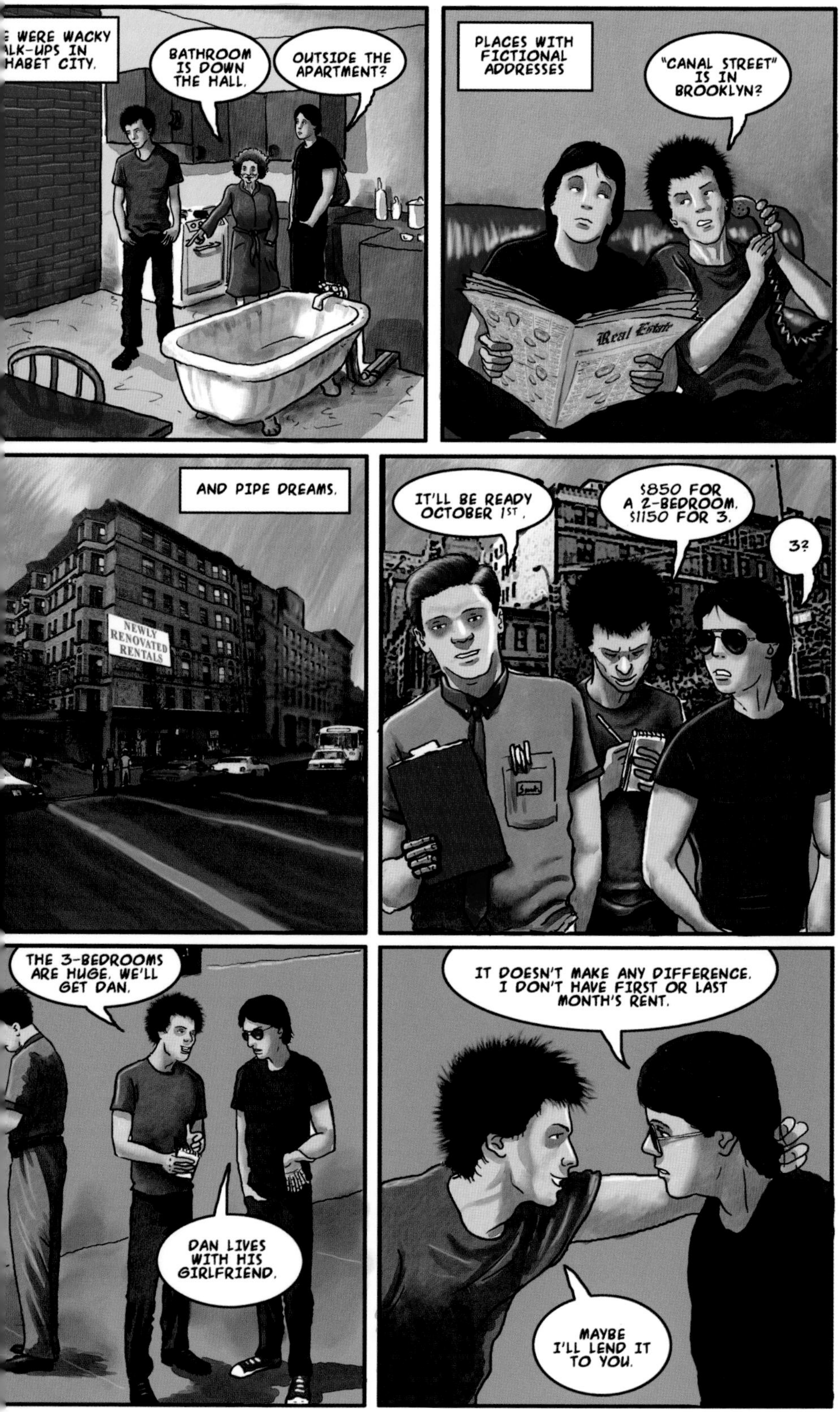
E WERE WACKY
ALK-UPS IN
HABET CITY.
BATHROOM IS DOWN THE HALL.
OUTSIDE THE APARTMENT?
PLACES WITH FICTIONAL ADDRESSES
"CANAL STREET" IS IN BROOKLYN?
Real Estate
AND PIPE DREAMS.
NEWLY RENOVATED RENTALS
IT'LL BE READY OCTOBER 1ST.
$850 FOR A 2-BEDROOM. $1150 FOR 3.
3?
THE 3-BEDROOMS ARE HUGE. WE'LL GET DAN.
DAN LIVES WITH HIS GIRLFRIEND.
IT DOESN'T MAKE ANY DIFFERENCE. I DON'T HAVE FIRST OR LAST MONTH'S RENT.
MAYBE I'LL LEND IT TO YOU.

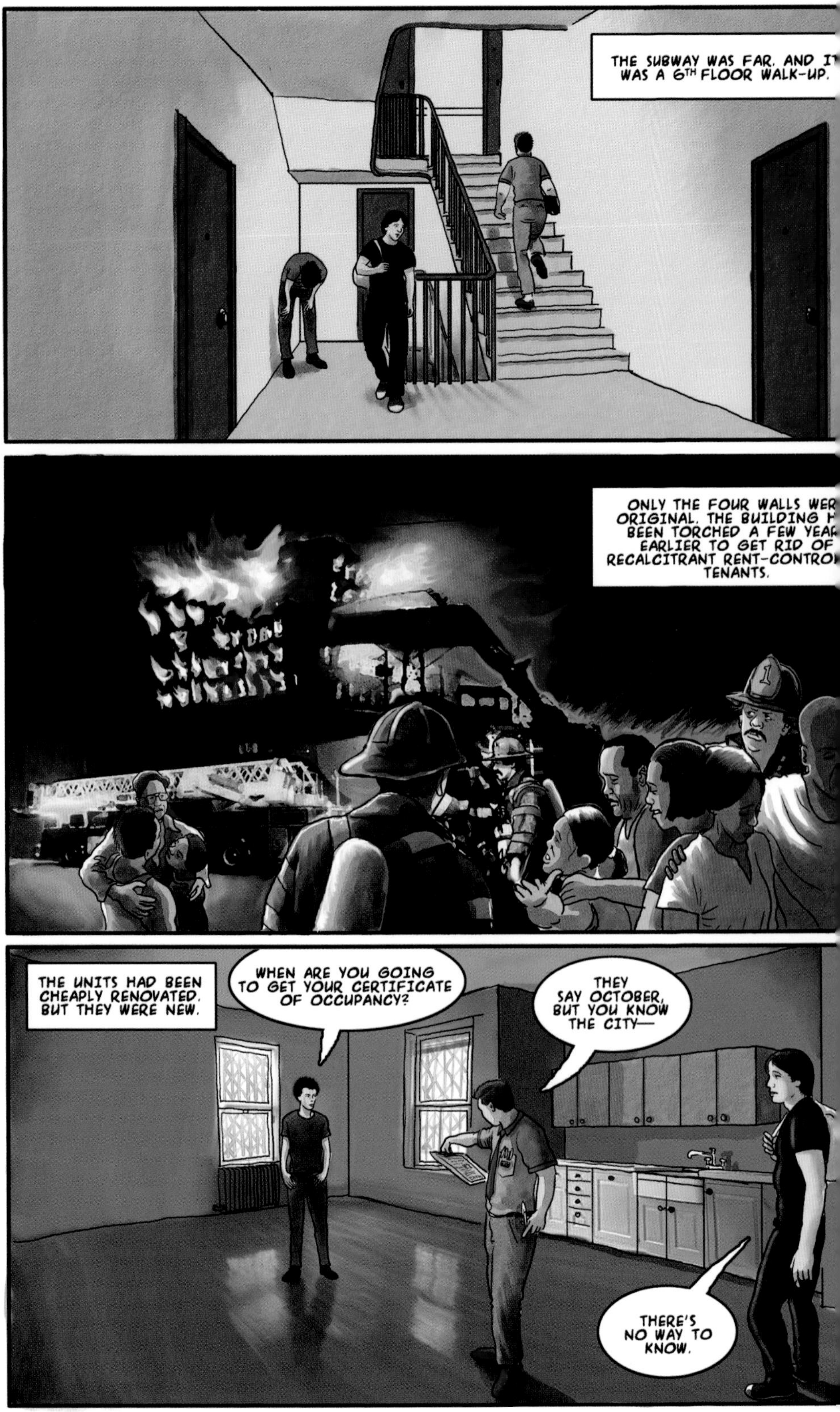
THE SUBWAY WAS FAR. AND I
WAS A 6TH FLOOR WALK-UP.
ONLY THE FOUR WALLS WER
ORIGINAL. THE BUILDING H
BEEN TORCHED A FEW YEAR
EARLIER TO GET RID OF
RECALCITRANT RENT-CONTRO
TENANTS.
THE UNITS HAD BEEN CHEAPLY RENOVATED, BUT THEY WERE NEW.
WHEN ARE YOU GOING TO GET YOUR CERTIFICATE OF OCCUPANCY?
THEY SAY OCTOBER, BUT YOU KNOW THE CITY—
THERE'S NO WAY TO KNOW.

CHRIS WAS EXCITED
[AB]OUT THE APARTMENT.

[T]HE
[D]OOR
[J]UST NEXT
[D]OOR!

THE BLUE DOOR, ON THE WEST SIDE OF AMSTERDAM BETWEEN 106TH
AND 107TH STREETS, WAS A STOREFRONT WITH A BLUE SECURITY GATE.
IT HOUSED THE DRUG OPERATION SERVING THE NEIGHBORHOOD
SOUTH OF THE COLUMBIA CAMPUS.

[WH]EN THE GATE WAS OPEN, YOU WALKED IN,
[PUT] YOUR MONEY THROUGH A WAIST-HIGH HOLE
[CUT]ED IN A WALL OF PLYWOOD, AND SAID WHAT
YOU WANTED TO BUY.

YO.
DIME.

WHEN THE STORE WAS "CLOSED," YOU WAITED BELOW
THE FIRE ESCAPE UNTIL SOMEONE LOWERED A
WICKER BASKET FROM THE WINDOW. THE STORE
OWNERS COULDN'T HAVE DRUGGIES YELLING THEIR
ORDERS FROM THE SIDEWALK, SO THE MENU WAS
LIMITED DURING OFF-HOURS: $5 FOR A NICKEL
BAG OF POT, $10 FOR A DIME, $100 FOR A TIN
OF COKE.

SOUNDED GREAT. BUT I WORRIED ABOUT SHARING
[A]N APARTMENT WITH CHRIS. CRAZY SHIT FOLLOWED
HIM WHEREVER HE WENT.

HAPPENED
RIGHT HERE.

"THE DUDES SHOT THE MOTHER-FUCKER WHILE HE WAS SITTING IN HIS CAR. BLEW OUT HIS FUCKING STOMACH".

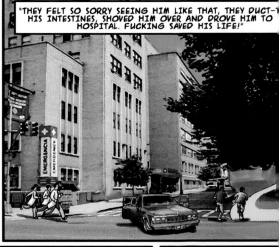

"THEY FELT SO SORRY SEEING HIM LIKE THAT, THEY DUCT-TAPED HIS INTESTINES, SHOVED HIM OVER AND DROVE HIM TO HOSPITAL. FUCKING SAVED HIS LIFE!"

NO SHIT!

FUCKED UP.

I DIDN'T TRUST CHRIS. THE ONLY PERSON I COULD COUNT ON WAS ME. ALAS, I HADN'T BEEN DOING THE MOST KICK-ASS JOB OF COMING THROUGH FOR MYSELF.

NOTHING NEW. WE'LL BE IN TOUCH.

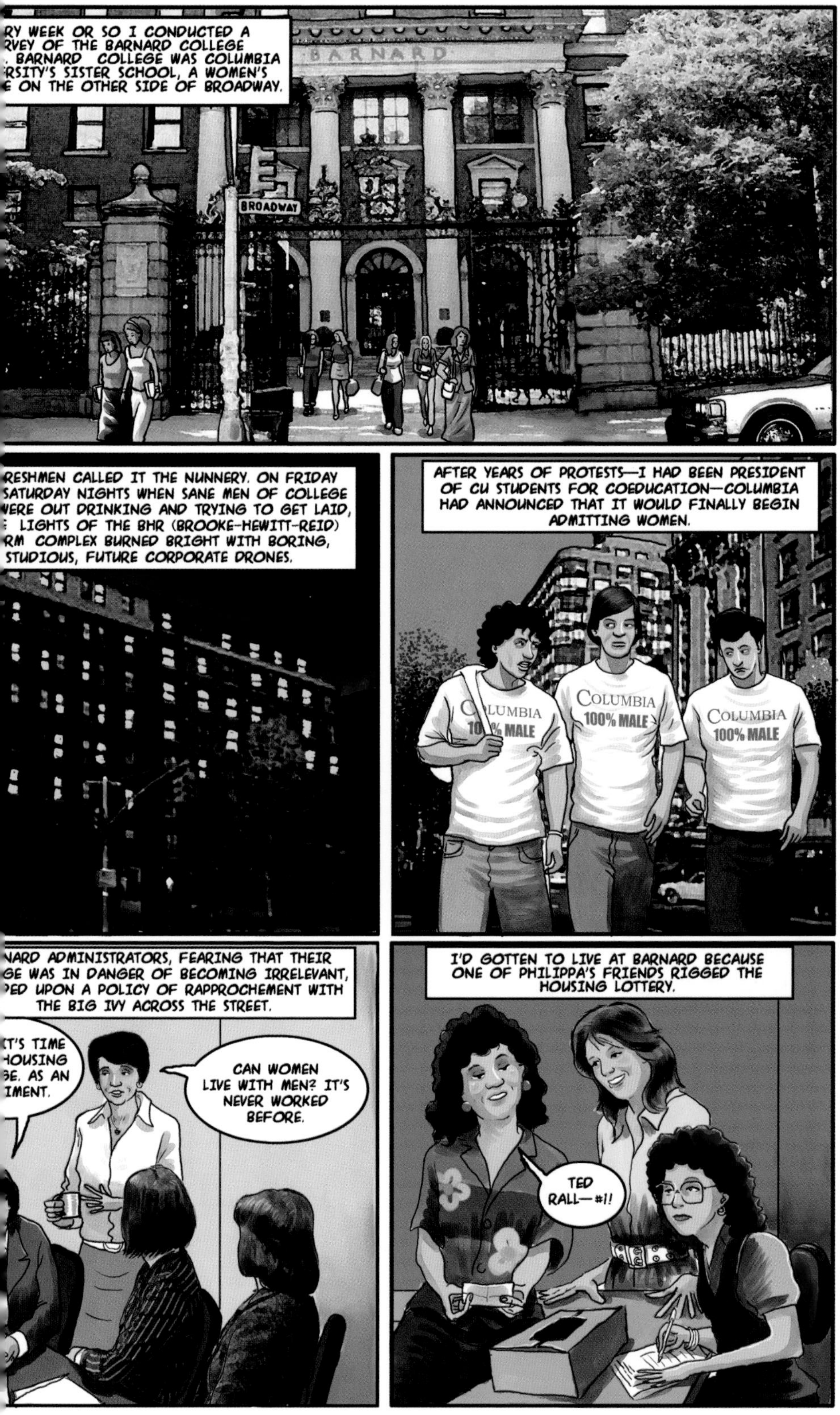

RY WEEK OR SO I CONDUCTED A RVEY OF THE BARNARD COLLEGE . BARNARD COLLEGE WAS COLUMBIA RSITY'S SISTER SCHOOL, A WOMEN'S E ON THE OTHER SIDE OF BROADWAY.
BARNARD
BROADWAY
RESHMEN CALLED IT THE NUNNERY. ON FRIDAY SATURDAY NIGHTS WHEN SANE MEN OF COLLEGE WERE OUT DRINKING AND TRYING TO GET LAID, E LIGHTS OF THE BHR (BROOKE-HEWITT-REID) RM COMPLEX BURNED BRIGHT WITH BORING, STUDIOUS, FUTURE CORPORATE DRONES.
AFTER YEARS OF PROTESTS—I HAD BEEN PRESIDENT OF CU STUDENTS FOR COEDUCATION—COLUMBIA HAD ANNOUNCED THAT IT WOULD FINALLY BEGIN ADMITTING WOMEN.
COLUMBIA 100% MALE
COLUMBIA 100% MALE
COLUMBIA 100% MALE
NARD ADMINISTRATORS, FEARING THAT THEIR GE WAS IN DANGER OF BECOMING IRRELEVANT, PED UPON A POLICY OF RAPPROCHEMENT WITH THE BIG IVY ACROSS THE STREET.
T'S TIME HOUSING GE. AS AN IMENT.
CAN WOMEN LIVE WITH MEN? IT'S NEVER WORKED BEFORE.
I'D GOTTEN TO LIVE AT BARNARD BECAUSE ONE OF PHILIPPA'S FRIENDS RIGGED THE HOUSING LOTTERY.
TED RALL—#1!

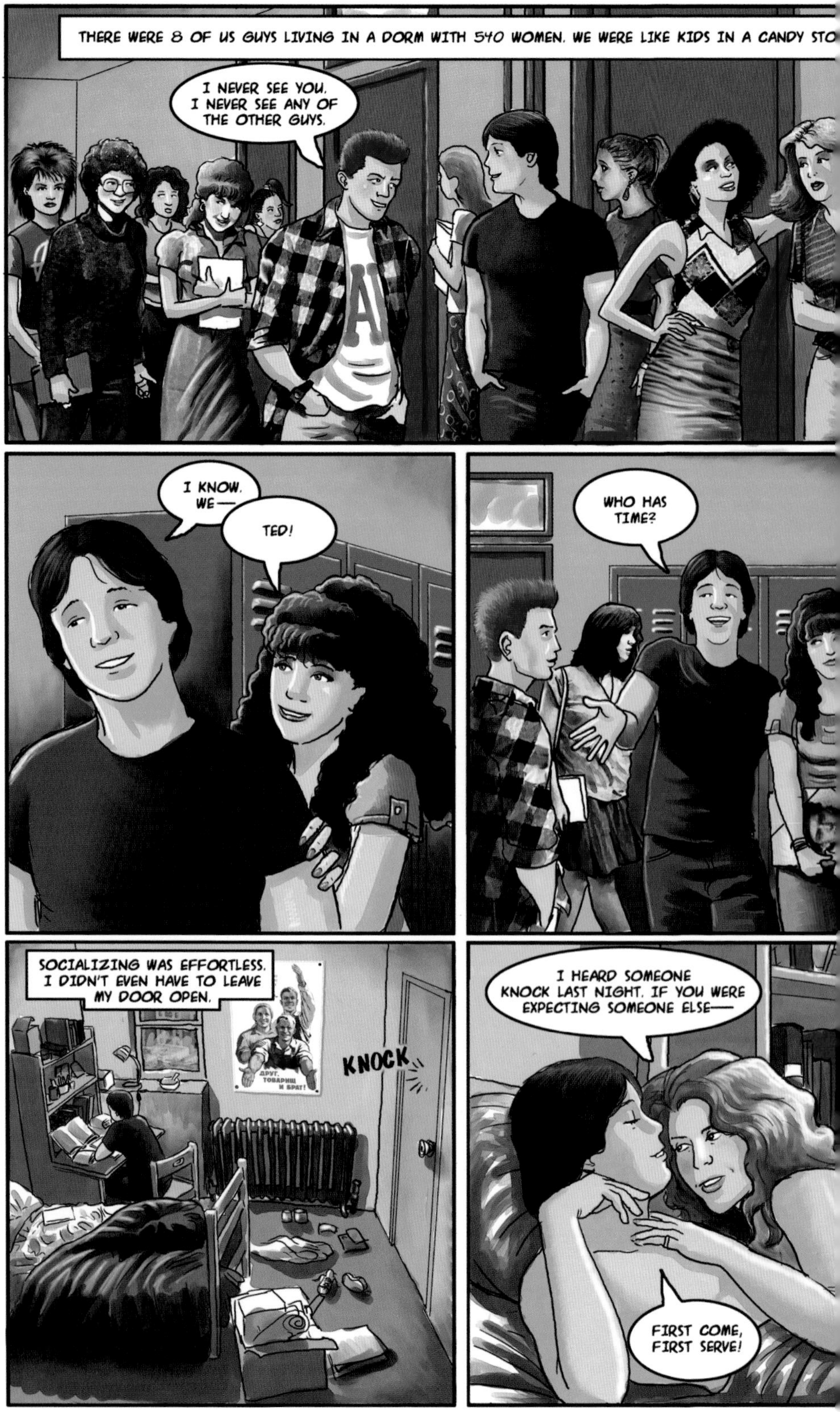
THERE WERE 8 OF US GUYS LIVING IN A DORM WITH 540 WOMEN. WE WERE LIKE KIDS IN A CANDY STO
I NEVER SEE YOU. I NEVER SEE ANY OF THE OTHER GUYS.
I KNOW. WE—
TED!
WHO HAS TIME?
SOCIALIZING WAS EFFORTLESS. I DIDN'T EVEN HAVE TO LEAVE MY DOOR OPEN.
ДРУГ, ТОВАРИЩ И БРАТ!
KNOCK
I HEARD SOMEONE KNOCK LAST NIGHT. IF YOU WERE EXPECTING SOMEONE ELSE—
FIRST COME, FIRST SERVE!

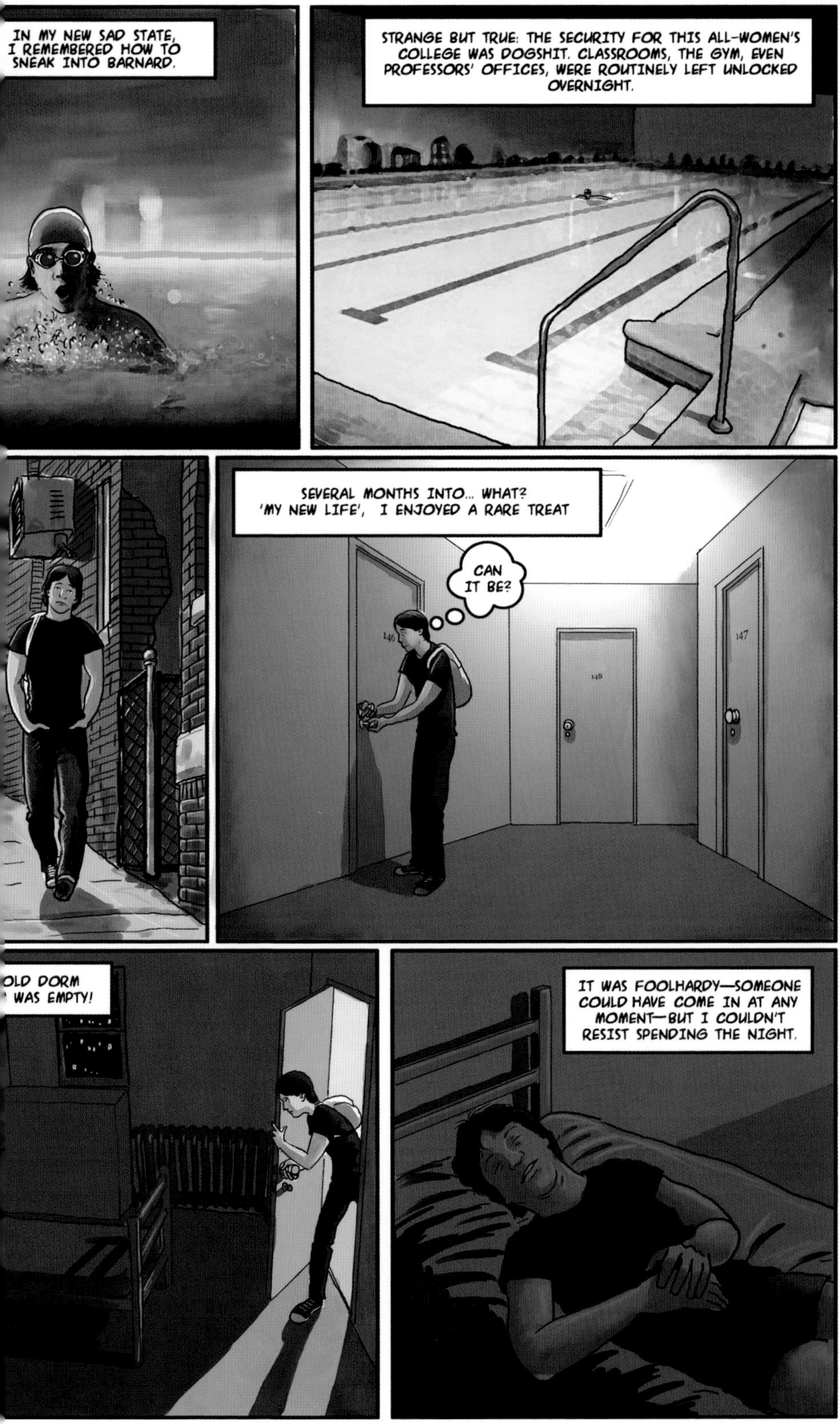
IN MY NEW SAD STATE, I REMEMBERED HOW TO SNEAK INTO BARNARD.
STRANGE BUT TRUE: THE SECURITY FOR THIS ALL-WOMEN'S COLLEGE WAS DOGSHIT. CLASSROOMS, THE GYM, EVEN PROFESSORS' OFFICES, WERE ROUTINELY LEFT UNLOCKED OVERNIGHT.
SEVERAL MONTHS INTO... WHAT? 'MY NEW LIFE', I ENJOYED A RARE TREAT
CAN IT BE?
OLD DORM
WAS EMPTY!
IT WAS FOOLHARDY—SOMEONE COULD HAVE COME IN AT ANY MOMENT—BUT I COULDN'T RESIST SPENDING THE NIGHT.

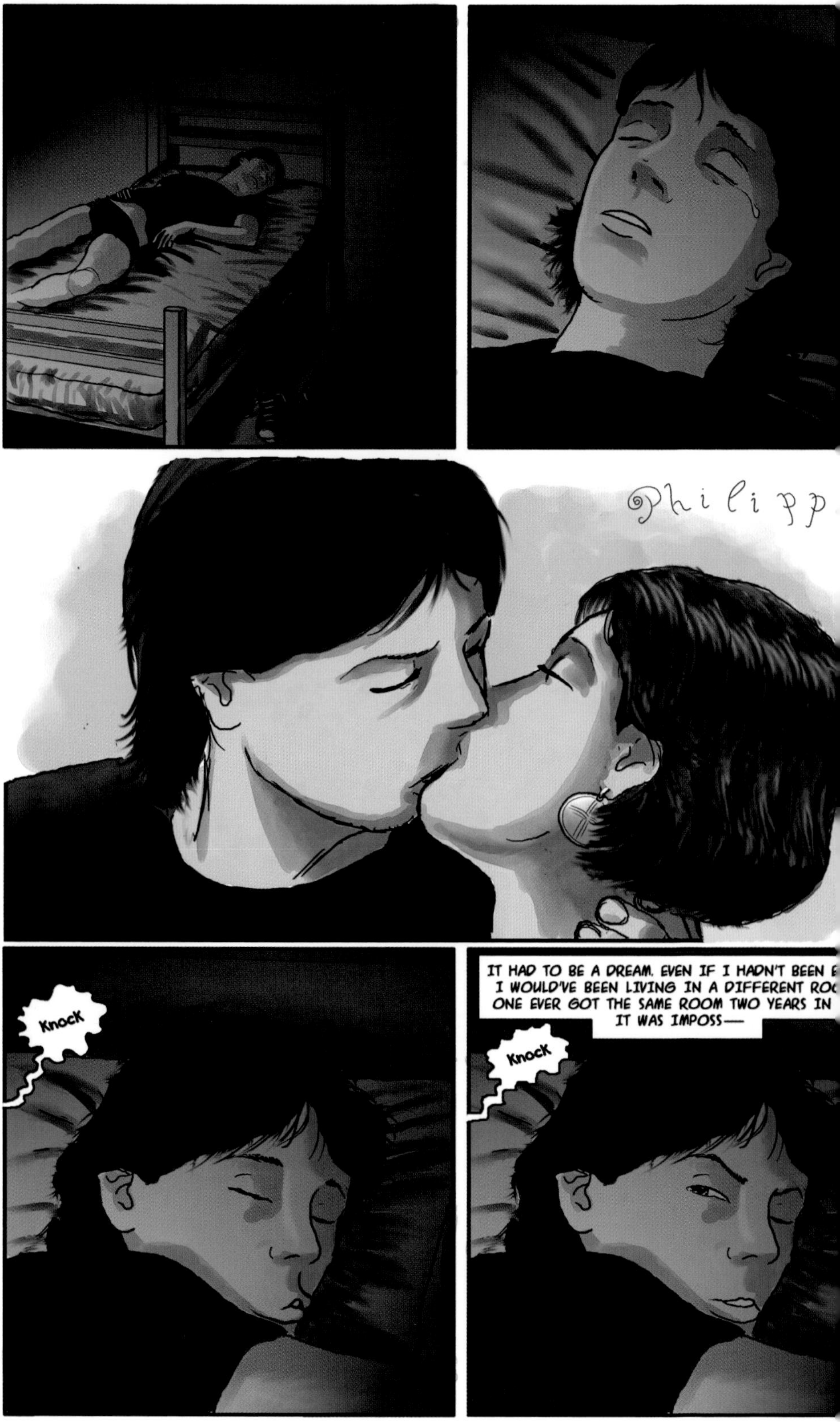
Philipp
Knock
IT HAD TO BE A DREAM. EVEN IF I HADN'T BEEN
I WOULD'VE BEEN LIVING IN A DIFFERENT RO
ONE EVER GOT THE SAME ROOM TWO YEARS IN
IT WAS IMPOSS—
Knock

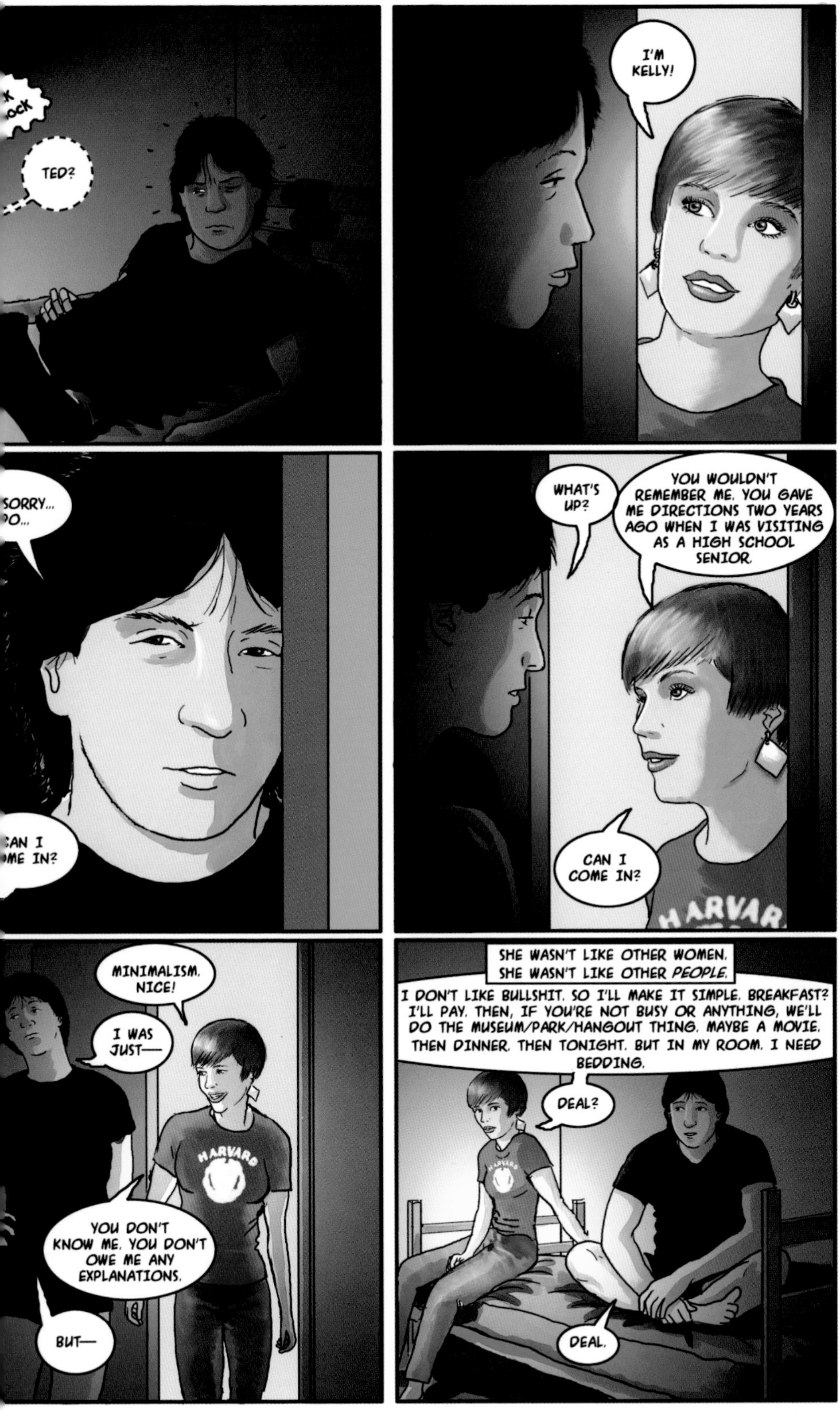

TED?
I'M KELLY!
SORRY...
ME IN?
WHAT'S UP?
YOU WOULDN'T REMEMBER ME. YOU GAVE ME DIRECTIONS TWO YEARS AGO WHEN I WAS VISITING AS A HIGH SCHOOL SENIOR.
CAN I COME IN?
MINIMALISM. NICE!
I WAS JUST—
YOU DON'T KNOW ME. YOU DON'T OWE ME ANY EXPLANATIONS.
BUT—
SHE WASN'T LIKE OTHER WOMEN. SHE WASN'T LIKE OTHER *PEOPLE*.
I DON'T LIKE BULLSHIT. SO I'LL MAKE IT SIMPLE. BREAKFAST? I'LL PAY. THEN, IF YOU'RE NOT BUSY OR ANYTHING, WE'LL DO THE MUSEUM/PARK/HANGOUT THING. MAYBE A MOVIE. THEN DINNER. THEN TONIGHT. BUT IN MY ROOM. I NEED BEDDING.
DEAL?
DEAL.

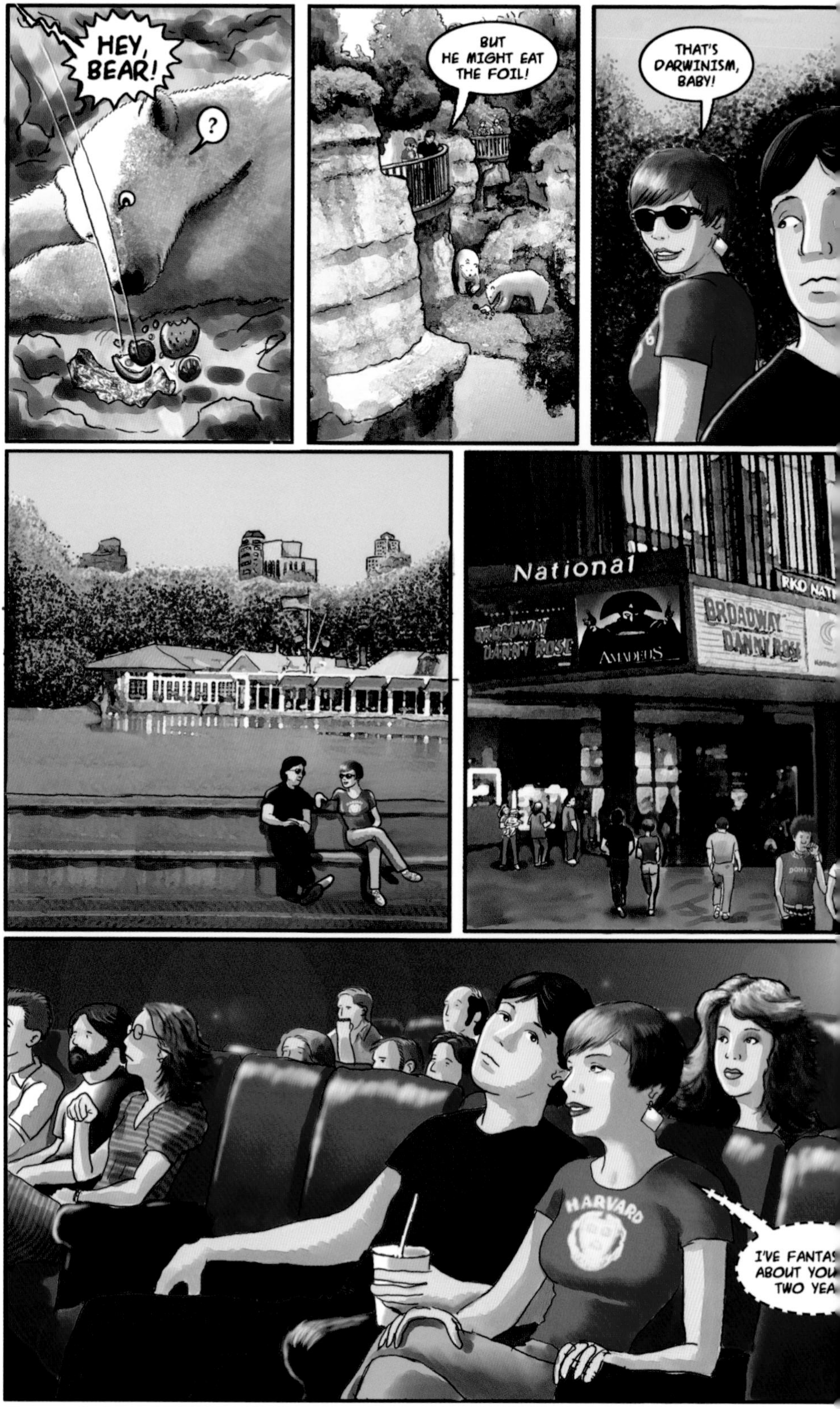
HEY, BEAR!
?
BUT HE MIGHT EAT THE FOIL!
THAT'S DARWINISM, BABY!
National
BROADWAY DANNY ROSE
AMADEUS
RKO NATI
BROADWAY DANNY ROSE
HARVARD
I'VE FANTAS
ABOUT YOU
TWO YEA

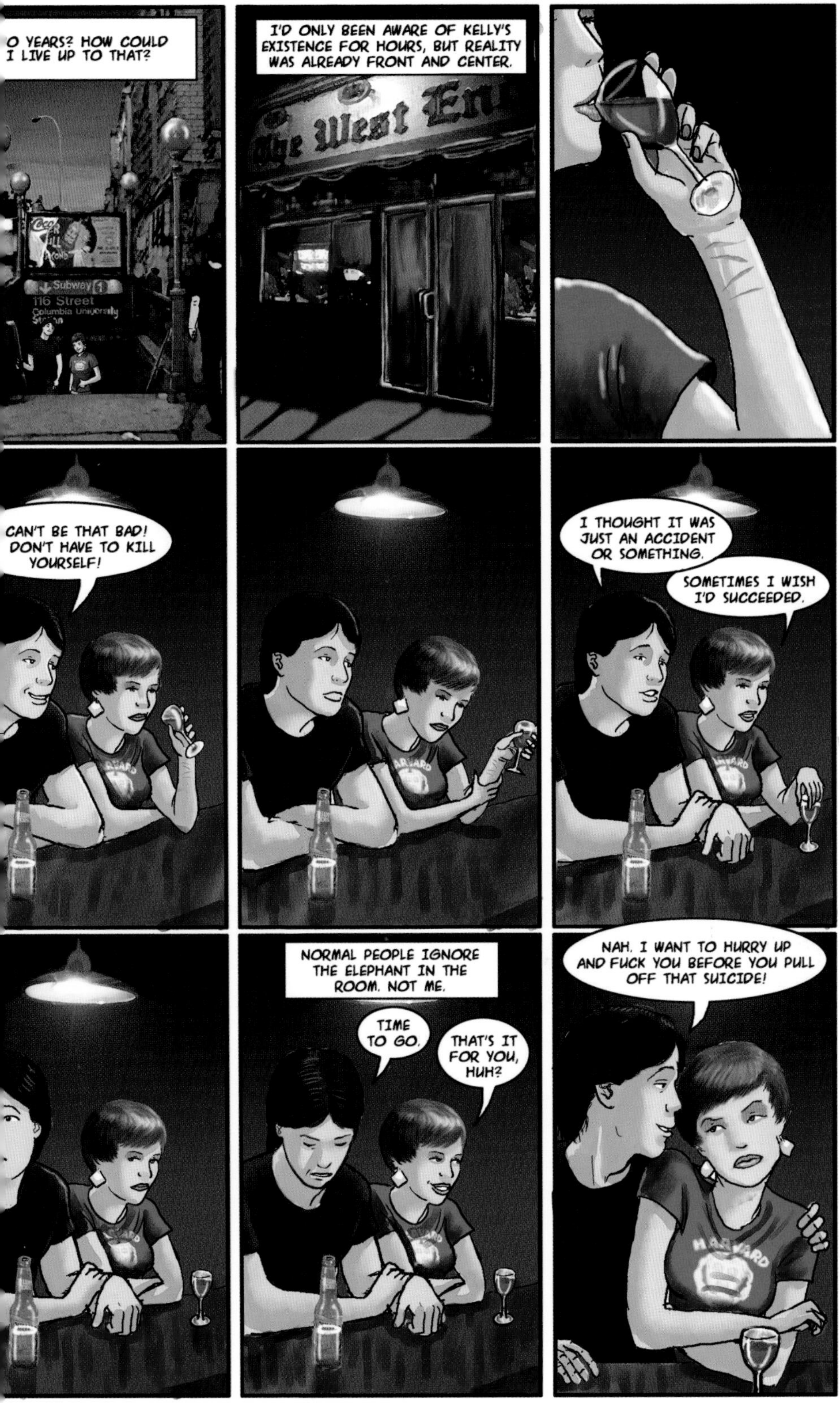
O YEARS? HOW COULD I LIVE UP TO THAT?
I'D ONLY BEEN AWARE OF KELLY'S EXISTENCE FOR HOURS, BUT REALITY WAS ALREADY FRONT AND CENTER.
CAN'T BE THAT BAD! DON'T HAVE TO KILL YOURSELF!
I THOUGHT IT WAS JUST AN ACCIDENT OR SOMETHING.
SOMETIMES I WISH I'D SUCCEEDED.
NORMAL PEOPLE IGNORE THE ELEPHANT IN THE ROOM. NOT ME.
TIME TO GO.
THAT'S IT FOR YOU, HUH?
NAH. I WANT TO HURRY UP AND FUCK YOU BEFORE YOU PULL OFF THAT SUICIDE!

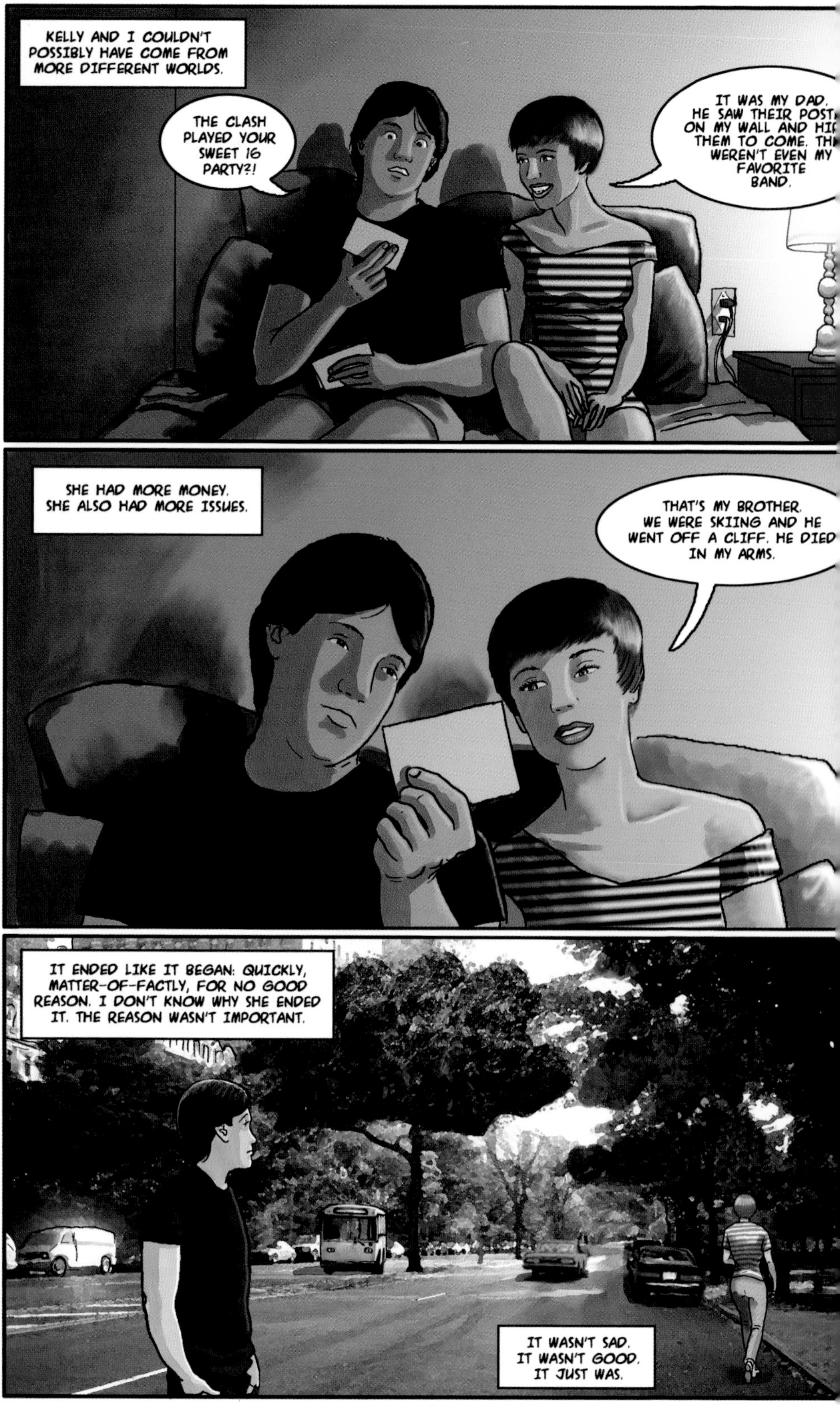
KELLY AND I COULDN'T POSSIBLY HAVE COME FROM MORE DIFFERENT WORLDS.
THE CLASH PLAYED YOUR SWEET 16 PARTY?!
IT WAS MY DAD. HE SAW THEIR POST ON MY WALL AND HI THEM TO COME. TH WEREN'T EVEN MY FAVORITE BAND.
SHE HAD MORE MONEY. SHE ALSO HAD MORE ISSUES.
THAT'S MY BROTHER. WE WERE SKIING AND HE WENT OFF A CLIFF. HE DIED IN MY ARMS.
IT ENDED LIKE IT BEGAN: QUICKLY, MATTER-OF-FACTLY, FOR NO GOOD REASON. I DON'T KNOW WHY SHE ENDED IT. THE REASON WASN'T IMPORTANT.
IT WASN'T SAD. IT WASN'T GOOD. IT JUST WAS.

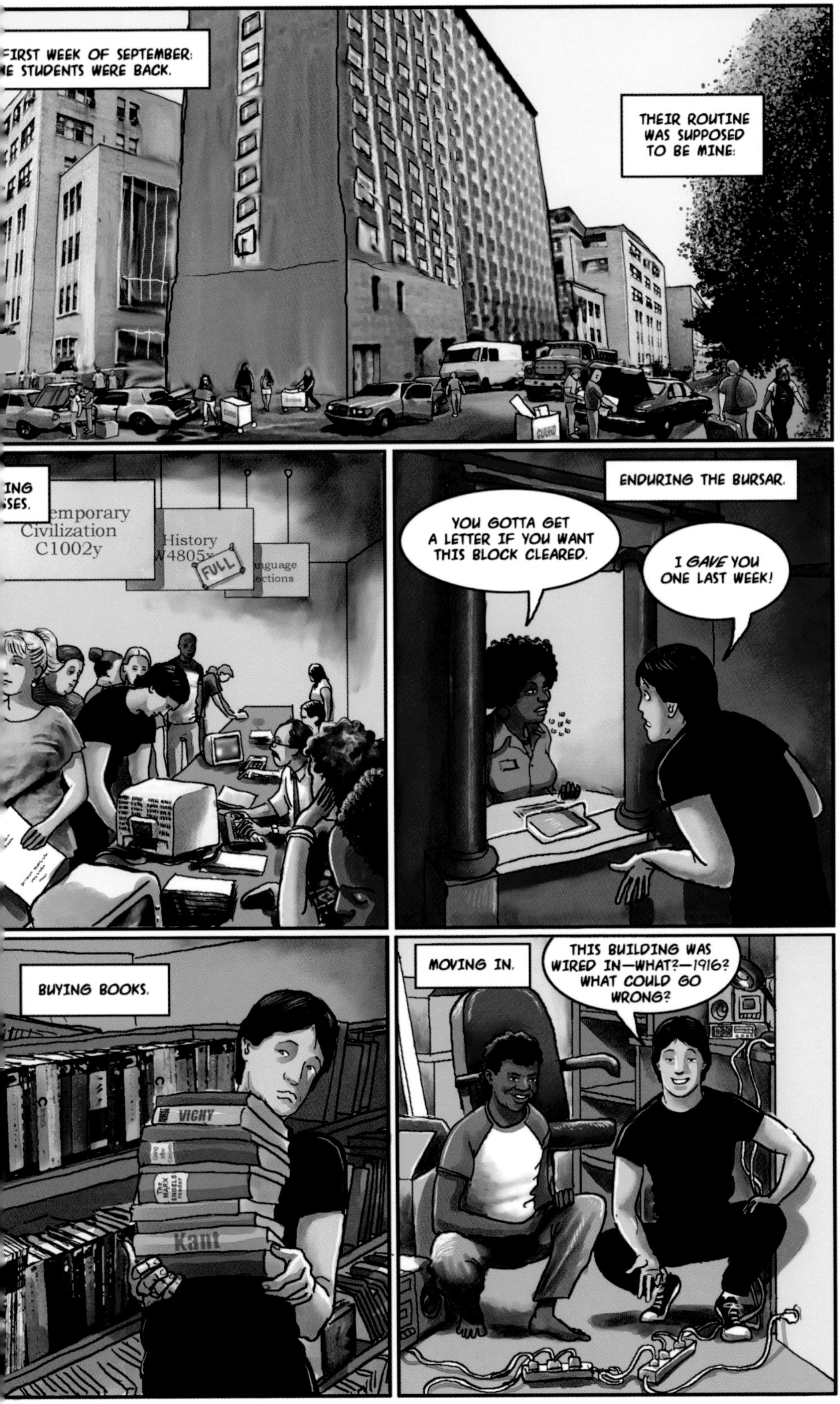
FIRST WEEK OF SEPTEMBER:
E STUDENTS WERE BACK.
THEIR ROUTINE WAS SUPPOSED TO BE MINE:
ING
SSES.
emporary Civilization C1002y
History W4805x
FULL
nguage ections
ENDURING THE BURSAR.
YOU GOTTA GET A LETTER IF YOU WANT THIS BLOCK CLEARED.
I GAVE YOU ONE LAST WEEK!
BUYING BOOKS.
VICHY
Kant
MOVING IN.
THIS BUILDING WAS WIRED IN—WHAT?—1916? WHAT COULD GO WRONG?

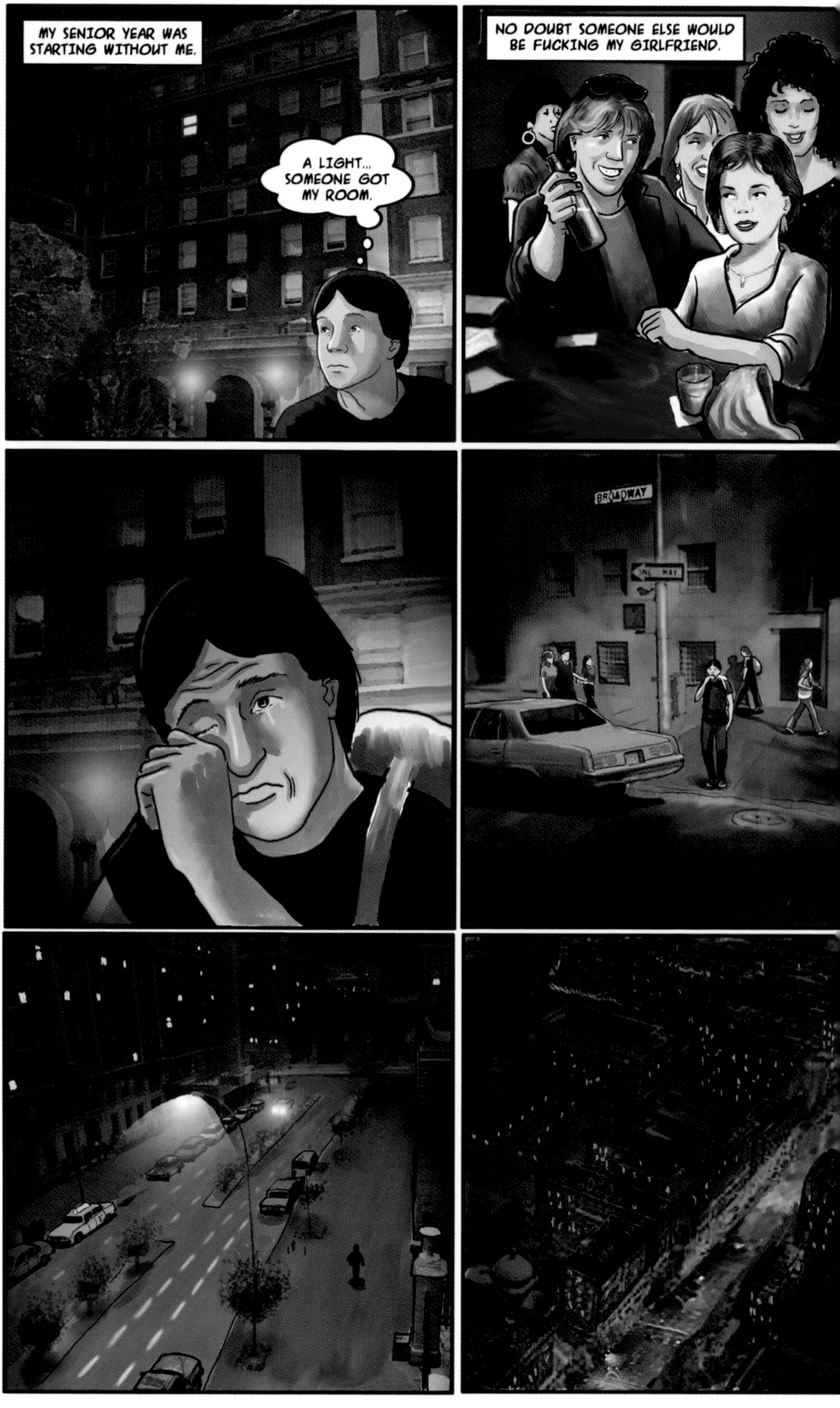
MY SENIOR YEAR WAS STARTING WITHOUT ME.
A LIGHT... SOMEONE GOT MY ROOM.
NO DOUBT SOMEONE ELSE WOULD BE FUCKING MY GIRLFRIEND.
BROADWAY

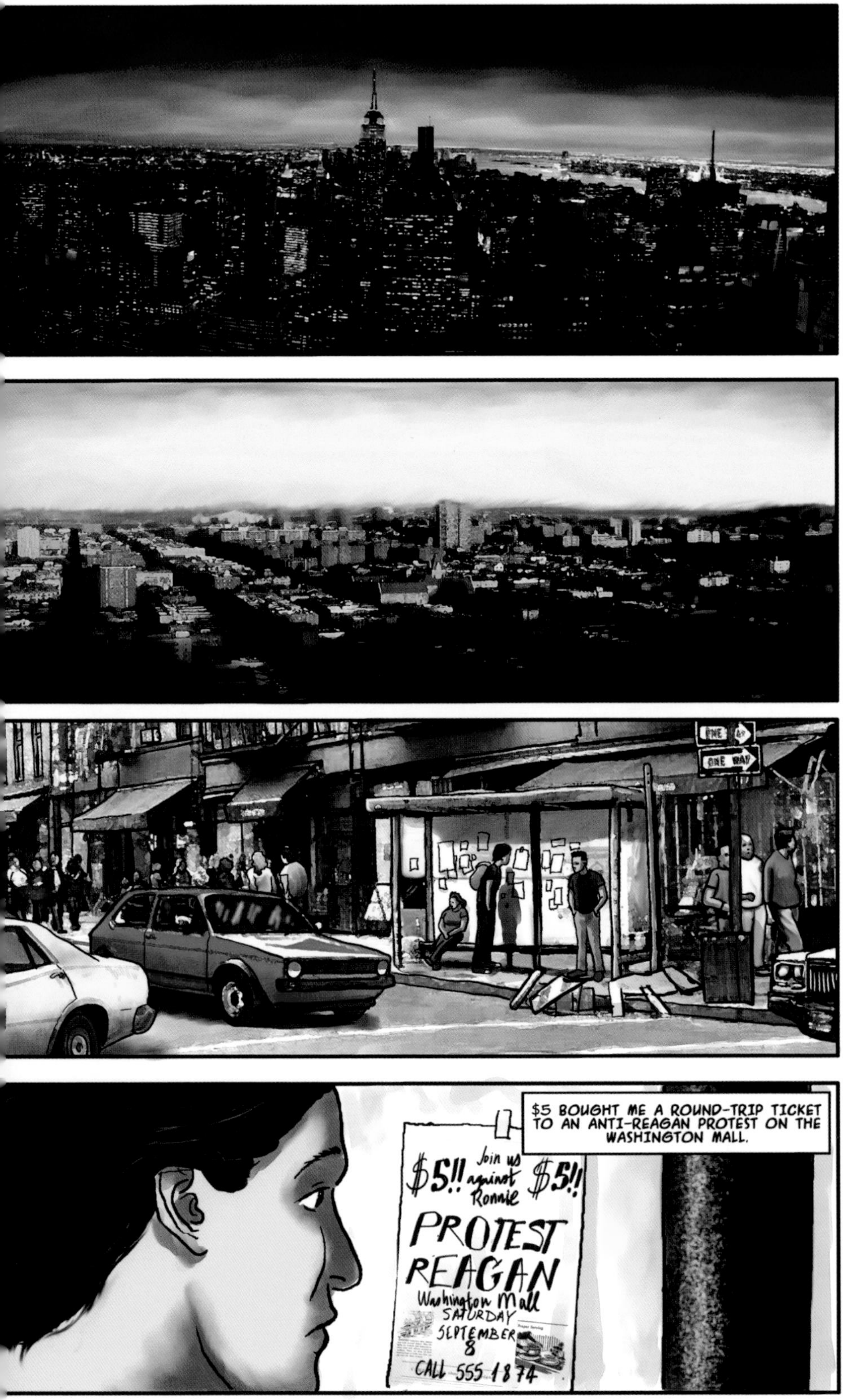

$5 BOUGHT ME A ROUND-TRIP TICKET TO AN ANTI-REAGAN PROTEST ON THE WASHINGTON MALL.
$5!! Join us against Ronnie $5!!
PROTEST REAGAN
Washington Mall
SATURDAY
SEPTEMBER 8
CALL 555 1874

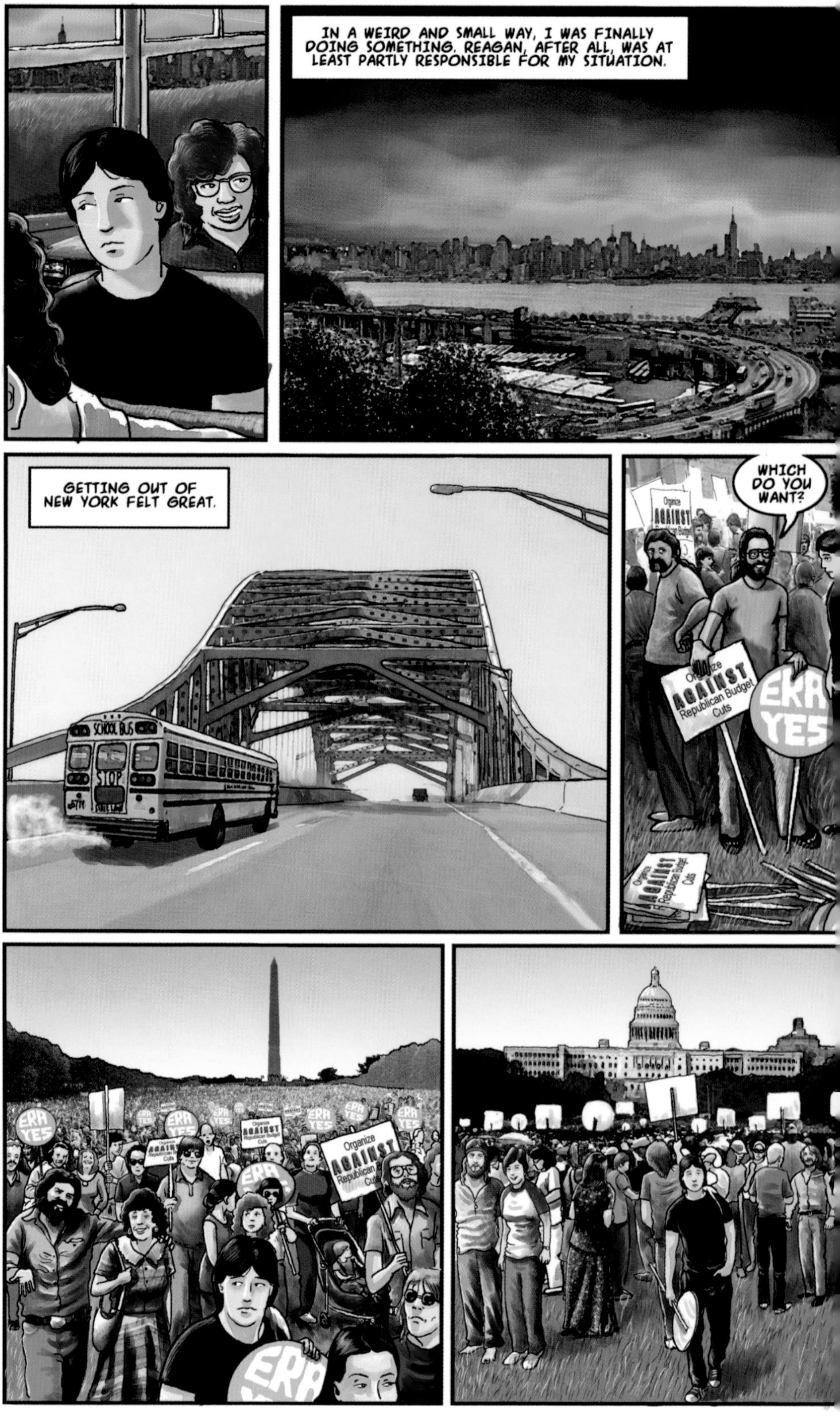
IN A WEIRD AND SMALL WAY, I WAS FINALLY DOING SOMETHING. REAGAN, AFTER ALL, WAS AT LEAST PARTLY RESPONSIBLE FOR MY SITUATION.
GETTING OUT OF NEW YORK FELT GREAT.
SCHOOL BUS
STOP
WHICH DO YOU WANT?
Organize AGAINST Republican Budget Cuts
ERA YES

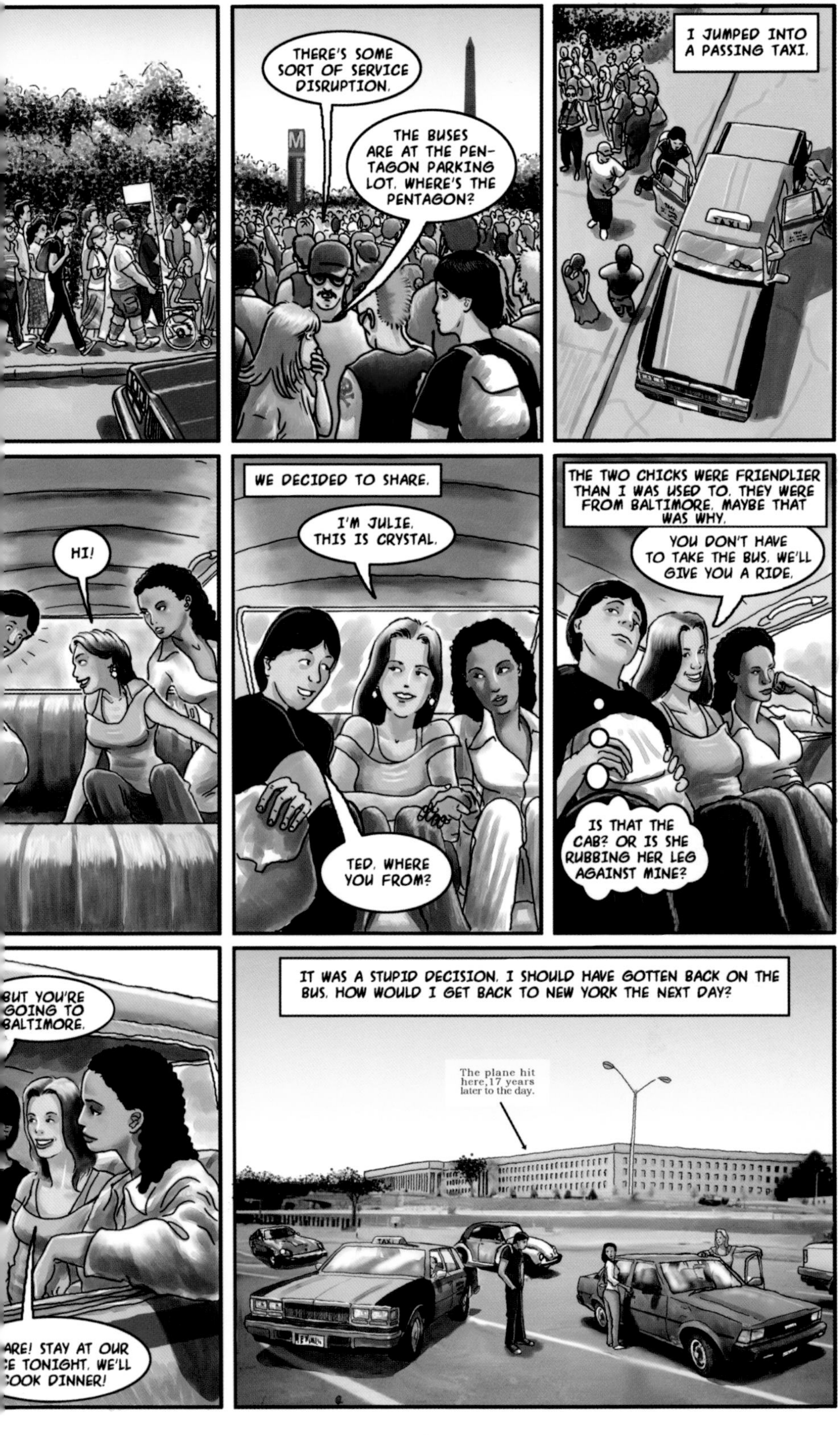
THERE'S SOME SORT OF SERVICE DISRUPTION.
THE BUSES ARE AT THE PENTAGON PARKING LOT. WHERE'S THE PENTAGON?
I JUMPED INTO A PASSING TAXI.
HI!
WE DECIDED TO SHARE.
I'M JULIE. THIS IS CRYSTAL.
TED, WHERE YOU FROM?
THE TWO CHICKS WERE FRIENDLIER THAN I WAS USED TO. THEY WERE FROM BALTIMORE. MAYBE THAT WAS WHY.
YOU DON'T HAVE TO TAKE THE BUS. WE'LL GIVE YOU A RIDE.
IS THAT THE CAB? OR IS SHE RUBBING HER LEG AGAINST MINE?
BUT YOU'RE GOING TO BALTIMORE.
ARE! STAY AT OUR
E TONIGHT. WE'LL
COOK DINNER!
IT WAS A STUPID DECISION. I SHOULD HAVE GOTTEN BACK ON THE BUS. HOW WOULD I GET BACK TO NEW YORK THE NEXT DAY?
The plane hit here, 17 years later to the day.

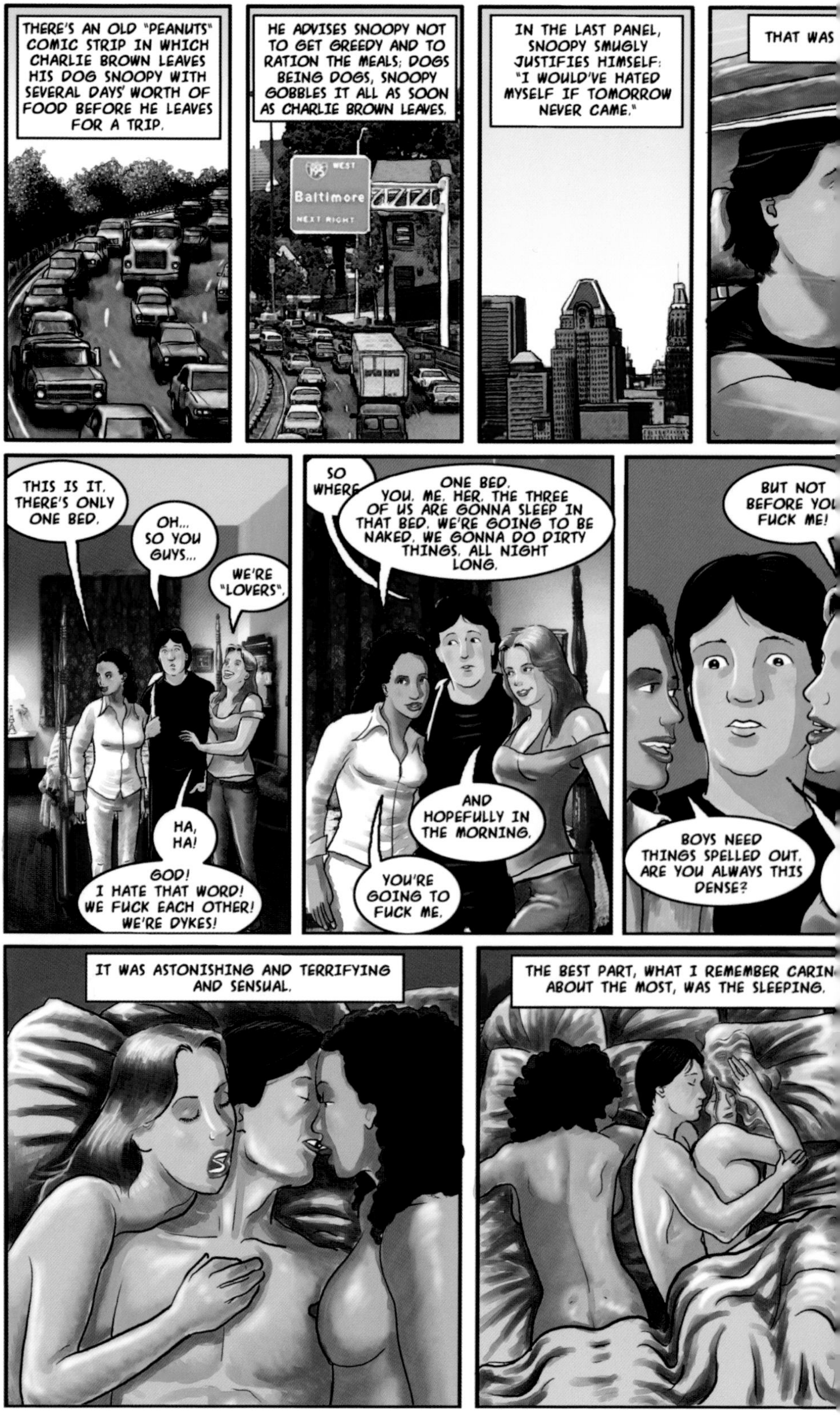

THERE'S AN OLD "PEANUTS" COMIC STRIP IN WHICH CHARLIE BROWN LEAVES HIS DOG SNOOPY WITH SEVERAL DAYS' WORTH OF FOOD BEFORE HE LEAVES FOR A TRIP.
HE ADVISES SNOOPY NOT TO GET GREEDY AND TO RATION THE MEALS; DOGS BEING DOGS, SNOOPY GOBBLES IT ALL AS SOON AS CHARLIE BROWN LEAVES.
95 WEST
Baltimore
NEXT RIGHT
IN THE LAST PANEL, SNOOPY SMUGLY JUSTIFIES HIMSELF: "I WOULD'VE HATED MYSELF IF TOMORROW NEVER CAME."
THAT WAS
THIS IS IT. THERE'S ONLY ONE BED.
OH... SO YOU GUYS...
WE'RE "LOVERS".
HA, HA!
GOD! I HATE THAT WORD! WE FUCK EACH OTHER! WE'RE DYKES!
SO WHERE
ONE BED. YOU. ME. HER. THE THREE OF US ARE GONNA SLEEP IN THAT BED. WE'RE GOING TO BE NAKED. WE GONNA DO DIRTY THINGS. ALL NIGHT LONG.
AND HOPEFULLY IN THE MORNING.
YOU'RE GOING TO FUCK ME.
BUT NOT BEFORE YO
FUCK ME!
BOYS NEED THINGS SPELLED OUT. ARE YOU ALWAYS THIS DENSE?
IT WAS ASTONISHING AND TERRIFYING AND SENSUAL.
THE BEST PART, WHAT I REMEMBER CARIN
ABOUT THE MOST, WAS THE SLEEPING.

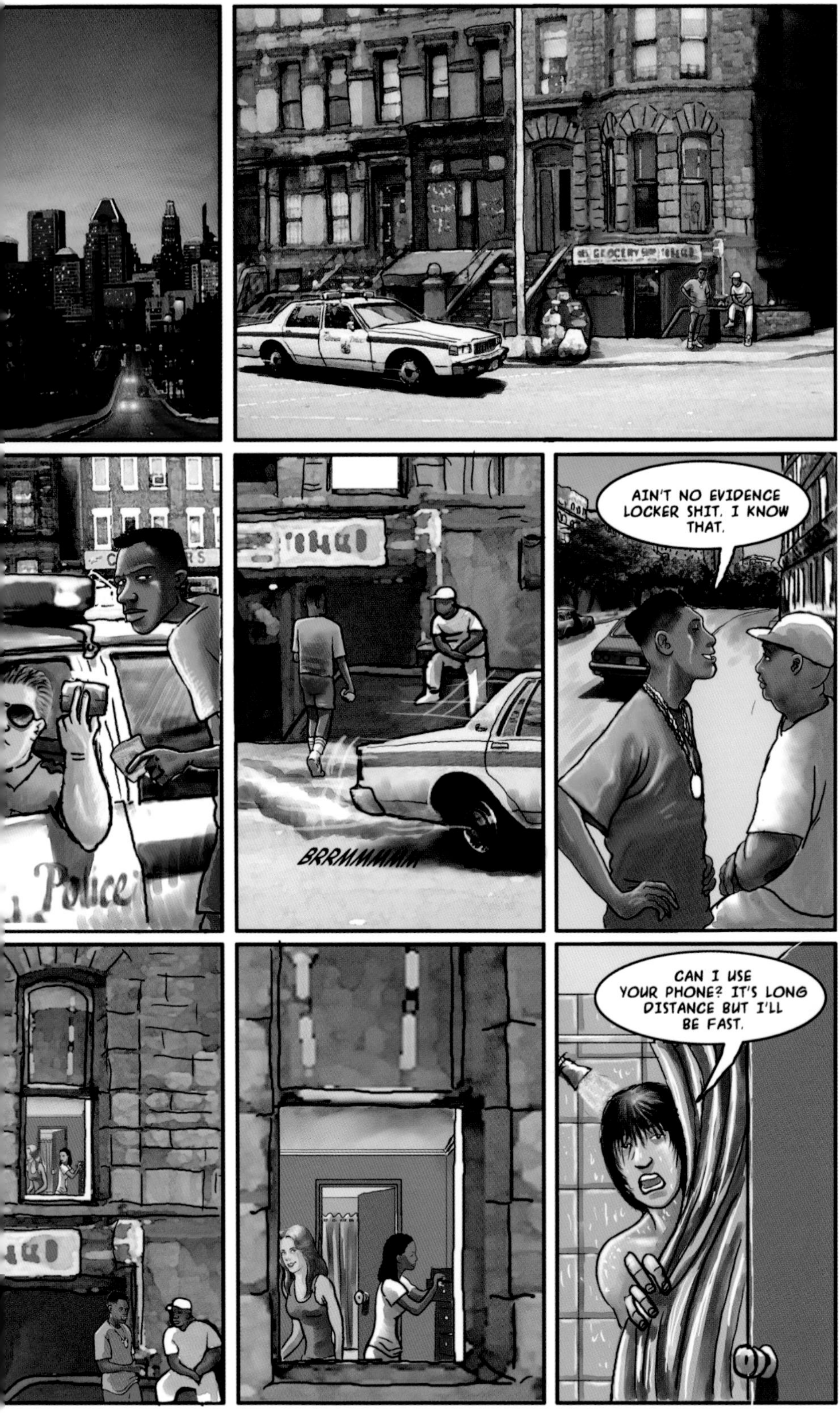
GROCERY
Police
BRRMMMMM
AIN'T NO EVIDENCE LOCKER SHIT. I KNOW THAT.
CAN I USE YOUR PHONE? IT'S LONG DISTANCE BUT I'LL BE FAST.

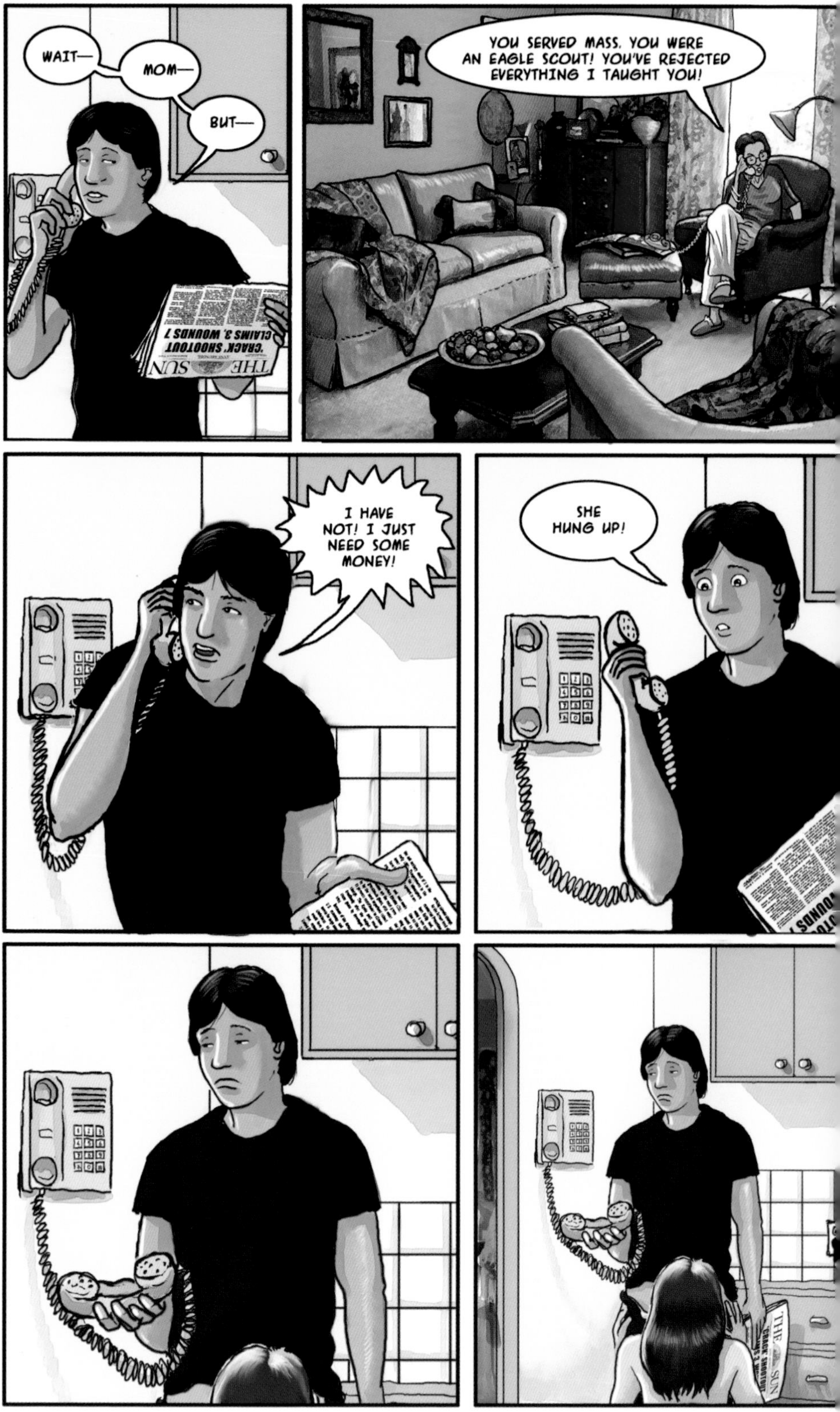
WAIT—
MOM—
BUT—
THE SUN
'CRACK' SHOOTOUT CLAIMS 3, WOUNDS 7
YOU SERVED MASS. YOU WERE AN EAGLE SCOUT! YOU'VE REJECTED EVERYTHING I TAUGHT YOU!
I HAVE NOT! I JUST NEED SOME MONEY!
SHE HUNG UP!

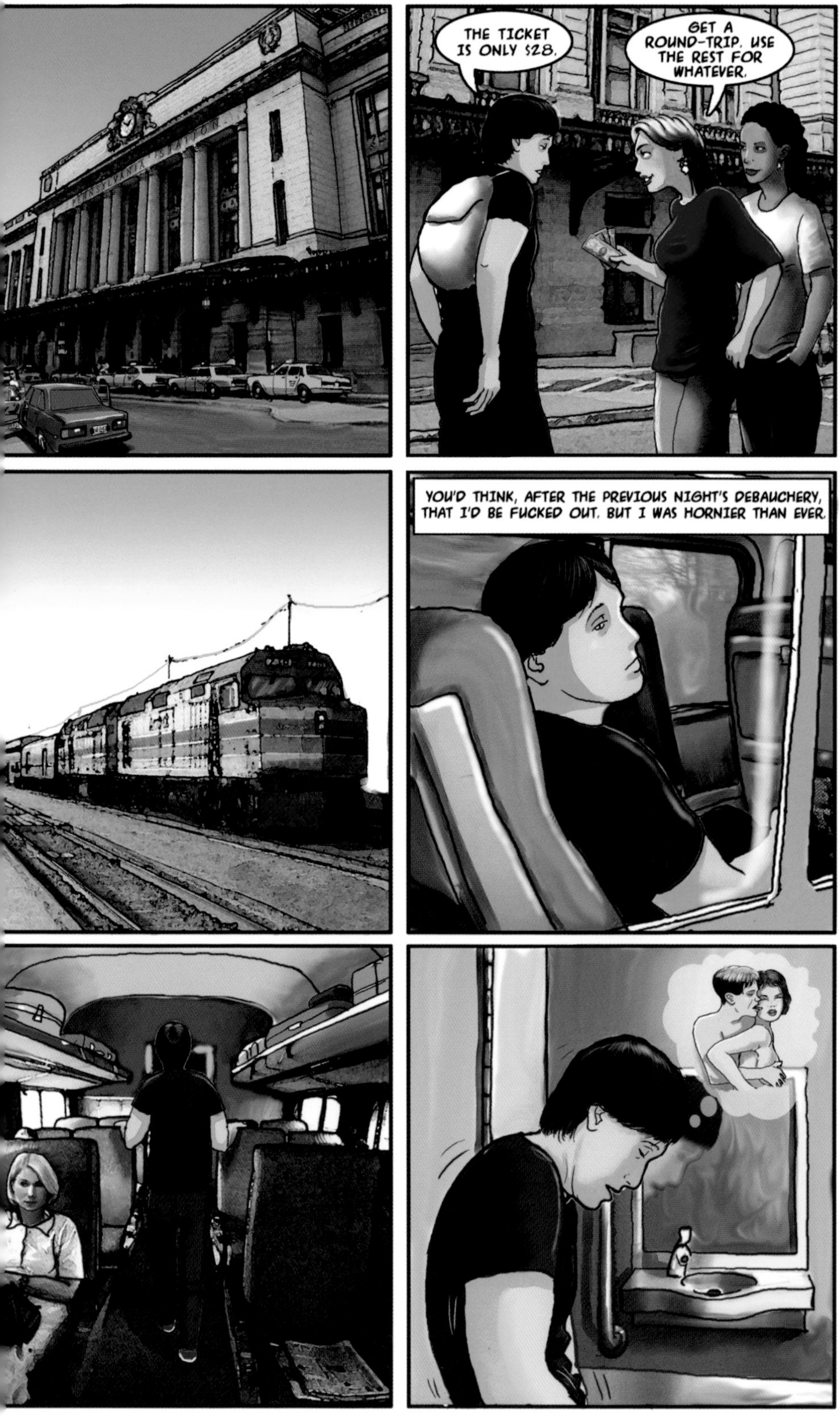
THE TICKET IS ONLY $28.
GET A ROUND-TRIP, USE THE REST FOR WHATEVER.
YOU'D THINK, AFTER THE PREVIOUS NIGHT'S DEBAUCHERY, THAT I'D BE FUCKED OUT. BUT I WAS HORNIER THAN EVER.

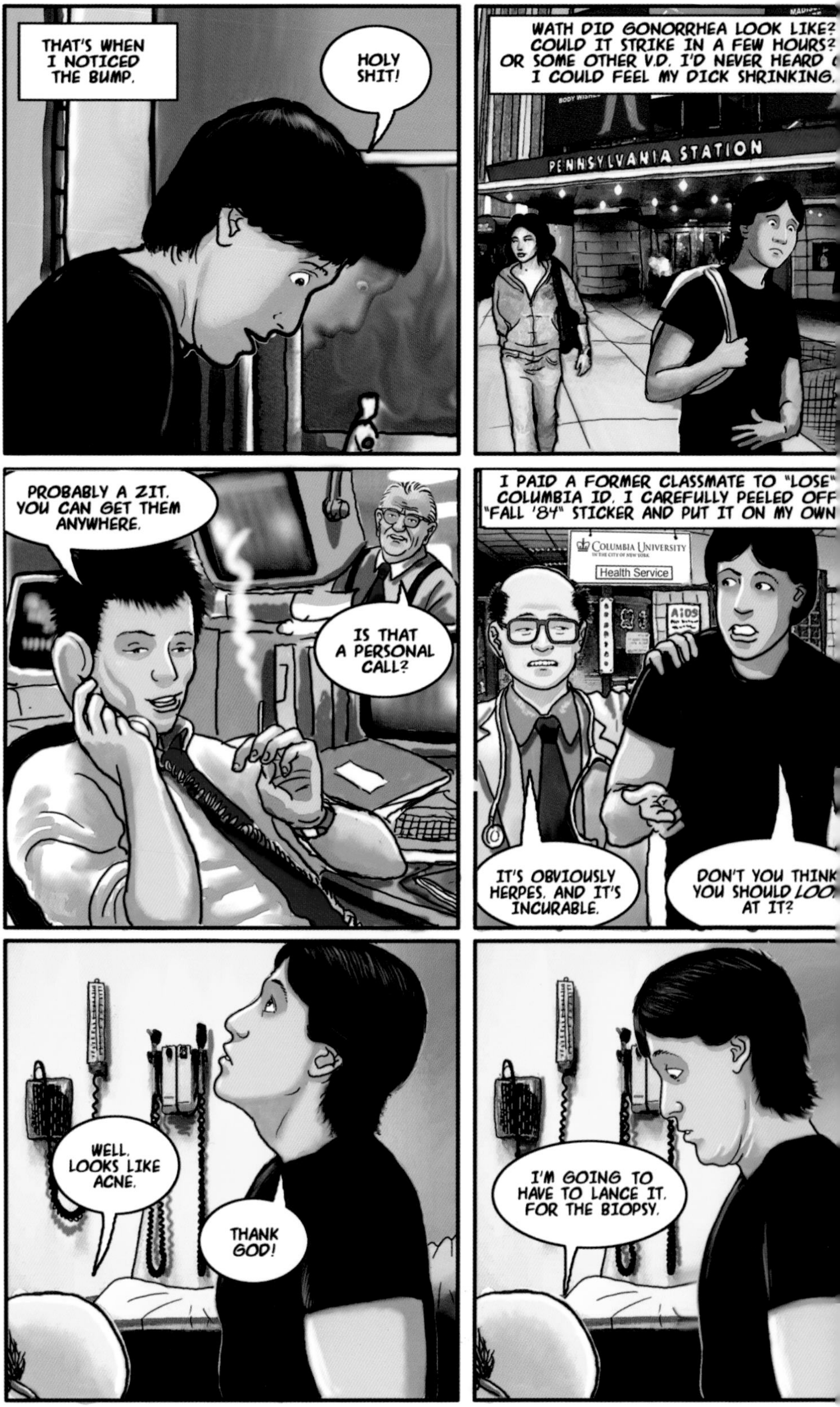
THAT'S WHEN I NOTICED THE BUMP.
HOLY SHIT!
WATH DID GONORRHEA LOOK LIKE? COULD IT STRIKE IN A FEW HOURS? OR SOME OTHER V.D. I'D NEVER HEARD
I COULD FEEL MY DICK SHRINKING.
PENNSYLVANIA STATION
PROBABLY A ZIT. YOU CAN GET THEM ANYWHERE.
IS THAT A PERSONAL CALL?
I PAID A FORMER CLASSMATE TO "LOSE"
COLUMBIA ID. I CAREFULLY PEELED OFF
"FALL '84" STICKER AND PUT IT ON MY OWN
COLUMBIA UNIVERSITY
Health Service
AIDS
IT'S OBVIOUSLY HERPES. AND IT'S INCURABLE.
DON'T YOU THINK YOU SHOULD LOO AT IT?
WELL, LOOKS LIKE ACNE.
THANK GOD!
I'M GOING TO HAVE TO LANCE IT. FOR THE BIOPSY.

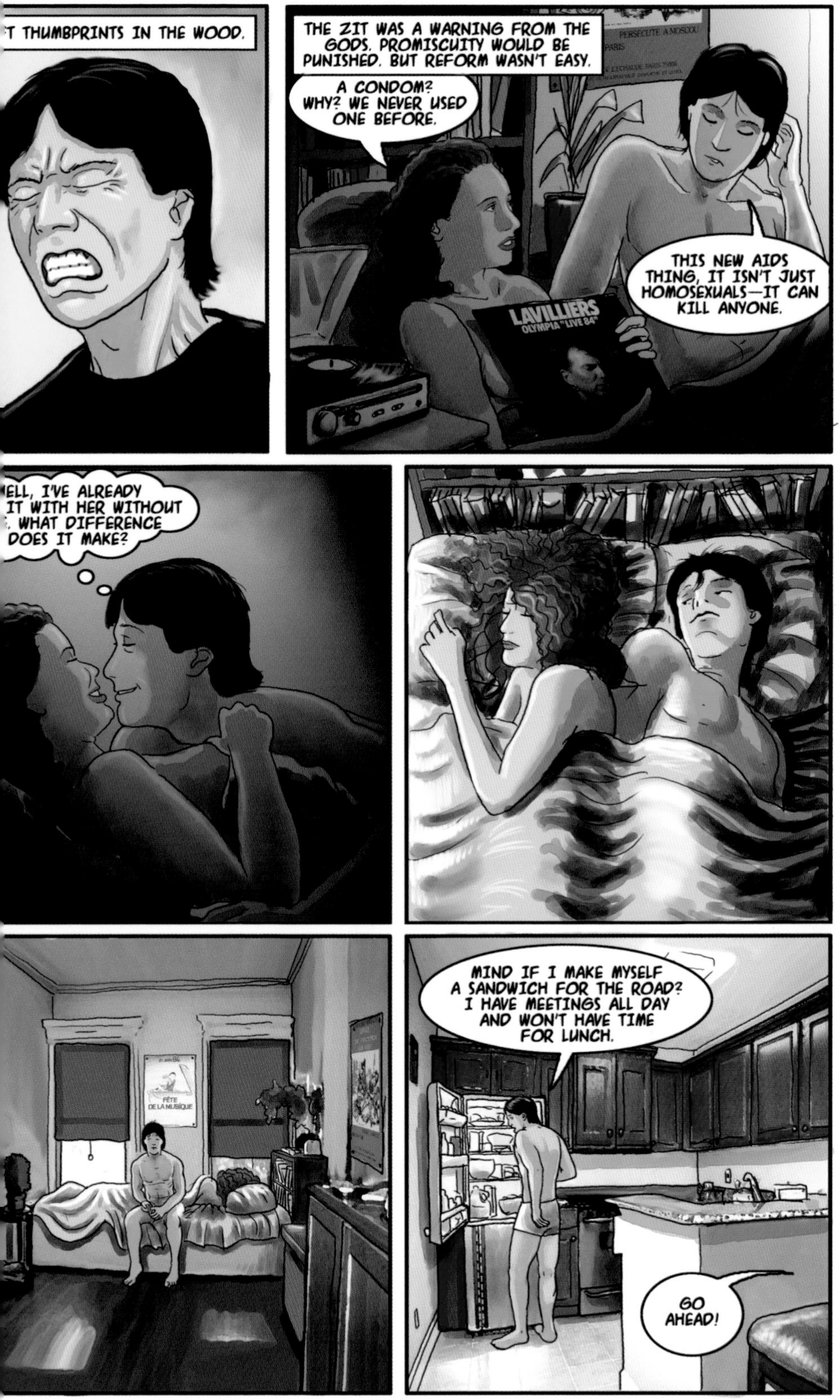
T THUMBPRINTS IN THE WOOD.
THE ZIT WAS A WARNING FROM THE GODS. PROMISCUITY WOULD BE PUNISHED. BUT REFORM WASN'T EASY.
A CONDOM? WHY? WE NEVER USED ONE BEFORE.
THIS NEW AIDS THING, IT ISN'T JUST HOMOSEXUALS—IT CAN KILL ANYONE.
LAVILLIERS OLYMPIA "LIVE 84"
ELL, I'VE ALREADY IT WITH HER WITHOUT . WHAT DIFFERENCE DOES IT MAKE?
FÊTE DE LA MUSIQUE
MIND IF I MAKE MYSELF A SANDWICH FOR THE ROAD? I HAVE MEETINGS ALL DAY AND WON'T HAVE TIME FOR LUNCH.
GO AHEAD!

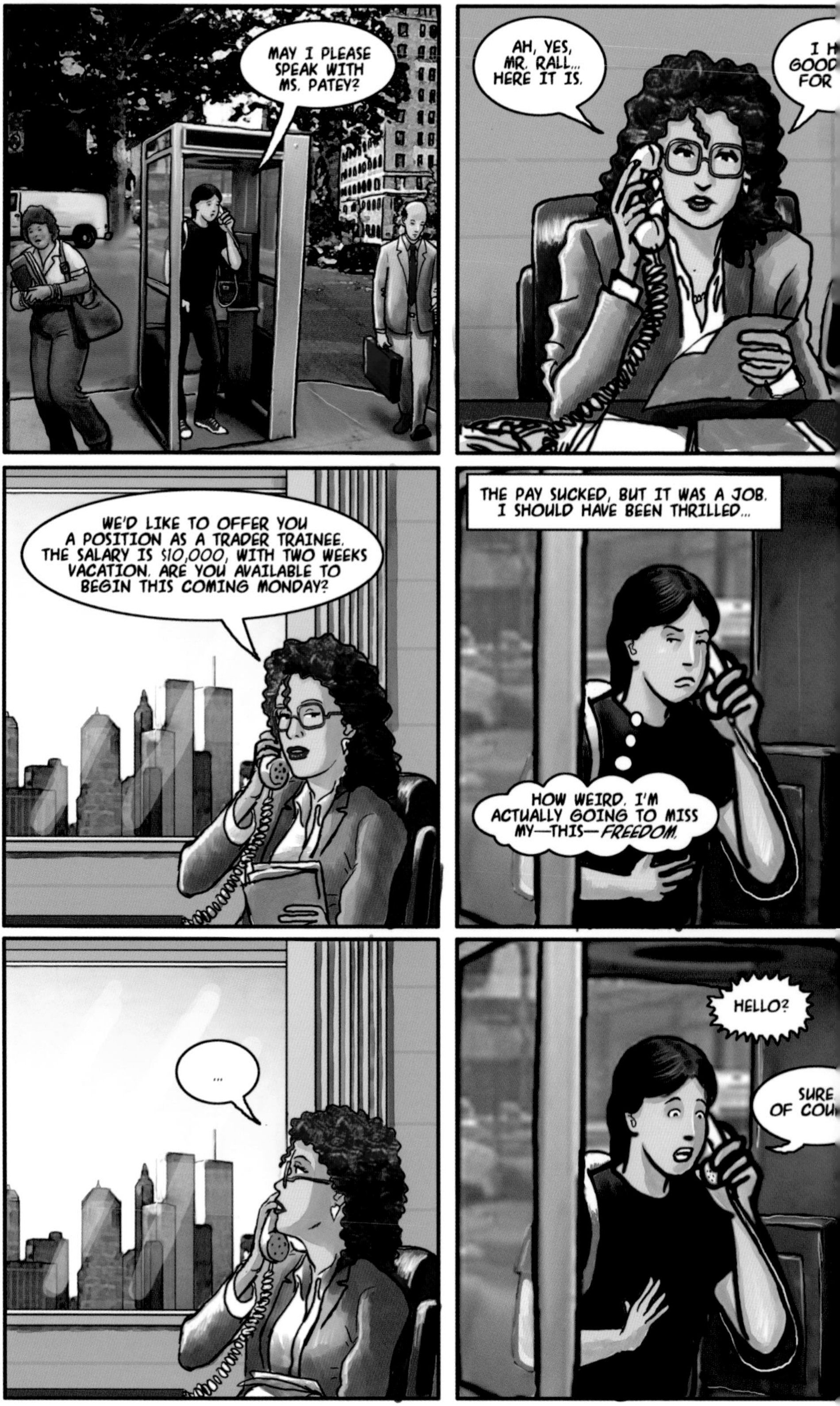
MAY I PLEASE SPEAK WITH MS. PATEY?
AH, YES, MR. RALL... HERE IT IS.
WE'D LIKE TO OFFER YOU A POSITION AS A TRADER TRAINEE. THE SALARY IS $10,000, WITH TWO WEEKS VACATION. ARE YOU AVAILABLE TO BEGIN THIS COMING MONDAY?
THE PAY SUCKED, BUT IT WAS A JOB. I SHOULD HAVE BEEN THRILLED...
HOW WEIRD. I'M ACTUALLY GOING TO MISS MY—THIS—*FREEDOM.*
...
HELLO?

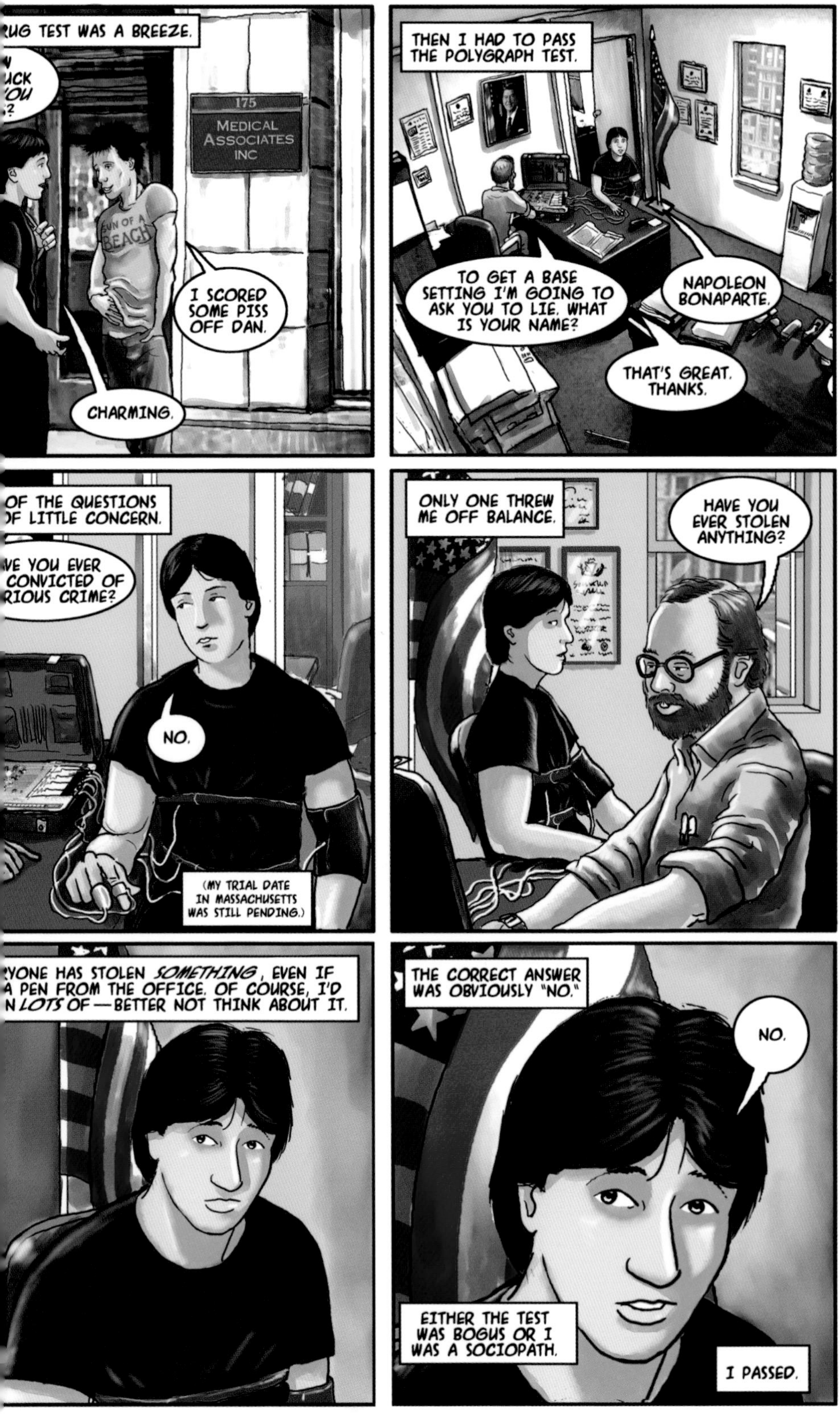
RUG TEST WAS A BREEZE.
175
MEDICAL ASSOCIATES INC
I SCORED SOME PISS OFF DAN.
CHARMING.
THEN I HAD TO PASS THE POLYGRAPH TEST.
TO GET A BASE SETTING I'M GOING TO ASK YOU TO LIE. WHAT IS YOUR NAME?
NAPOLEON BONAPARTE.
THAT'S GREAT. THANKS.
OF THE QUESTIONS
F LITTLE CONCERN.
VE YOU EVER
CONVICTED OF
RIOUS CRIME?
NO.
(MY TRIAL DATE IN MASSACHUSETTS WAS STILL PENDING.)
ONLY ONE THREW ME OFF BALANCE.
HAVE YOU EVER STOLEN ANYTHING?
YONE HAS STOLEN *SOMETHING*, EVEN IF
A PEN FROM THE OFFICE. OF COURSE, I'D
N *LOTS* OF—BETTER NOT THINK ABOUT IT.
THE CORRECT ANSWER WAS OBVIOUSLY "NO."
NO.
EITHER THE TEST WAS BOGUS OR I WAS A SOCIOPATH.
I PASSED.

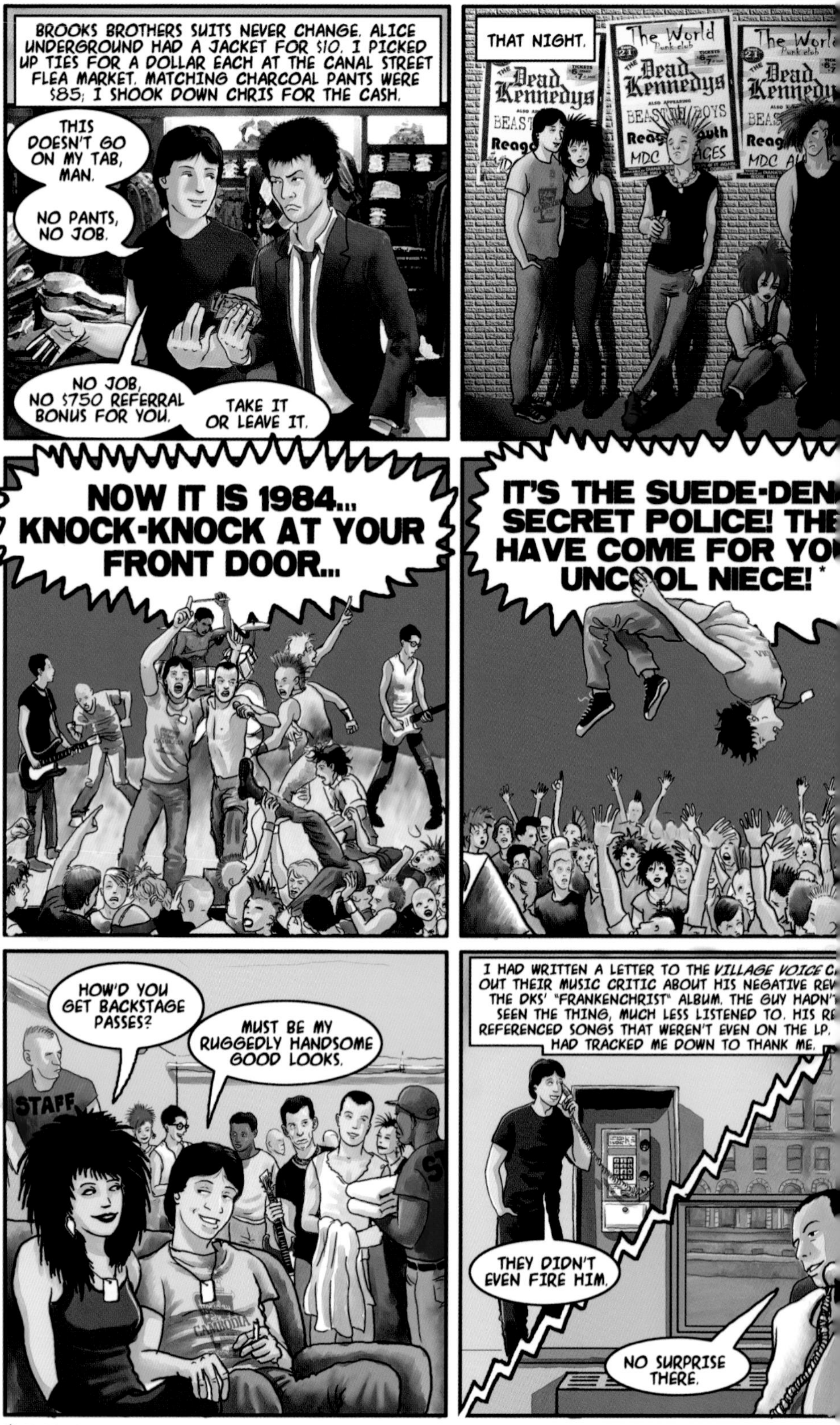

BROOKS BROTHERS SUITS NEVER CHANGE. ALICE UNDERGROUND HAD A JACKET FOR $10. I PICKED UP TIES FOR A DOLLAR EACH AT THE CANAL STREET FLEA MARKET. MATCHING CHARCOAL PANTS WERE $85; I SHOOK DOWN CHRIS FOR THE CASH.
THIS DOESN'T GO ON MY TAB, MAN.
NO PANTS, NO JOB.
NO JOB, NO $750 REFERRAL BONUS FOR YOU.
TAKE IT OR LEAVE IT.
THAT NIGHT.
The World
Punk club
THE Dead Kennedys
NOW IT IS 1984... KNOCK-KNOCK AT YOUR FRONT DOOR...
IT'S THE SUEDE-DEN SECRET POLICE! THE HAVE COME FOR YO UNCOOL NIECE! *
HOW'D YOU GET BACKSTAGE PASSES?
MUST BE MY RUGGEDLY HANDSOME GOOD LOOKS.
STAFF
I HAD WRITTEN A LETTER TO THE VILLAGE VOICE C OUT THEIR MUSIC CRITIC ABOUT HIS NEGATIVE REV THE DKS' "FRANKENCHRIST" ALBUM. THE GUY HADN' SEEN THE THING, MUCH LESS LISTENED TO. HIS R REFERENCED SONGS THAT WEREN'T EVEN ON THE LP. HAD TRACKED ME DOWN TO THANK ME.
THEY DIDN'T EVEN FIRE HIM.
NO SURPRISE THERE.

* *"California Uber Alles"*, by the Dead Kennedys (1979)

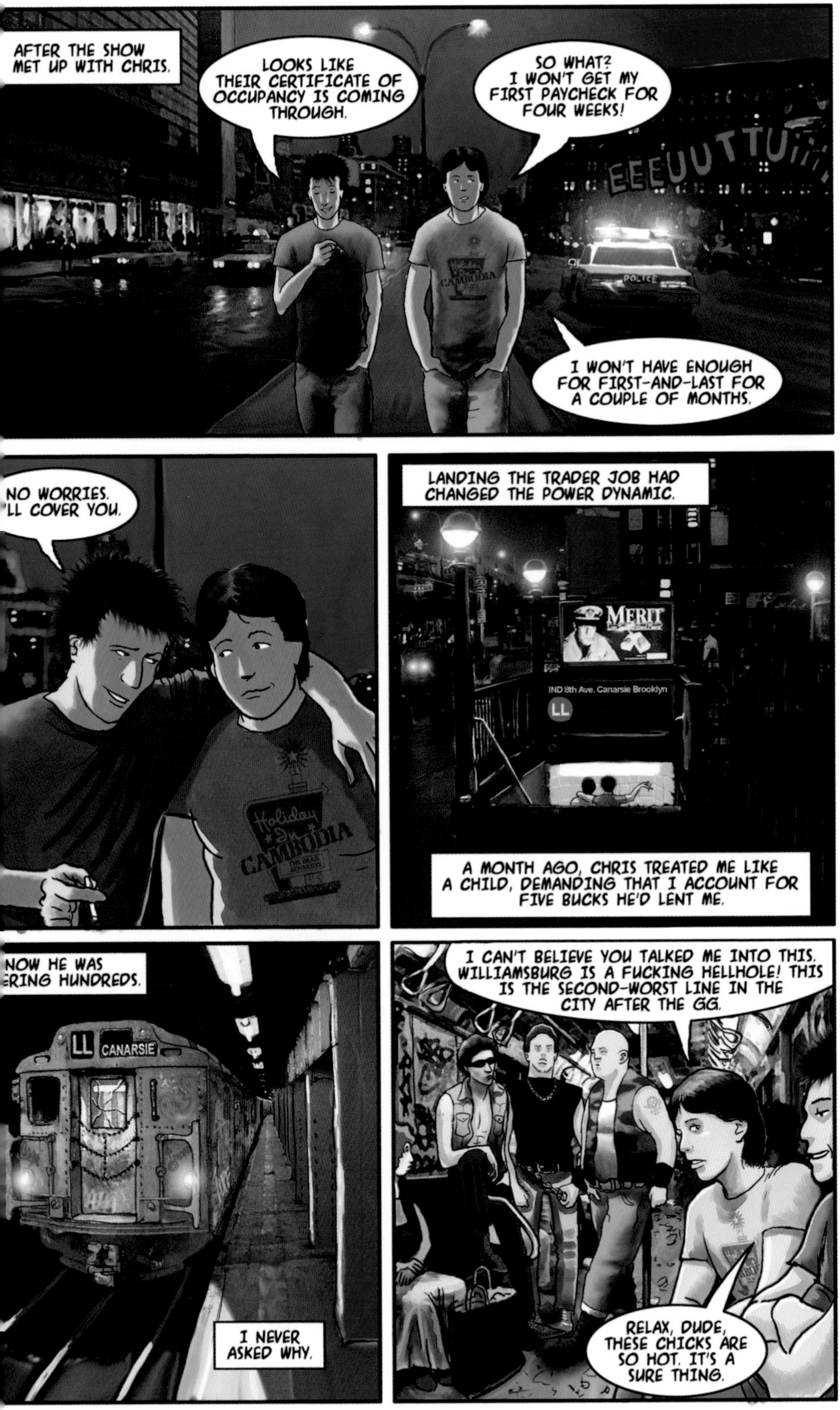
AFTER THE SHOW MET UP WITH CHRIS.
LOOKS LIKE THEIR CERTIFICATE OF OCCUPANCY IS COMING THROUGH.
SO WHAT? I WON'T GET MY FIRST PAYCHECK FOR FOUR WEEKS!
EEEUUTTTU
POLICE
CAMBODIA
I WON'T HAVE ENOUGH FOR FIRST-AND-LAST FOR A COUPLE OF MONTHS.
NO WORRIES. 'LL COVER YOU.
CAMBODIA
LANDING THE TRADER JOB HAD CHANGED THE POWER DYNAMIC.
MERIT
IND 8th Ave. Canarsie Brooklyn
LL
A MONTH AGO, CHRIS TREATED ME LIKE A CHILD, DEMANDING THAT I ACCOUNT FOR FIVE BUCKS HE'D LENT ME.
NOW HE WAS ERING HUNDREDS.
LL
CANARSIE
I NEVER ASKED WHY.
I CAN'T BELIEVE YOU TALKED ME INTO THIS. WILLIAMSBURG IS A FUCKING HELLHOLE! THIS IS THE SECOND-WORST LINE IN THE CITY AFTER THE GG.
RELAX, DUDE, THESE CHICKS ARE SO HOT. IT'S A SURE THING.

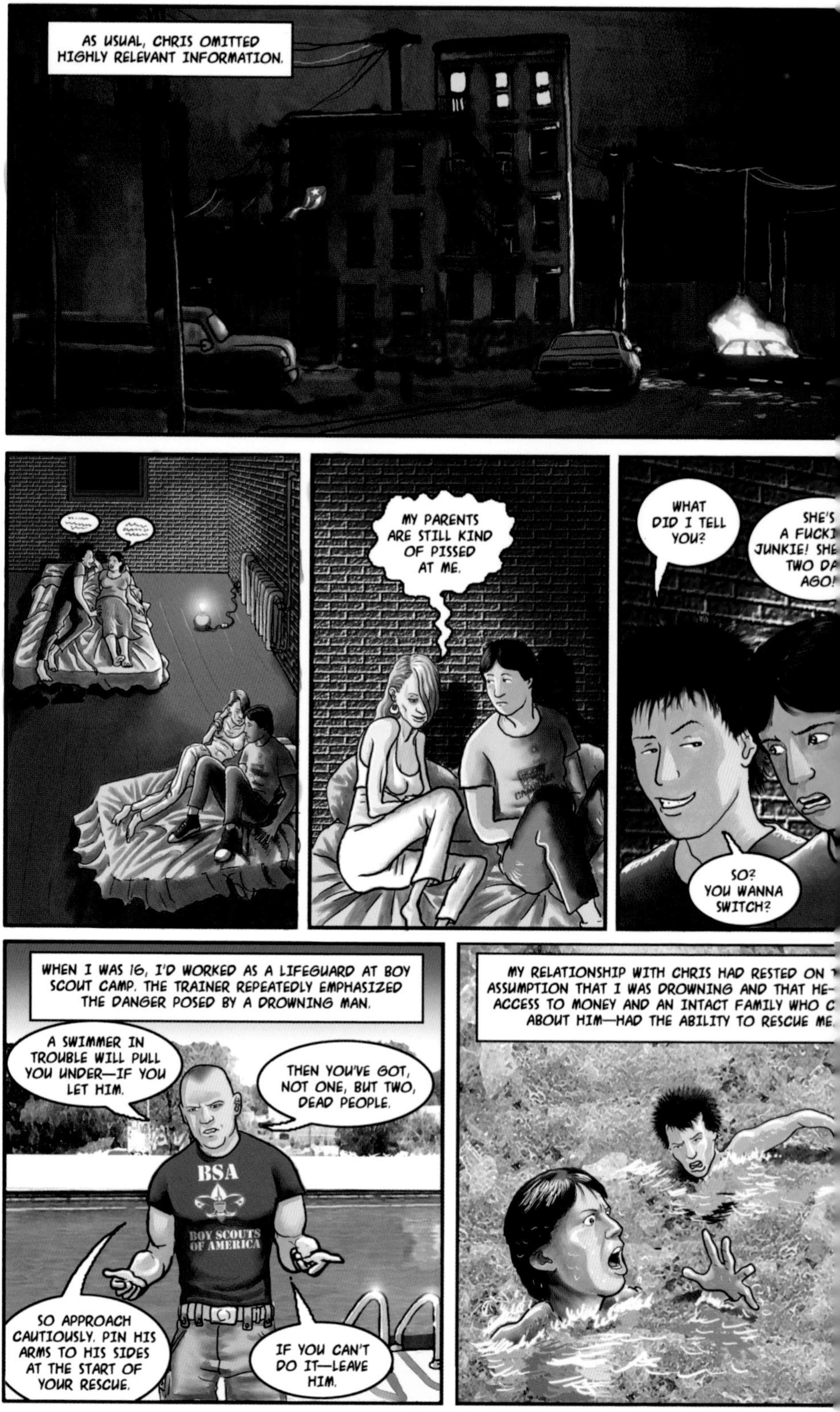
AS USUAL, CHRIS OMITTED HIGHLY RELEVANT INFORMATION.
MY PARENTS ARE STILL KIND OF PISSED AT ME.
WHAT DID I TELL YOU?
SHE'S A FUCKI JUNKIE! SHE TWO DA AGO!
SO? YOU WANNA SWITCH?
WHEN I WAS 16, I'D WORKED AS A LIFEGUARD AT BOY SCOUT CAMP. THE TRAINER REPEATEDLY EMPHASIZED THE DANGER POSED BY A DROWNING MAN.
A SWIMMER IN TROUBLE WILL PULL YOU UNDER—IF YOU LET HIM.
THEN YOU'VE GOT, NOT ONE, BUT TWO, DEAD PEOPLE.
BSA
BOY SCOUTS OF AMERICA
SO APPROACH CAUTIOUSLY. PIN HIS ARMS TO HIS SIDES AT THE START OF YOUR RESCUE.
IF YOU CAN'T DO IT—LEAVE HIM.
MY RELATIONSHIP WITH CHRIS HAD RESTED ON
ASSUMPTION THAT I WAS DROWNING AND THAT HE-
ACCESS TO MONEY AND AN INTACT FAMILY WHO C
ABOUT HIM—HAD THE ABILITY TO RESCUE ME.

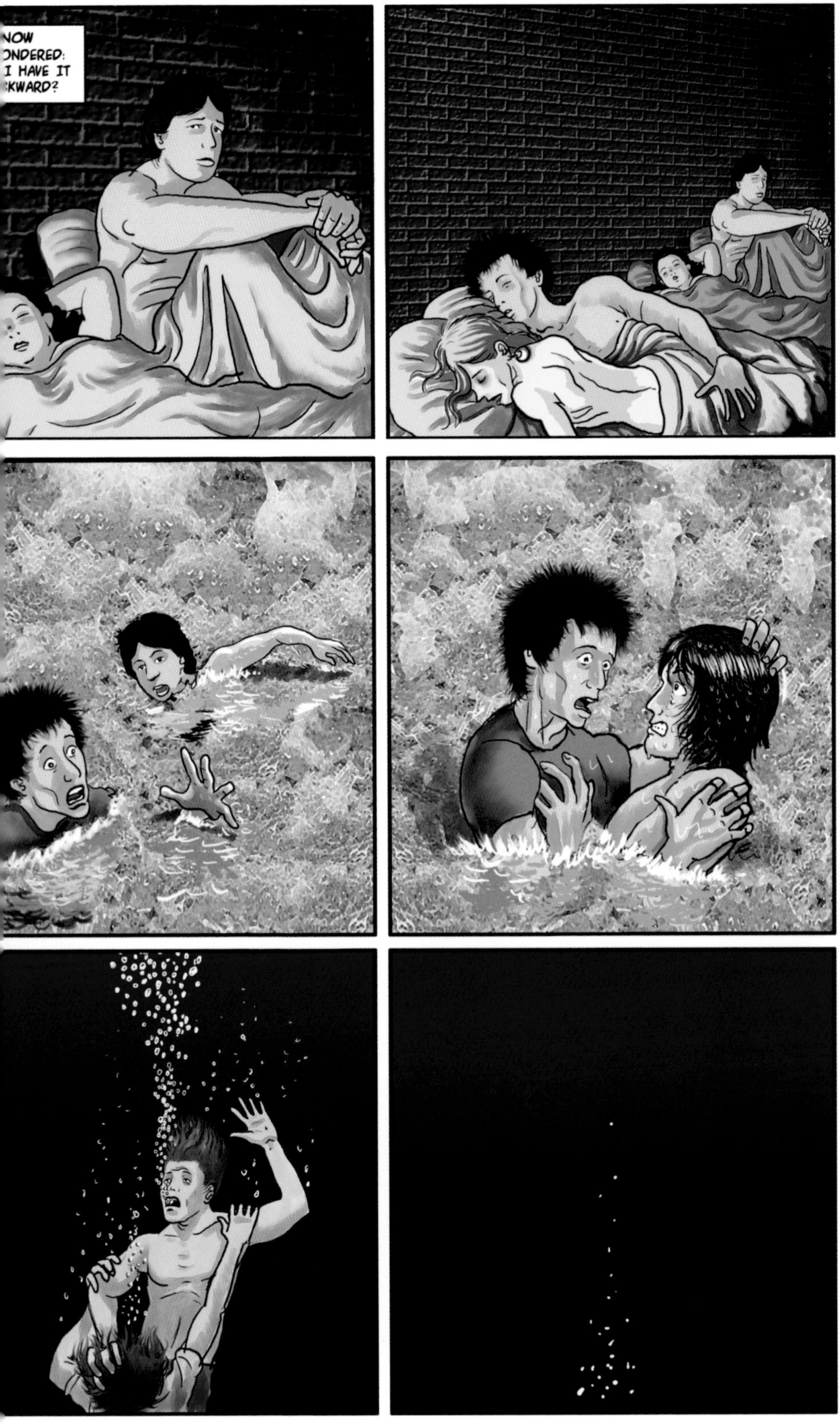
NOW
ONDERED:
I HAVE IT
KWARD?

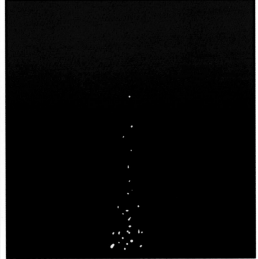

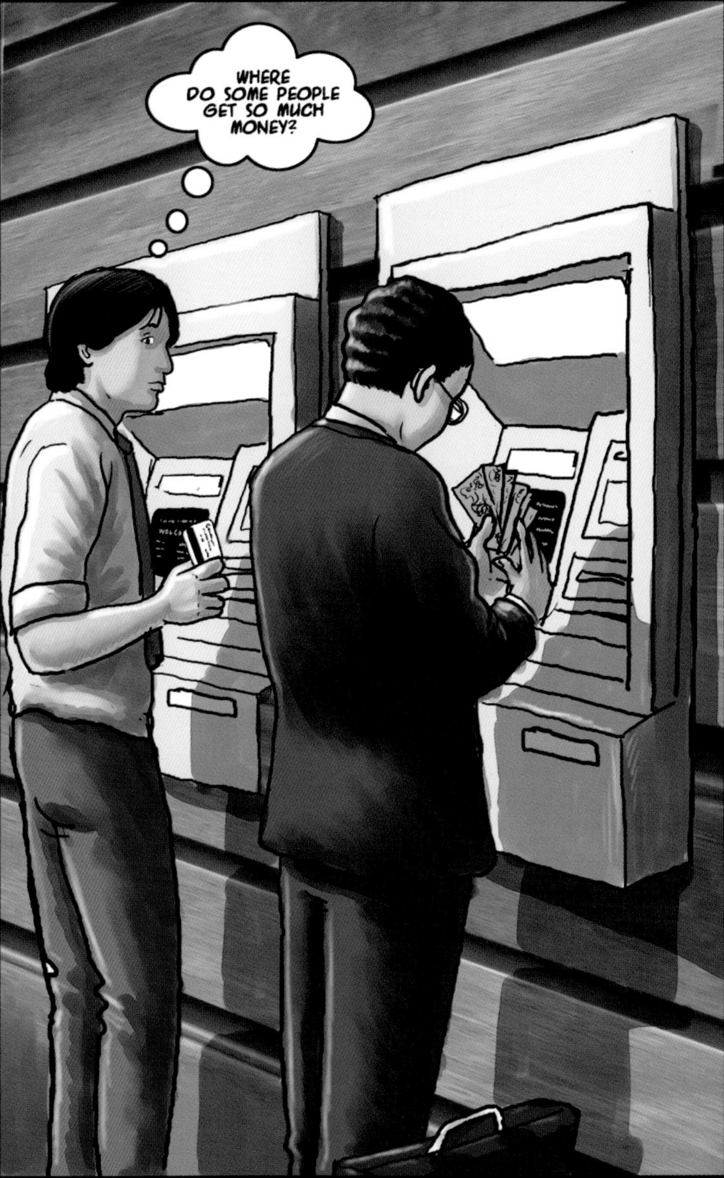
WHERE DO SOME PEOPLE GET SO MUCH MONEY?

III

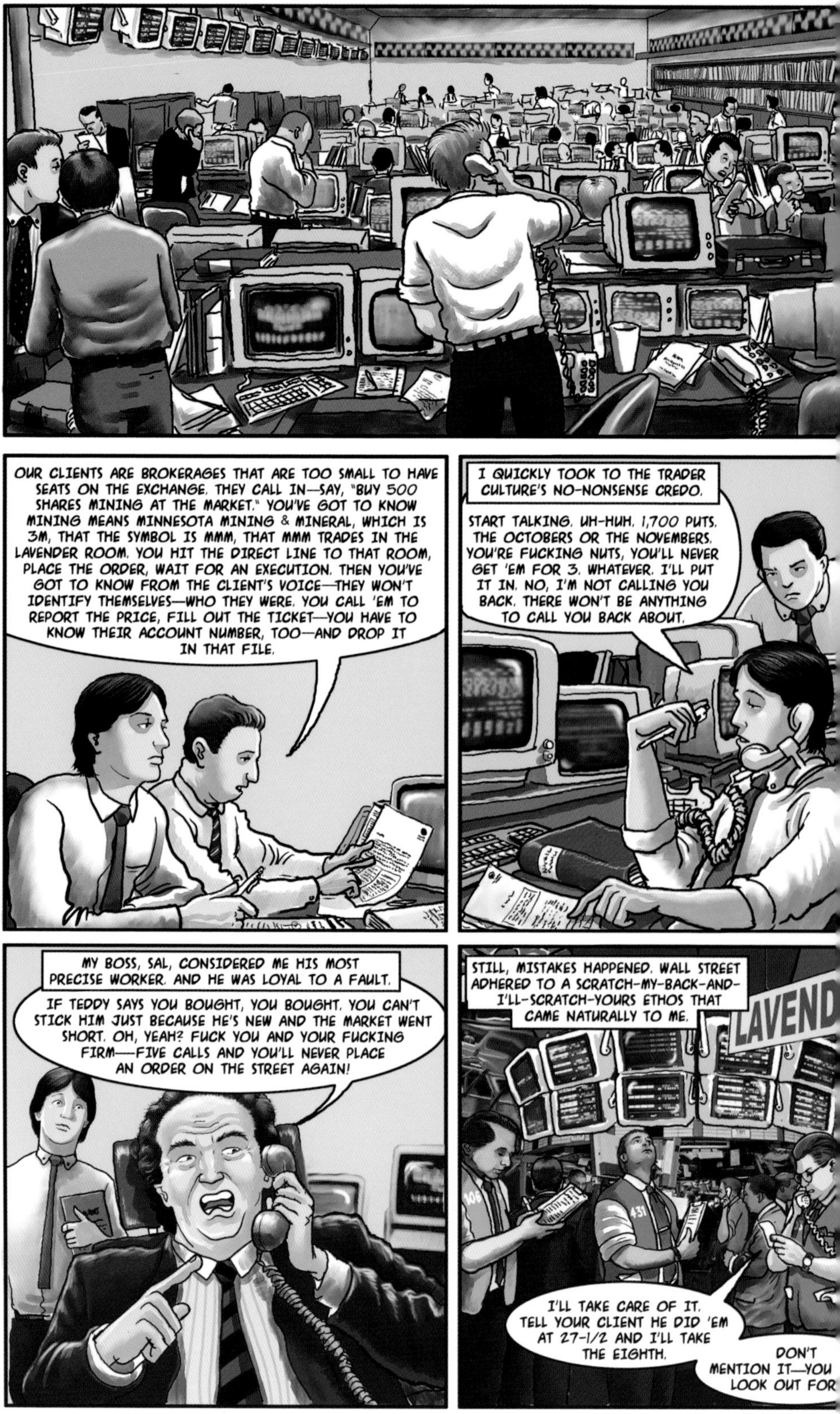
OUR CLIENTS ARE BROKERAGES THAT ARE TOO SMALL TO HAVE SEATS ON THE EXCHANGE. THEY CALL IN—SAY, "BUY 500 SHARES MINING AT THE MARKET." YOU'VE GOT TO KNOW MINING MEANS MINNESOTA MINING & MINERAL, WHICH IS 3M, THAT THE SYMBOL IS MMM, THAT MMM TRADES IN THE LAVENDER ROOM. YOU HIT THE DIRECT LINE TO THAT ROOM, PLACE THE ORDER, WAIT FOR AN EXECUTION. THEN YOU'VE GOT TO KNOW FROM THE CLIENT'S VOICE—THEY WON'T IDENTIFY THEMSELVES—WHO THEY WERE. YOU CALL 'EM TO REPORT THE PRICE, FILL OUT THE TICKET—YOU HAVE TO KNOW THEIR ACCOUNT NUMBER, TOO—AND DROP IT IN THAT FILE.
I QUICKLY TOOK TO THE TRADER CULTURE'S NO-NONSENSE CREDO.
START TALKING. UH-HUH. 1,700 PUTS. THE OCTOBERS OR THE NOVEMBERS. YOU'RE FUCKING NUTS, YOU'LL NEVER GET 'EM FOR 3. WHATEVER. I'LL PUT IT IN. NO, I'M NOT CALLING YOU BACK. THERE WON'T BE ANYTHING TO CALL YOU BACK ABOUT.
MY BOSS, SAL, CONSIDERED ME HIS MOST PRECISE WORKER. AND HE WAS LOYAL TO A FAULT.
IF TEDDY SAYS YOU BOUGHT, YOU BOUGHT. YOU CAN'T STICK HIM JUST BECAUSE HE'S NEW AND THE MARKET WENT SHORT. OH, YEAH? FUCK YOU AND YOUR FUCKING FIRM—FIVE CALLS AND YOU'LL NEVER PLACE AN ORDER ON THE STREET AGAIN!
STILL, MISTAKES HAPPENED. WALL STREET ADHERED TO A SCRATCH-MY-BACK-AND-I'LL-SCRATCH-YOURS ETHOS THAT CAME NATURALLY TO ME.
LAVEND
I'LL TAKE CARE OF IT. TELL YOUR CLIENT HE DID 'EM AT 27-1/2 AND I'LL TAKE THE EIGHTH.
DON'T MENTION IT—YOU LOOK OUT FOR

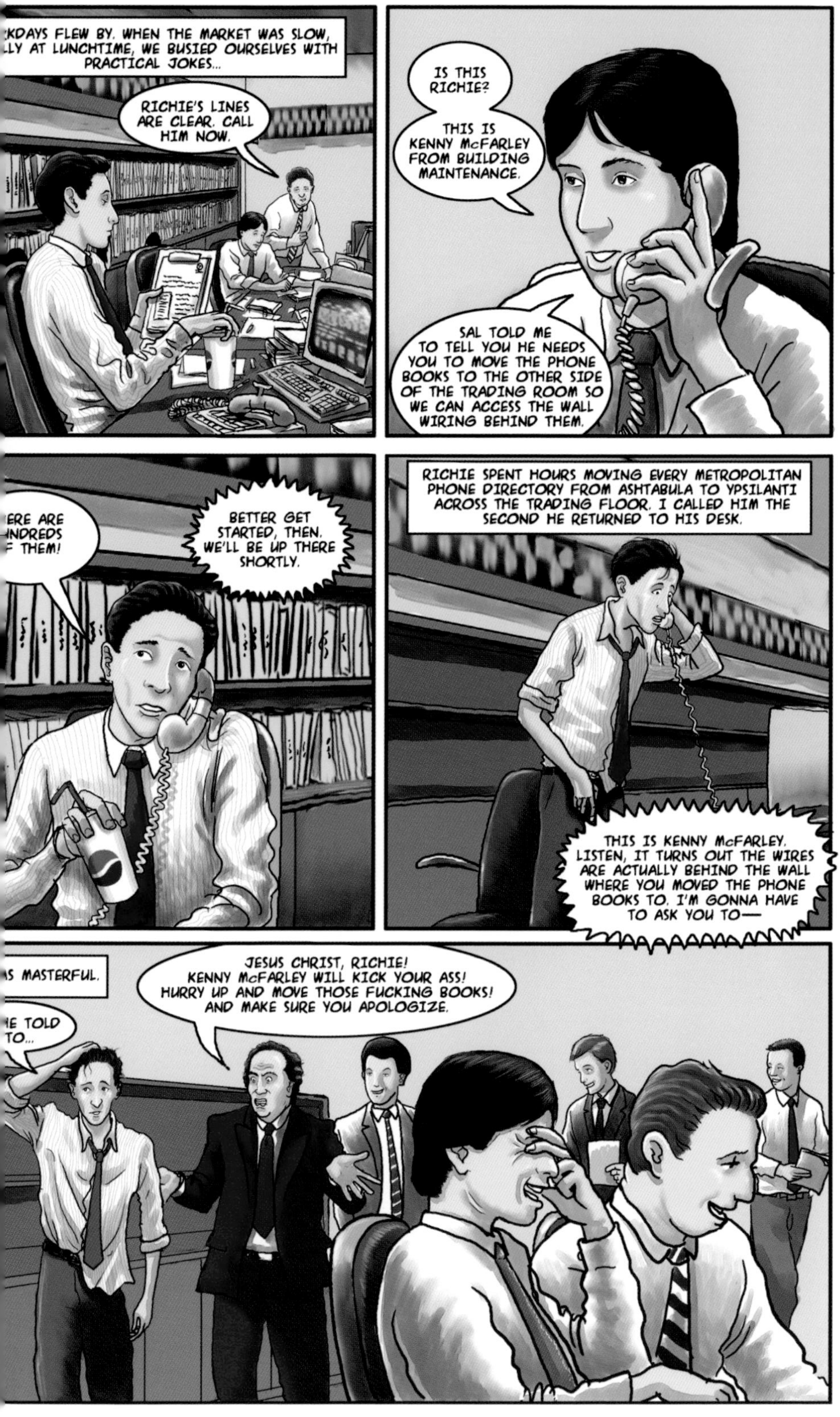
KDAYS FLEW BY. WHEN THE MARKET WAS SLOW, LLY AT LUNCHTIME, WE BUSIED OURSELVES WITH PRACTICAL JOKES...
RICHIE'S LINES ARE CLEAR. CALL HIM NOW.
IS THIS RICHIE?
THIS IS KENNY McFARLEY FROM BUILDING MAINTENANCE.
SAL TOLD ME TO TELL YOU HE NEEDS YOU TO MOVE THE PHONE BOOKS TO THE OTHER SIDE OF THE TRADING ROOM SO WE CAN ACCESS THE WALL WIRING BEHIND THEM.
ERE ARE NDREDS THEM!
BETTER GET STARTED, THEN. WE'LL BE UP THERE SHORTLY.
RICHIE SPENT HOURS MOVING EVERY METROPOLITAN PHONE DIRECTORY FROM ASHTABULA TO YPSILANTI ACROSS THE TRADING FLOOR. I CALLED HIM THE SECOND HE RETURNED TO HIS DESK.
THIS IS KENNY McFARLEY. LISTEN, IT TURNS OUT THE WIRES ARE ACTUALLY BEHIND THE WALL WHERE YOU MOVED THE PHONE BOOKS TO. I'M GONNA HAVE TO ASK YOU TO—
S MASTERFUL.
JESUS CHRIST, RICHIE! KENNY McFARLEY WILL KICK YOUR ASS! HURRY UP AND MOVE THOSE FUCKING BOOKS! AND MAKE SURE YOU APOLOGIZE.
E TOLD TO...

THERE WERE PERKS.

I'M SENDING OVER A CASE TOMORROW. BUT I THOUGHT YOU MIGHT NEED THIS FOR LATER.

HEY, DONNA! HERE'S TED, THE GUY I TOLD YOU ABOUT!

FOUR DIFFERENT CONDITIONERS AND NOT ONE SINGLE SHAMPOO?

IF I'D KNOWN YOU WERE... I WOULD'VE BOUGHT BAGELS.

BUZZ

MOM!

SHE ALWAYS TAKES FOREVER IN THE BATHROOM!

THANK SHE F BROUGH SOME DEC

YO SHOULD SOME OF SCU

96

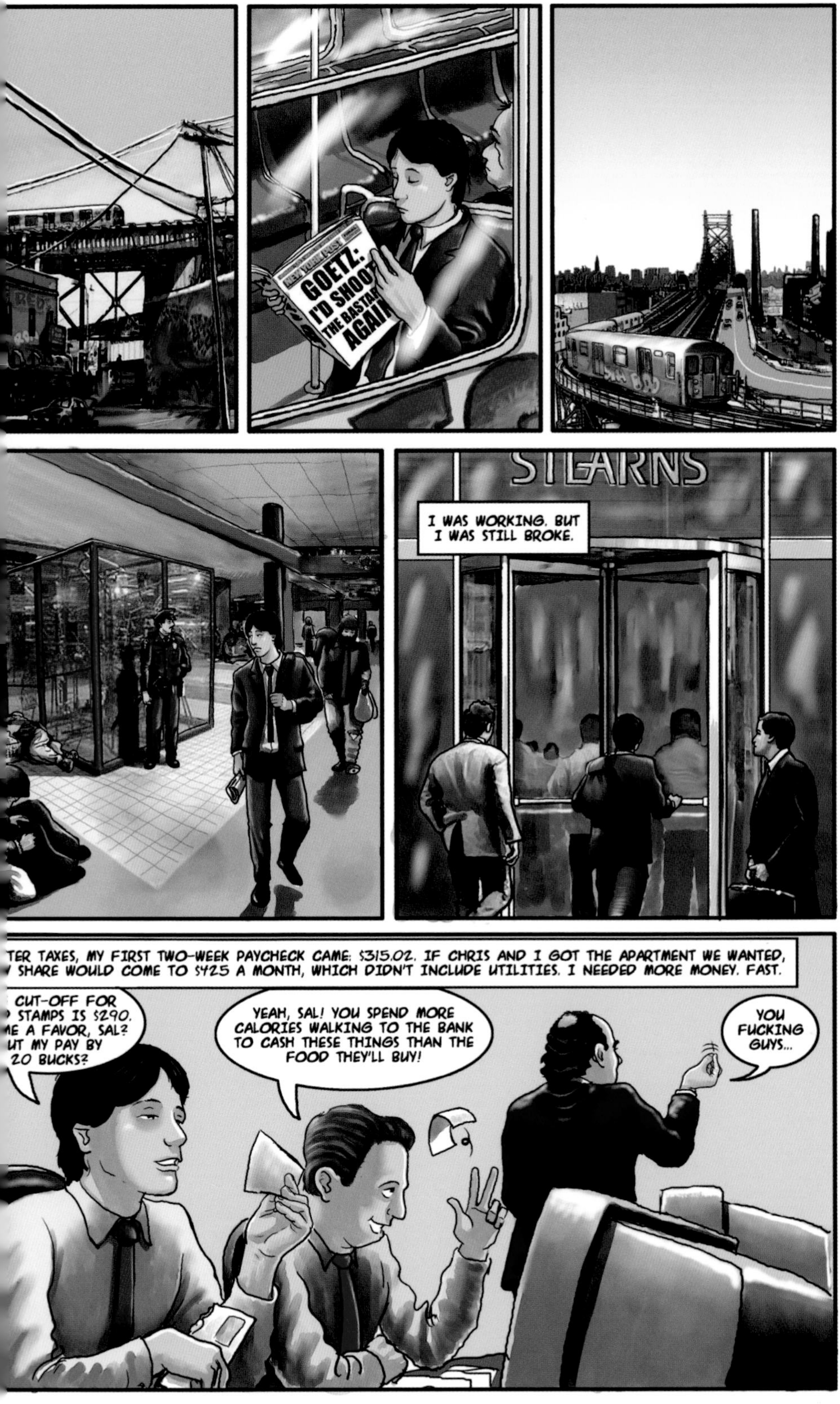
NEW YORK POST
GOETZ:
I'D SHOOT
THE BASTAR
AGAI
I WAS WORKING. BUT I WAS STILL BROKE.
TER TAXES, MY FIRST TWO-WEEK PAYCHECK CAME: $315.02. IF CHRIS AND I GOT THE APARTMENT WE WANTED, SHARE WOULD COME TO $425 A MONTH, WHICH DIDN'T INCLUDE UTILITIES. I NEEDED MORE MONEY. FAST.
CUT-OFF FOR STAMPS IS $290. ME A FAVOR, SAL? UT MY PAY BY 20 BUCKS?
YEAH, SAL! YOU SPEND MORE CALORIES WALKING TO THE BANK TO CASH THESE THINGS THAN THE FOOD THEY'LL BUY!
YOU FUCKING GUYS...

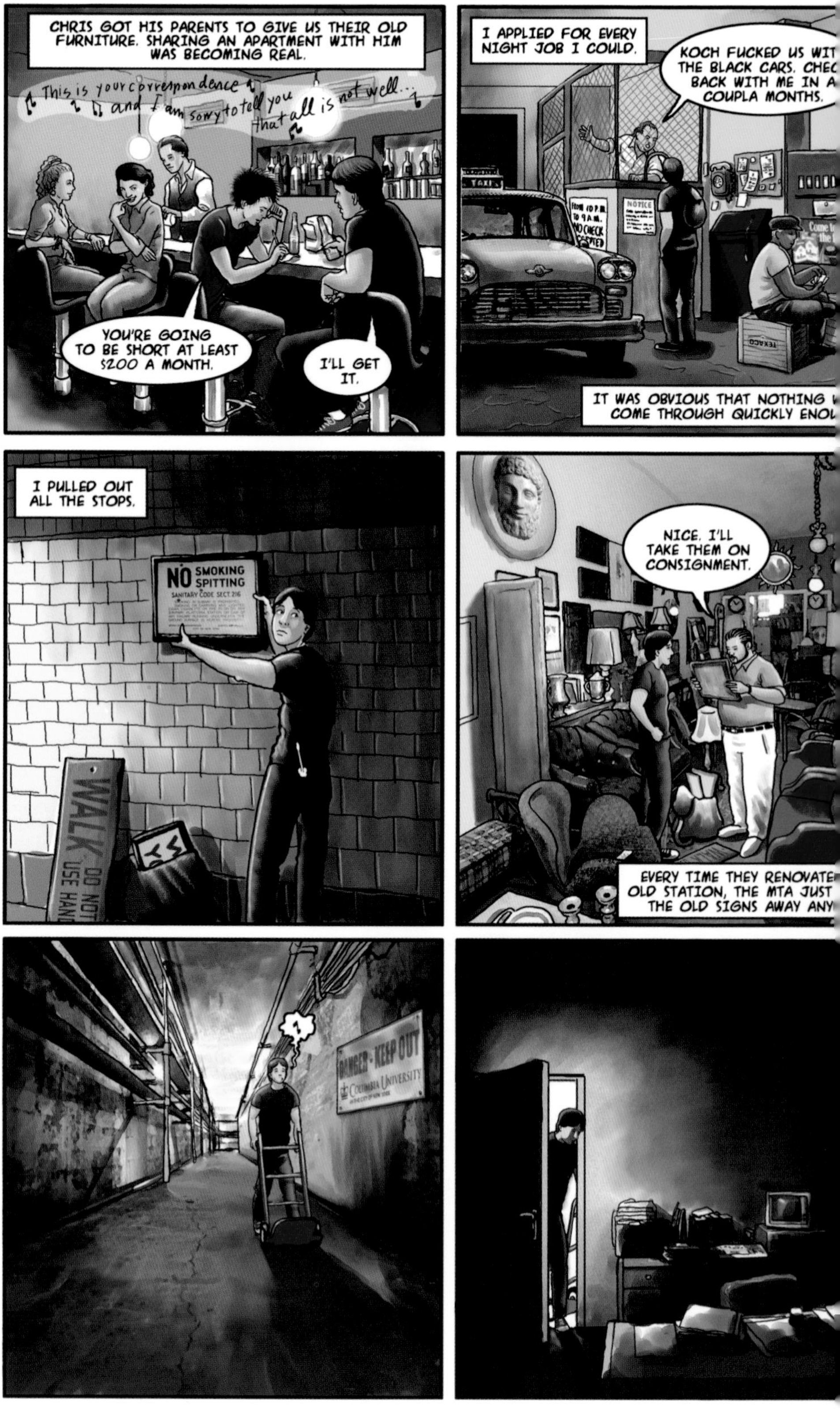

CHRIS GOT HIS PARENTS TO GIVE US THEIR OLD FURNITURE. SHARING AN APARTMENT WITH HIM WAS BECOMING REAL.
This is your correspondence and I am sorry to tell you that all is not well...
YOU'RE GOING TO BE SHORT AT LEAST $200 A MONTH.
I'LL GET IT.
I APPLIED FOR EVERY NIGHT JOB I COULD.
KOCH FUCKED US WIT THE BLACK CARS. CHEC BACK WITH ME IN A COUPLA MONTHS.
TAXI
NOTICE
IT WAS OBVIOUS THAT NOTHING W COME THROUGH QUICKLY ENOU
I PULLED OUT ALL THE STOPS.
NO SMOKING SPITTING
SANITARY CODE SECT. 216
WALK
DO NOT USE HAN
NICE. I'LL TAKE THEM ON CONSIGNMENT.
EVERY TIME THEY RENOVATE OLD STATION, THE MTA JUST THE OLD SIGNS AWAY ANY
DANGER - KEEP OUT
COLUMBIA UNIVERSITY

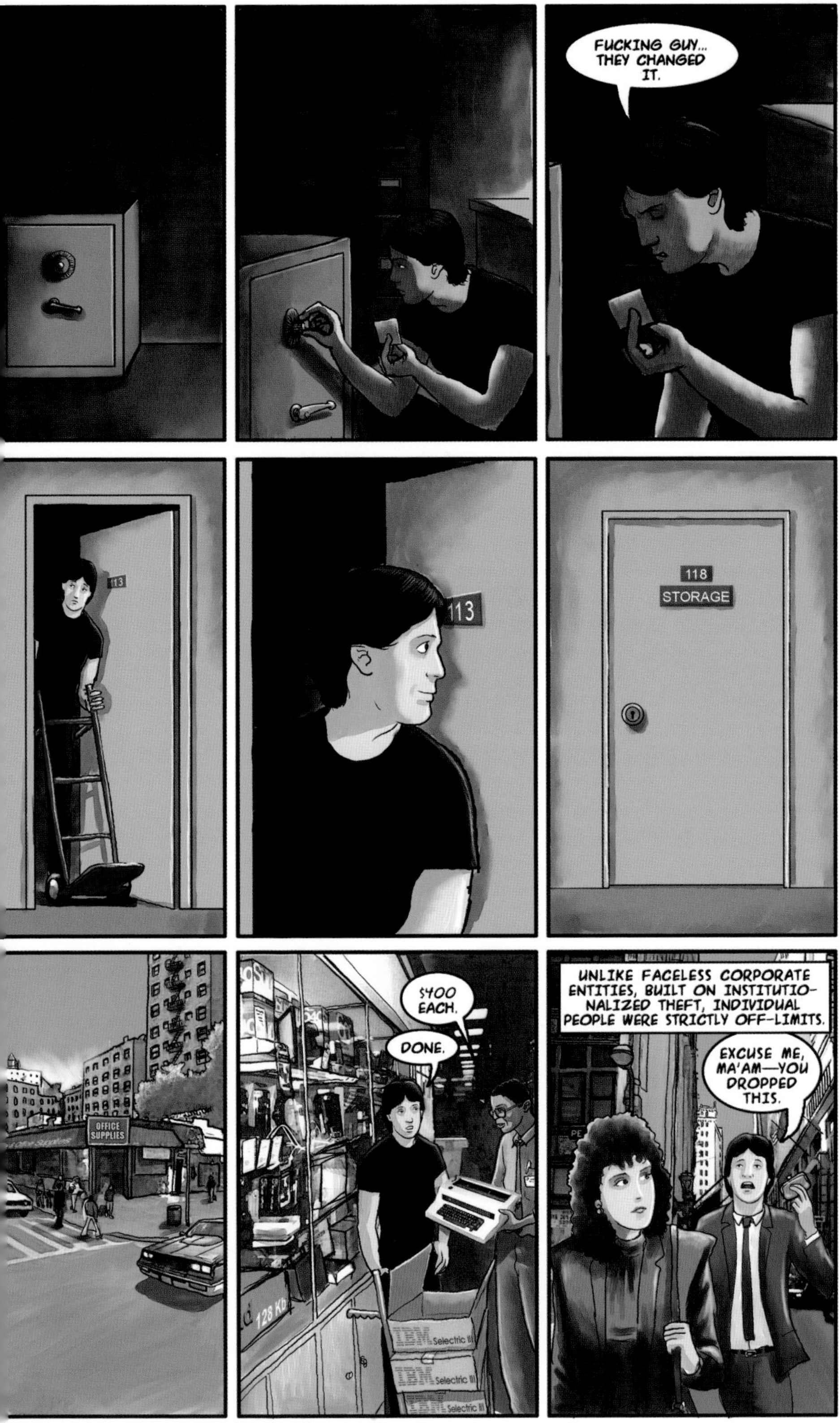
FUCKING GUY... THEY CHANGED IT.
113
113
118
STORAGE
OFFICE SUPPLIES
$400 EACH.
DONE.
128 Kb
IBM Selectric III
IBM Selectric III
IBM Selectric III
UNLIKE FACELESS CORPORATE ENTITIES, BUILT ON INSTITUTIONALIZED THEFT, INDIVIDUAL PEOPLE WERE STRICTLY OFF-LIMITS.
EXCUSE ME, MA'AM—YOU DROPPED THIS.

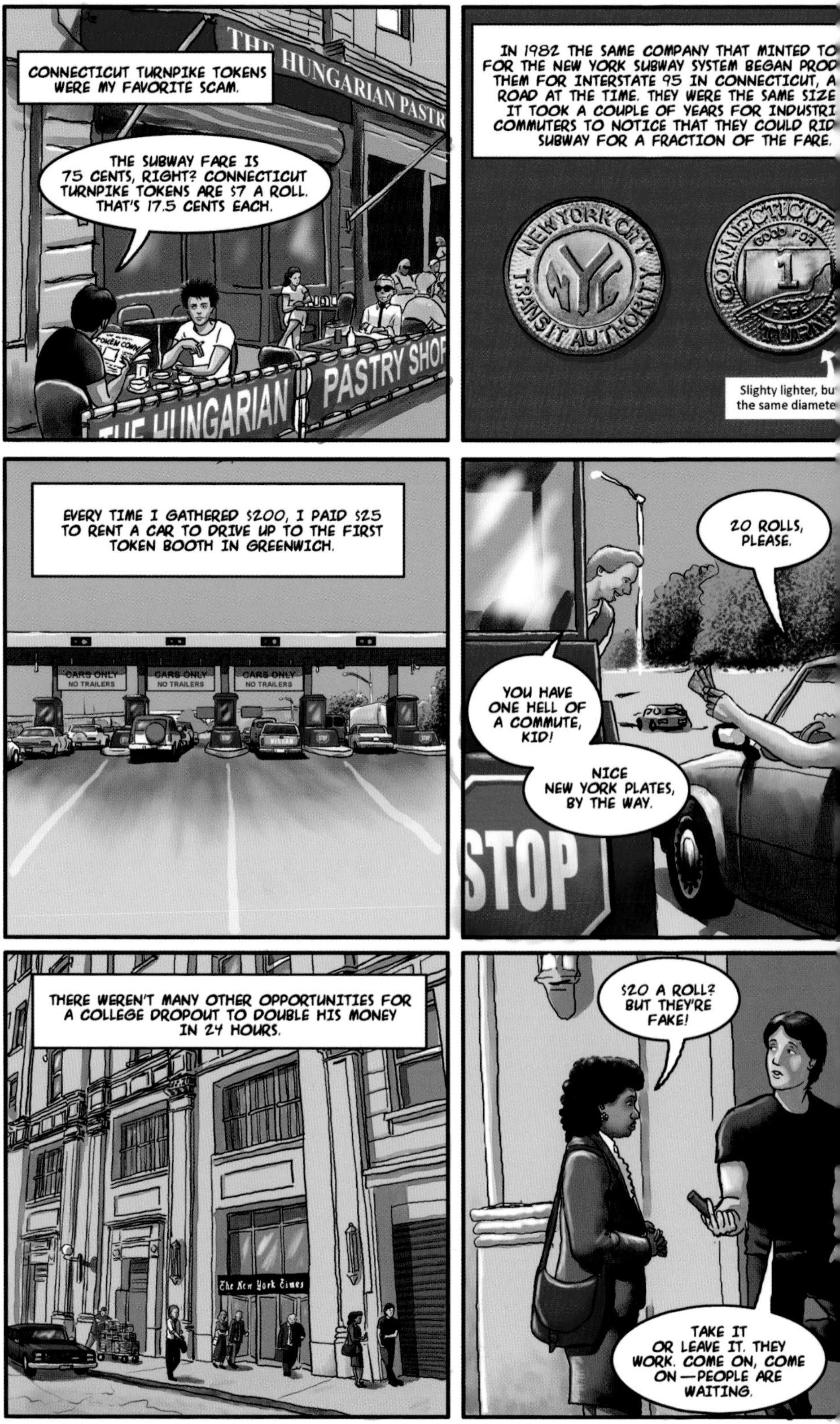
THE HUNGARIAN PASTR
CONNECTICUT TURNPIKE TOKENS WERE MY FAVORITE SCAM.
THE SUBWAY FARE IS 75 CENTS, RIGHT? CONNECTICUT TURNPIKE TOKENS ARE $7 A ROLL. THAT'S 17.5 CENTS EACH.
THE HUNGARIAN PASTRY SHOP
IN 1982 THE SAME COMPANY THAT MINTED TO
FOR THE NEW YORK SUBWAY SYSTEM BEGAN PROD
THEM FOR INTERSTATE 95 IN CONNECTICUT, A
ROAD AT THE TIME. THEY WERE THE SAME SIZE
IT TOOK A COUPLE OF YEARS FOR INDUSTRI
COMMUTERS TO NOTICE THAT THEY COULD RID
SUBWAY FOR A FRACTION OF THE FARE.
NEW YORK CITY TRANSIT AUTHORITY
NYC
GOOD FOR 1
Slighty lighter, bu
the same diamete
EVERY TIME I GATHERED $200, I PAID $25 TO RENT A CAR TO DRIVE UP TO THE FIRST TOKEN BOOTH IN GREENWICH.
CARS ONLY NO TRAILERS
CARS ONLY NO TRAILERS
CARS ONLY NO TRAILERS
20 ROLLS, PLEASE.
YOU HAVE ONE HELL OF A COMMUTE, KID!
NICE NEW YORK PLATES, BY THE WAY.
STOP
THERE WEREN'T MANY OTHER OPPORTUNITIES FOR A COLLEGE DROPOUT TO DOUBLE HIS MONEY IN 24 HOURS.
The New York Times
$20 A ROLL? BUT THEY'RE FAKE!
TAKE IT OR LEAVE IT. THEY WORK. COME ON, COME ON—PEOPLE ARE WAITING.

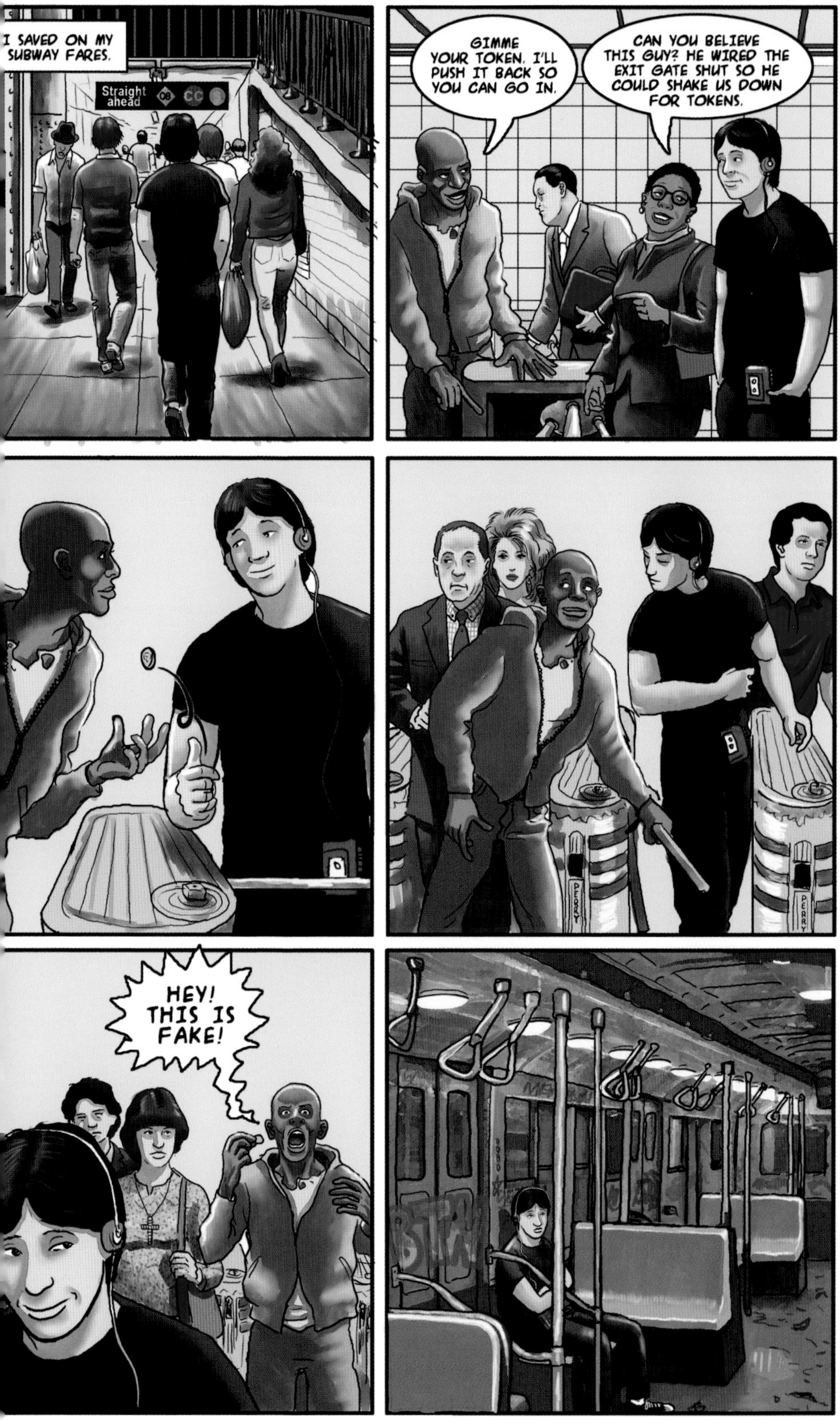
I SAVED ON MY SUBWAY FARES.
Straight ahead
GIMME YOUR TOKEN. I'LL PUSH IT BACK SO YOU CAN GO IN.
CAN YOU BELIEVE THIS GUY? HE WIRED THE EXIT GATE SHUT SO HE COULD SHAKE US DOWN FOR TOKENS.
PERRY
PERRY
HEY! THIS IS FAKE!

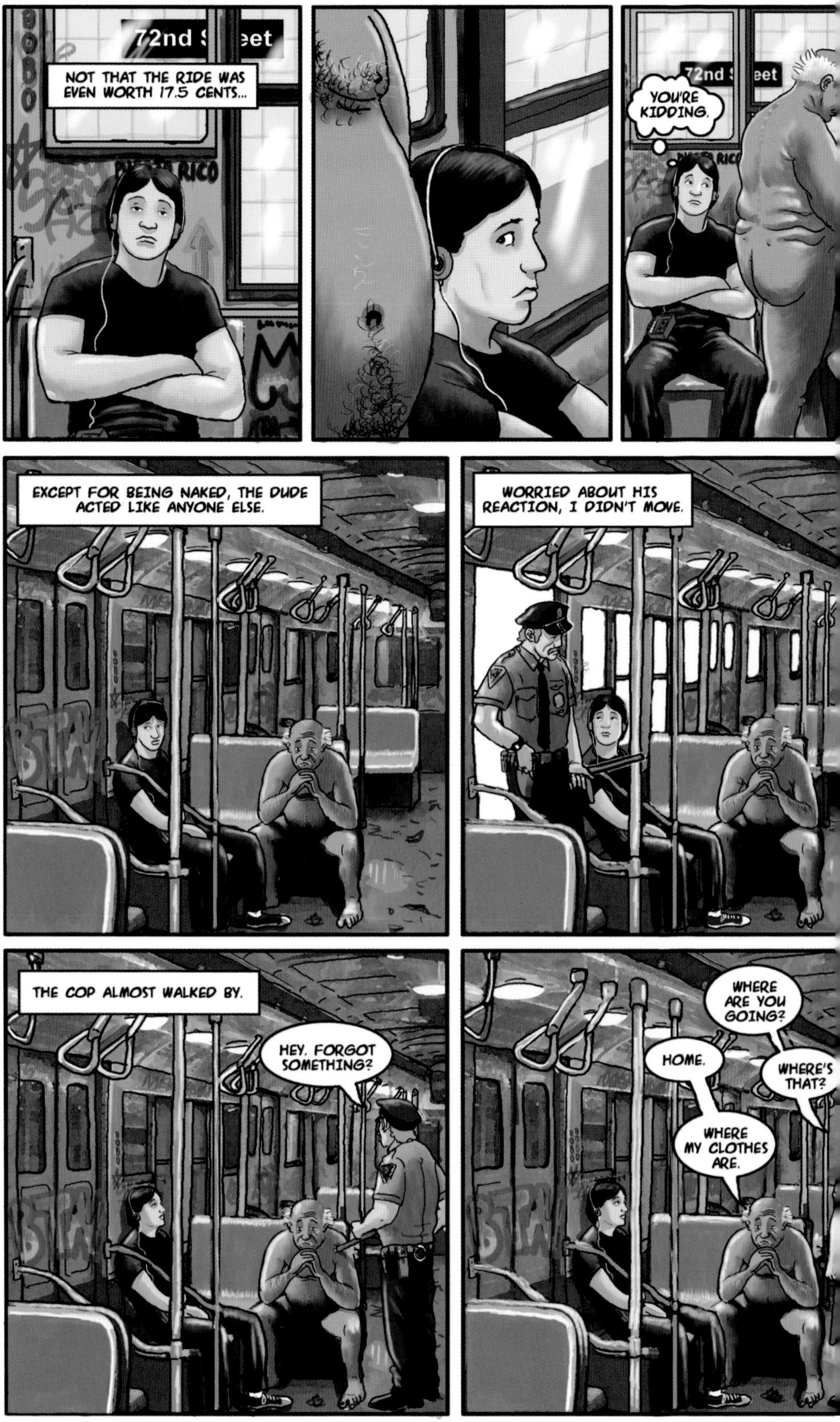
72nd Street
NOT THAT THE RIDE WAS EVEN WORTH 17.5 CENTS...
72nd Street
YOU'RE KIDDING.
EXCEPT FOR BEING NAKED, THE DUDE ACTED LIKE ANYONE ELSE.
WORRIED ABOUT HIS REACTION, I DIDN'T MOVE.
THE COP ALMOST WALKED BY.
HEY. FORGOT SOMETHING?
WHERE ARE YOU GOING?
HOME.
WHERE'S THAT?
WHERE MY CLOTHES ARE.

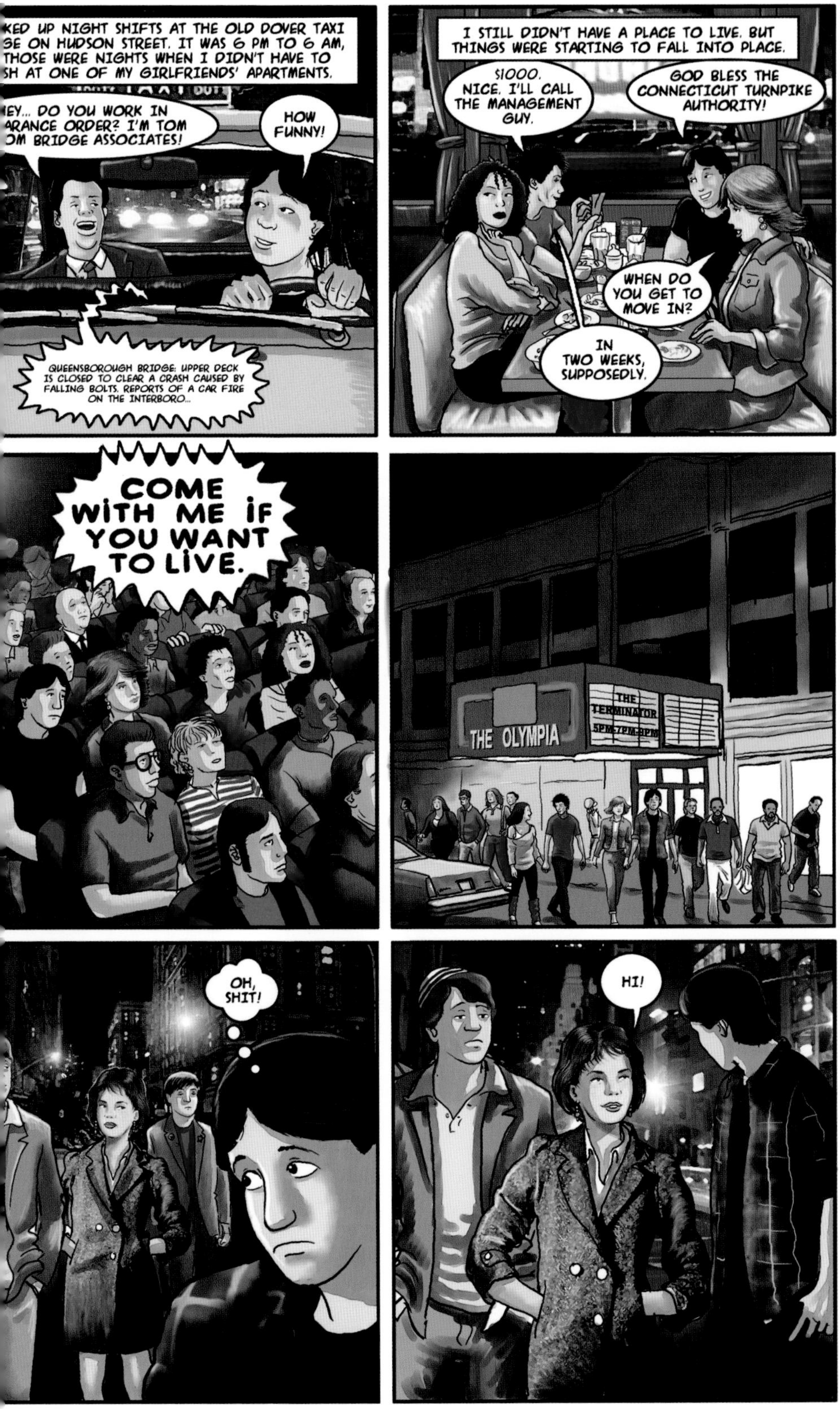
KED UP NIGHT SHIFTS AT THE OLD DOVER TAXI
GE ON HUDSON STREET. IT WAS 6 PM TO 6 AM,
THOSE WERE NIGHTS WHEN I DIDN'T HAVE TO
SH AT ONE OF MY GIRLFRIENDS' APARTMENTS.
EY... DO YOU WORK IN ARANCE ORDER? I'M TOM OM BRIDGE ASSOCIATES!
HOW FUNNY!
QUEENSBOROUGH BRIDGE: UPPER DECK IS CLOSED TO CLEAR A CRASH CAUSED BY FALLING BOLTS. REPORTS OF A CAR FIRE ON THE INTERBORO...
I STILL DIDN'T HAVE A PLACE TO LIVE. BUT THINGS WERE STARTING TO FALL INTO PLACE.
$1000. NICE. I'LL CALL THE MANAGEMENT GUY.
GOD BLESS THE CONNECTICUT TURNPIKE AUTHORITY!
WHEN DO YOU GET TO MOVE IN?
IN TWO WEEKS, SUPPOSEDLY.
COME WITH ME IF YOU WANT TO LIVE.
THE OLYMPIA
THE TERMINATOR
OH, SHIT!
HI!

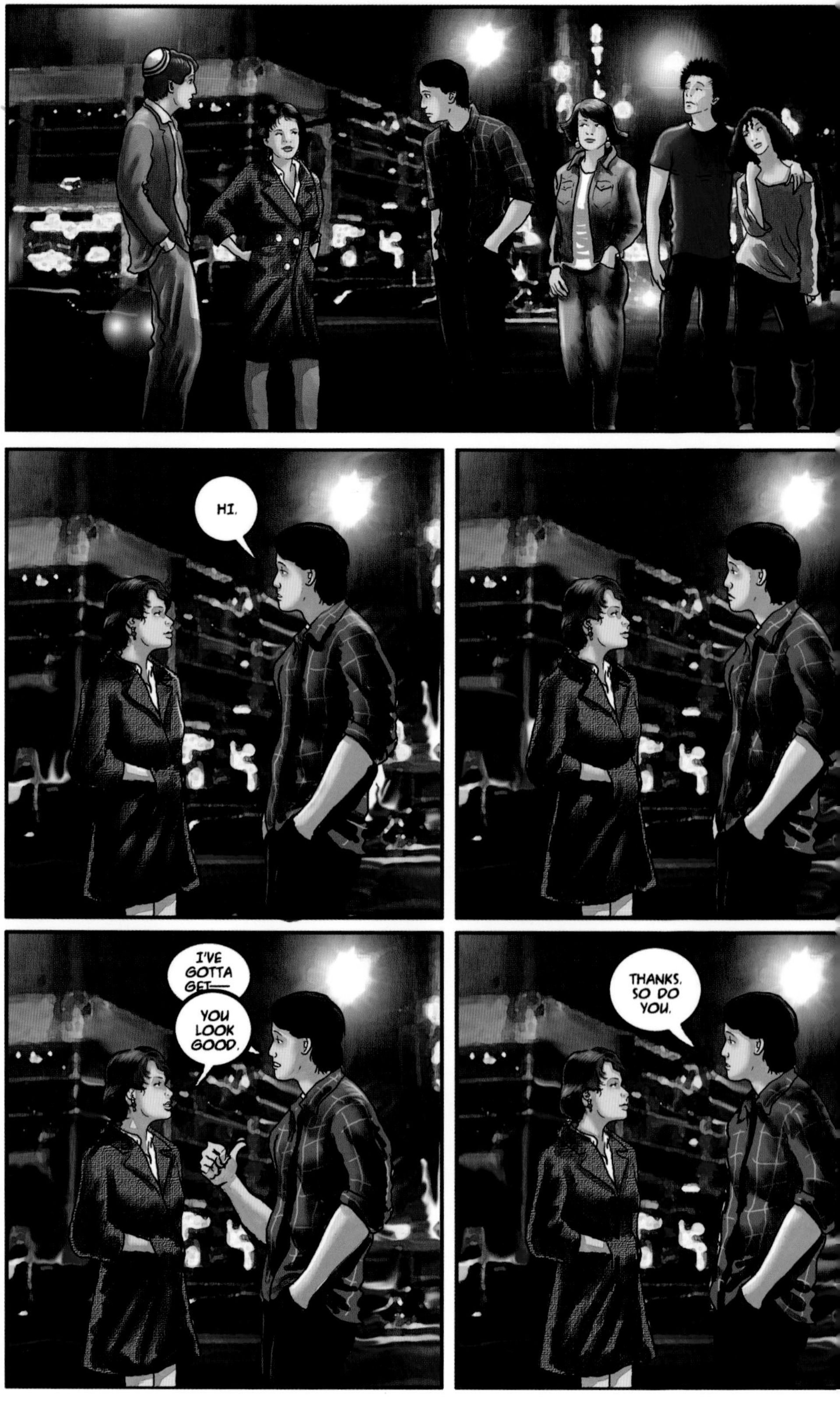
HI.
I'VE GOTTA GET—
YOU LOOK GOOD.
THANKS. SO DO YOU.

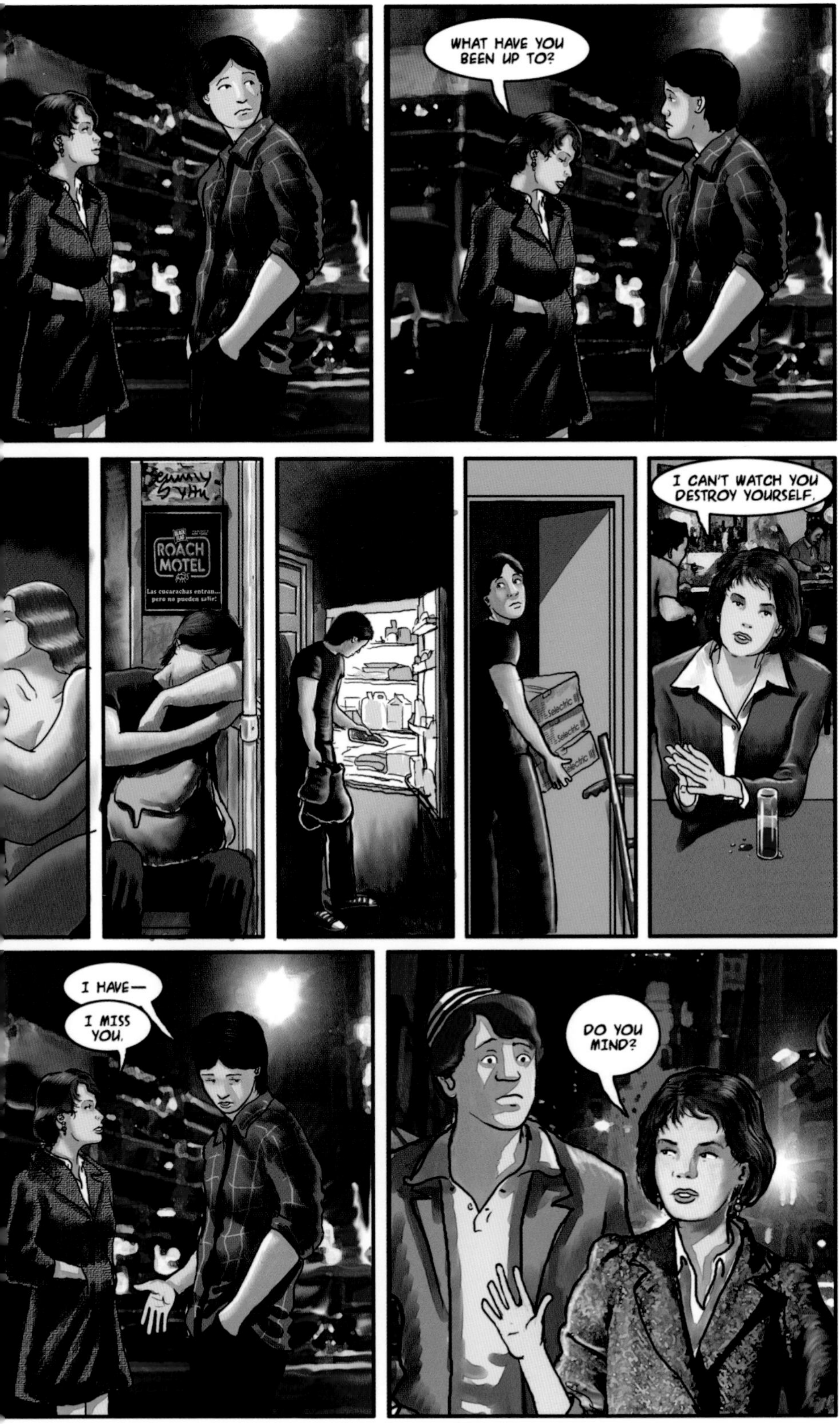
WHAT HAVE YOU BEEN UP TO?
ROACH MOTEL
Las cucarachas entran... pero no pueden salir!
I CAN'T WATCH YOU DESTROY YOURSELF.
I HAVE—
I MISS YOU.
DO YOU MIND?

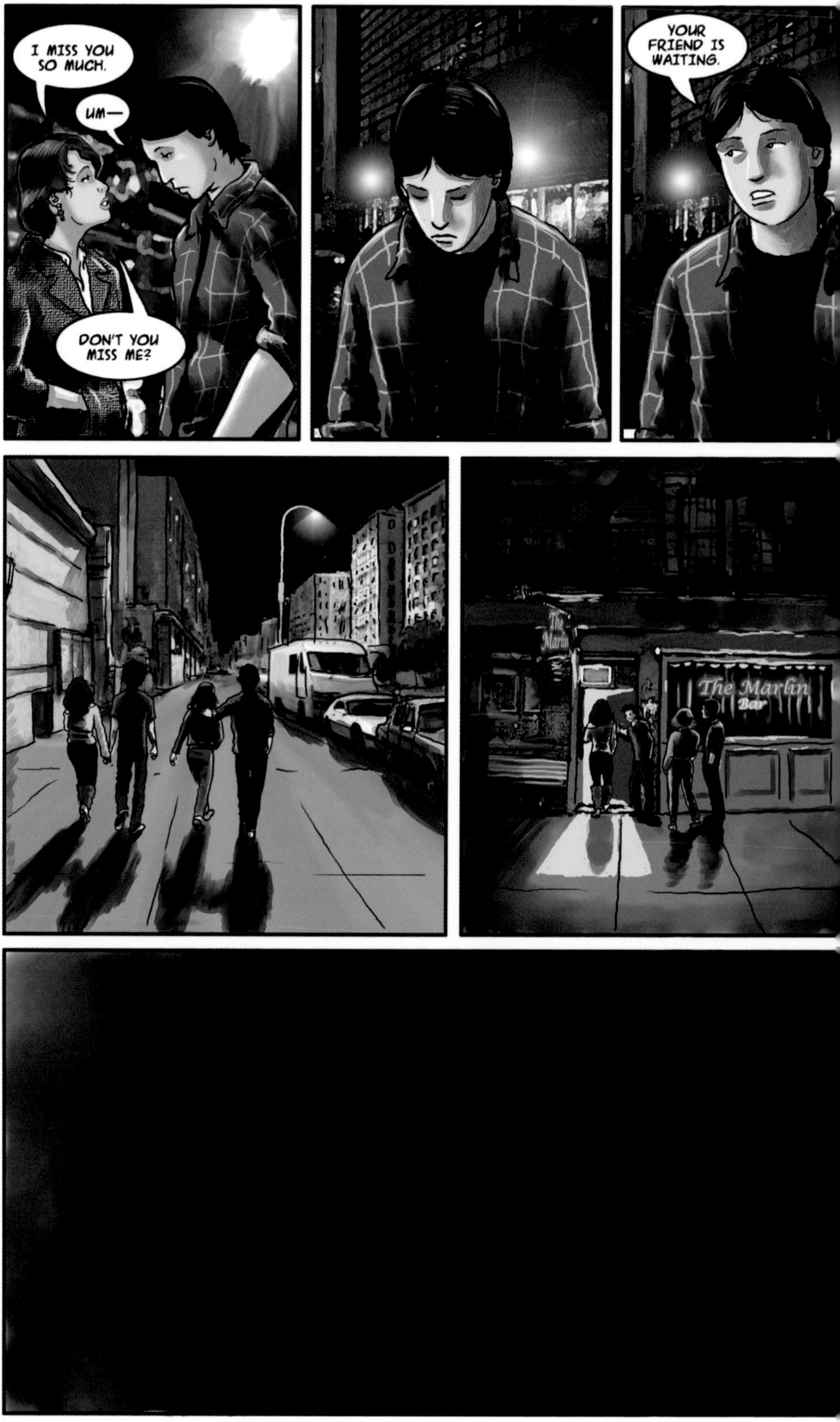
I MISS YOU SO MUCH.
UM—
DON'T YOU MISS ME?
YOUR FRIEND IS WAITING.
The Marlin Bar

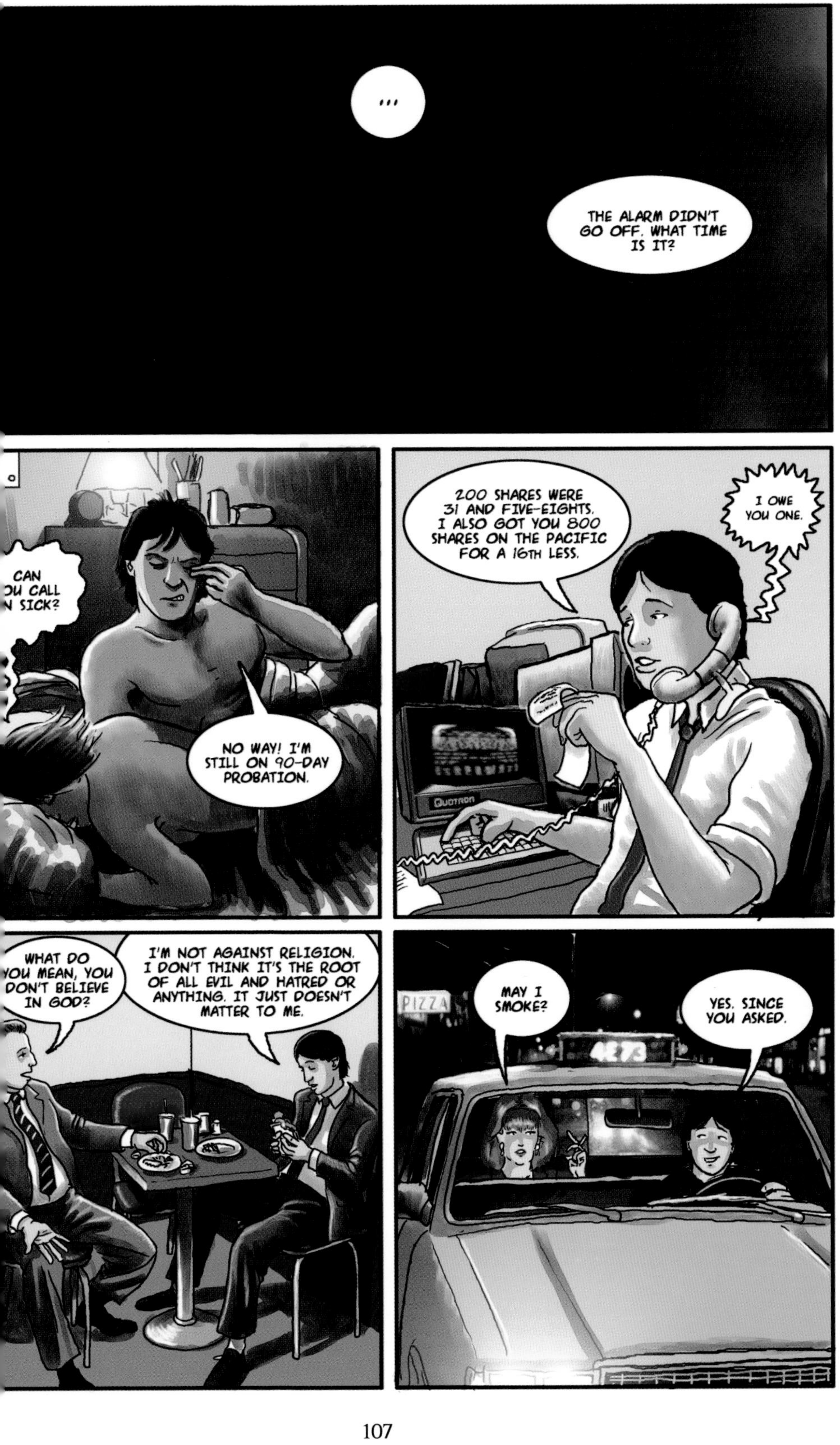
...
THE ALARM DIDN'T GO OFF. WHAT TIME IS IT?
CAN OU CALL N SICK?
NO WAY! I'M STILL ON 90-DAY PROBATION.
200 SHARES WERE 31 AND FIVE-EIGHTS. I ALSO GOT YOU 800 SHARES ON THE PACIFIC FOR A 16TH LESS.
I OWE YOU ONE.
QUOTRON
WHAT DO YOU MEAN, YOU DON'T BELIEVE IN GOD?
I'M NOT AGAINST RELIGION. I DON'T THINK IT'S THE ROOT OF ALL EVIL AND HATRED OR ANYTHING. IT JUST DOESN'T MATTER TO ME.
PIZZA
MAY I SMOKE?
YES. SINCE YOU ASKED.
4E73

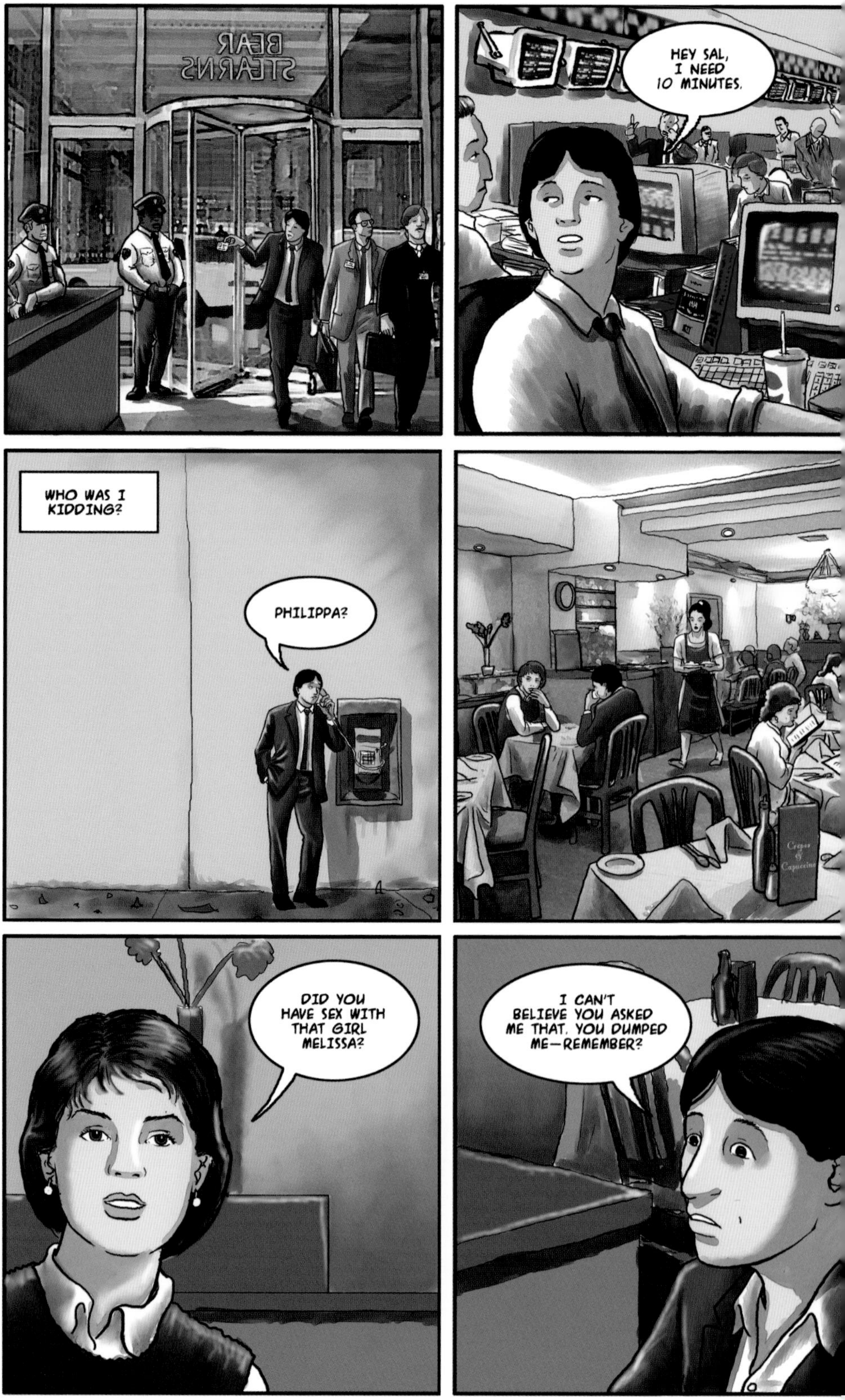
BEAR STEARNS
HEY SAL, I NEED 10 MINUTES.
WHO WAS I KIDDING?
PHILIPPA?
DID YOU HAVE SEX WITH THAT GIRL MELISSA?
I CAN'T BELIEVE YOU ASKED ME THAT. YOU DUMPED ME—REMEMBER?

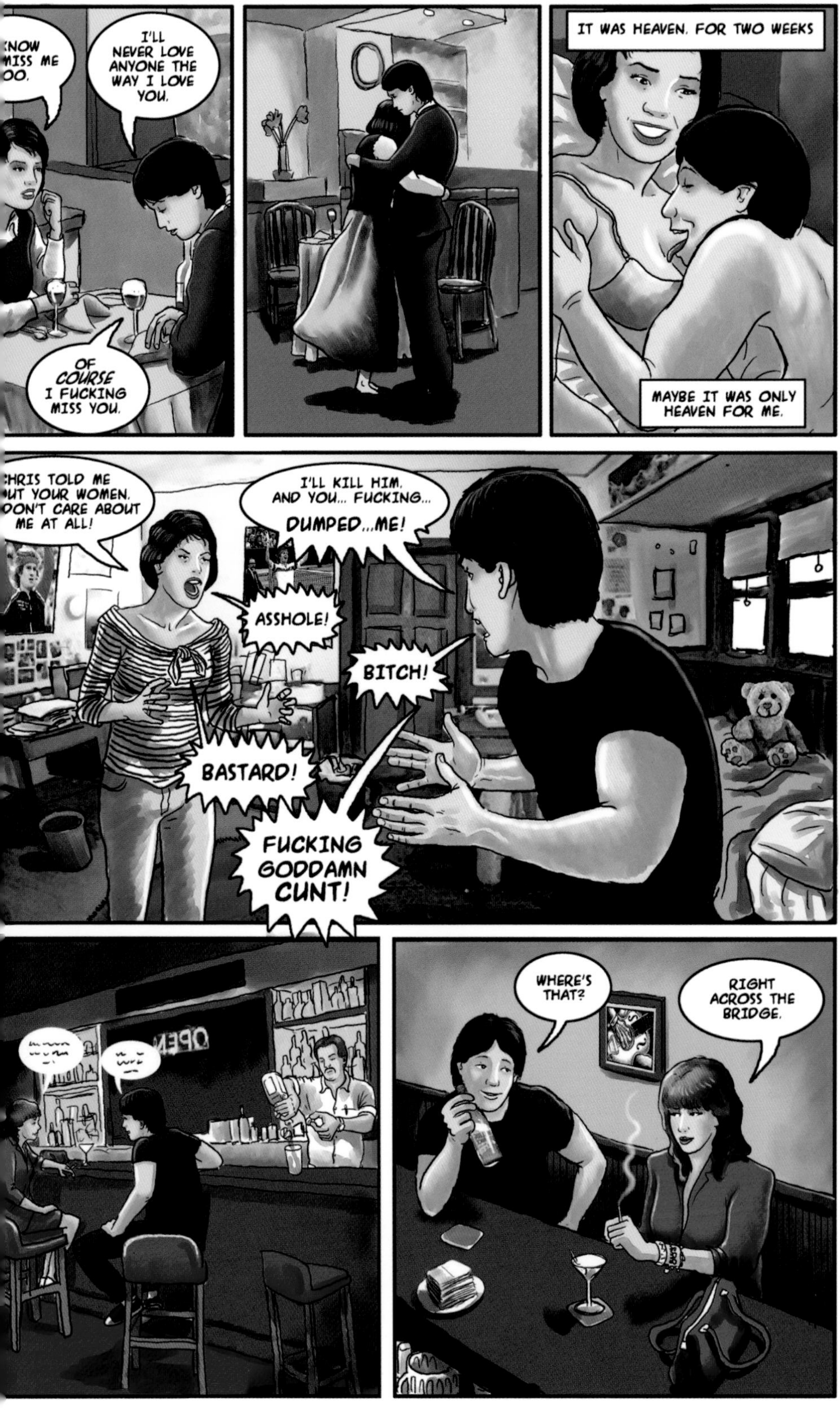
:NOW
MISS ME
OO.
I'LL NEVER LOVE ANYONE THE WAY I LOVE YOU.
OF COURSE I FUCKING MISS YOU.
IT WAS HEAVEN. FOR TWO WEEKS
MAYBE IT WAS ONLY HEAVEN FOR ME.
CHRIS TOLD ME
UT YOUR WOMEN.
ON'T CARE ABOUT
ME AT ALL!
I'LL KILL HIM. AND YOU... FUCKING... DUMPED...ME!
ASSHOLE!
BITCH!
BASTARD!
FUCKING GODDAMN CUNT!
OPEN
WHERE'S THAT?
RIGHT ACROSS THE BRIDGE.

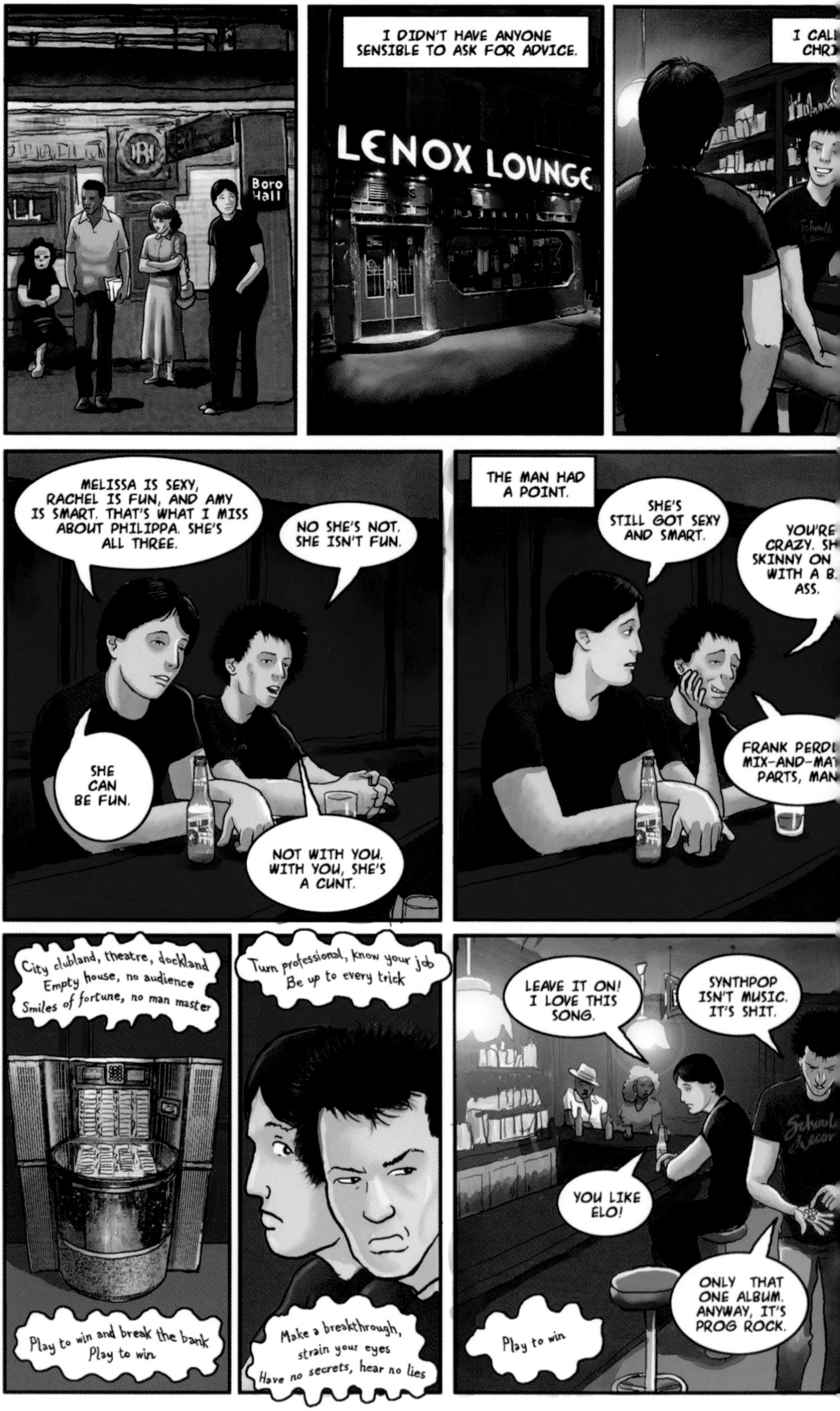
Boro Hall
I DIDN'T HAVE ANYONE SENSIBLE TO ASK FOR ADVICE.
LENOX LOUNGE
I CAL
CHRI
MELISSA IS SEXY, RACHEL IS FUN, AND AMY IS SMART. THAT'S WHAT I MISS ABOUT PHILIPPA. SHE'S ALL THREE.
NO SHE'S NOT. SHE ISN'T FUN.
SHE CAN BE FUN.
NOT WITH YOU. WITH YOU, SHE'S A CUNT.
THE MAN HAD A POINT.
SHE'S STILL GOT SEXY AND SMART.
YOU'RE CRAZY. SH SKINNY ON WITH A B ASS.
FRANK PERD MIX-AND-MA PARTS, MAN
City clubland, theatre, dockland
Empty house, no audience
Smiles of fortune, no man master
Play to win and break the bank
Play to win
Turn professional, know your job
Be up to every trick
Make a breakthrough, strain your eyes
Have no secrets, hear no lies
LEAVE IT ON! I LOVE THIS SONG.
SYNTHPOP ISN'T MUSIC. IT'S SHIT.
YOU LIKE ELO!
ONLY THAT ONE ALBUM. ANYWAY, IT'S PROG ROCK.
Play to win

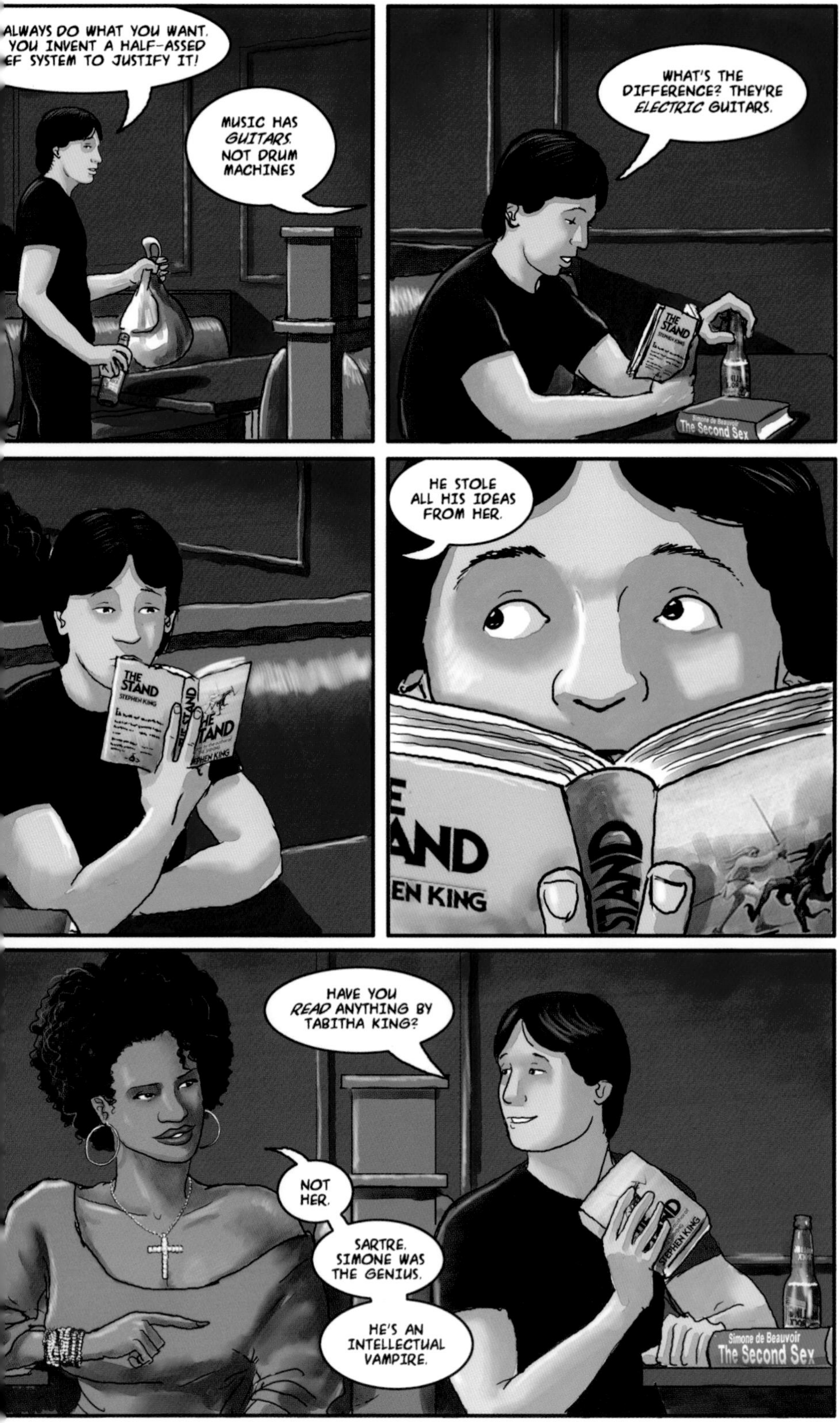
ALWAYS DO WHAT YOU WANT. YOU INVENT A HALF-ASSED EF SYSTEM TO JUSTIFY IT!
MUSIC HAS GUITARS. NOT DRUM MACHINES
WHAT'S THE DIFFERENCE? THEY'RE ELECTRIC GUITARS.
THE STAND
STEPHEN KING
Simone de Beauvoir
The Second Sex
HE STOLE ALL HIS IDEAS FROM HER.
HAVE YOU READ ANYTHING BY TABITHA KING?
NOT HER.
SARTRE. SIMONE WAS THE GENIUS.
HE'S AN INTELLECTUAL VAMPIRE.
Simone de Beauvoir
The Second Sex

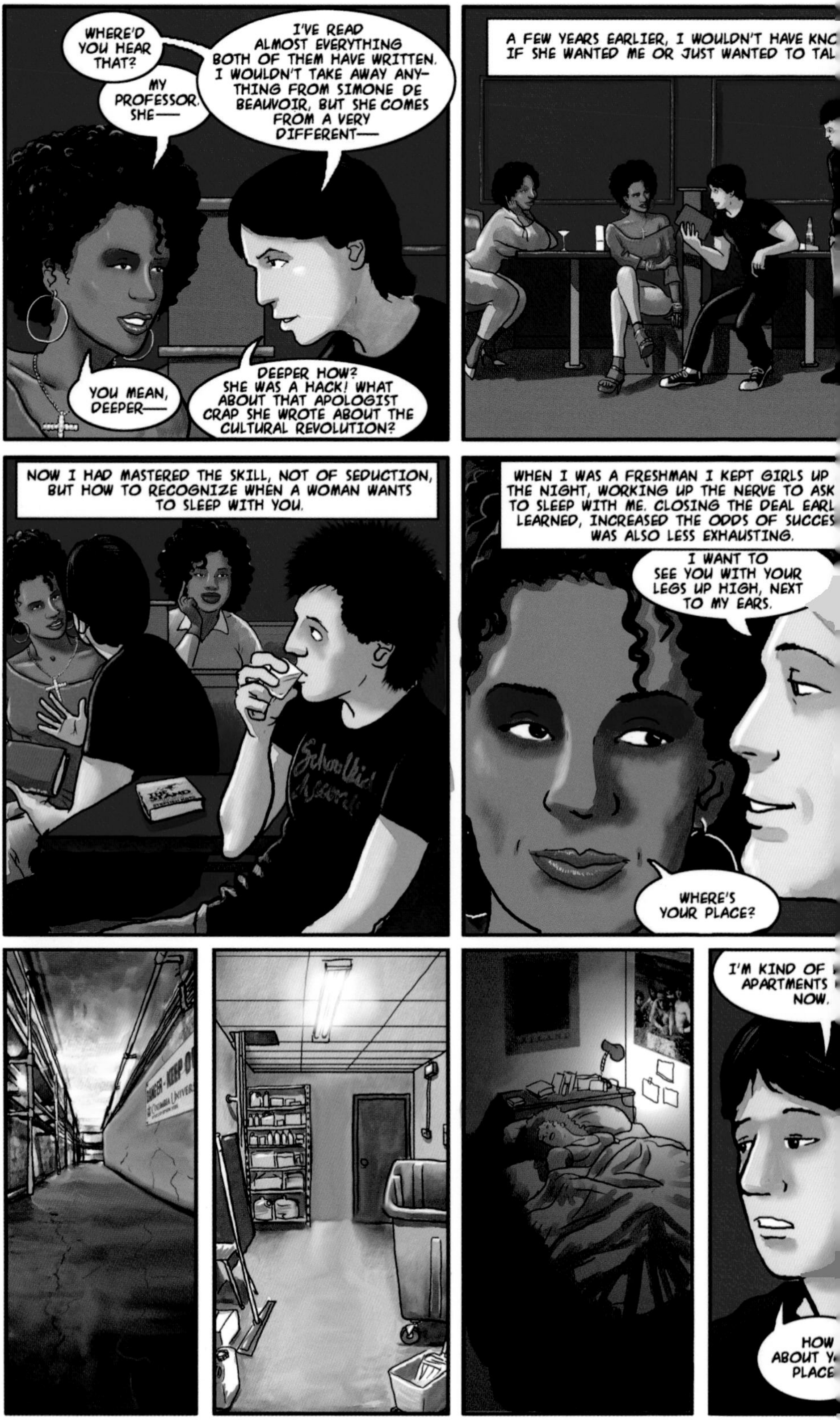
WHERE'D YOU HEAR THAT?
I'VE READ ALMOST EVERYTHING BOTH OF THEM HAVE WRITTEN. I WOULDN'T TAKE AWAY ANY-THING FROM SIMONE DE BEAUVOIR, BUT SHE COMES FROM A VERY DIFFERENT—
MY PROFESSOR. SHE—
YOU MEAN, DEEPER—
DEEPER HOW? SHE WAS A HACK! WHAT ABOUT THAT APOLOGIST CRAP SHE WROTE ABOUT THE CULTURAL REVOLUTION?
A FEW YEARS EARLIER, I WOULDN'T HAVE KNO
IF SHE WANTED ME OR JUST WANTED TO TAL
NOW I HAD MASTERED THE SKILL, NOT OF SEDUCTION, BUT HOW TO RECOGNIZE WHEN A WOMAN WANTS TO SLEEP WITH YOU.
WHEN I WAS A FRESHMAN I KEPT GIRLS UP
THE NIGHT, WORKING UP THE NERVE TO ASK
TO SLEEP WITH ME. CLOSING THE DEAL EARL
LEARNED, INCREASED THE ODDS OF SUCCES
WAS ALSO LESS EXHAUSTING.
I WANT TO SEE YOU WITH YOUR LEGS UP HIGH, NEXT TO MY EARS.
WHERE'S YOUR PLACE?
I'M KIND OF
APARTMENTS
NOW.
HOW
ABOUT Y
PLACE

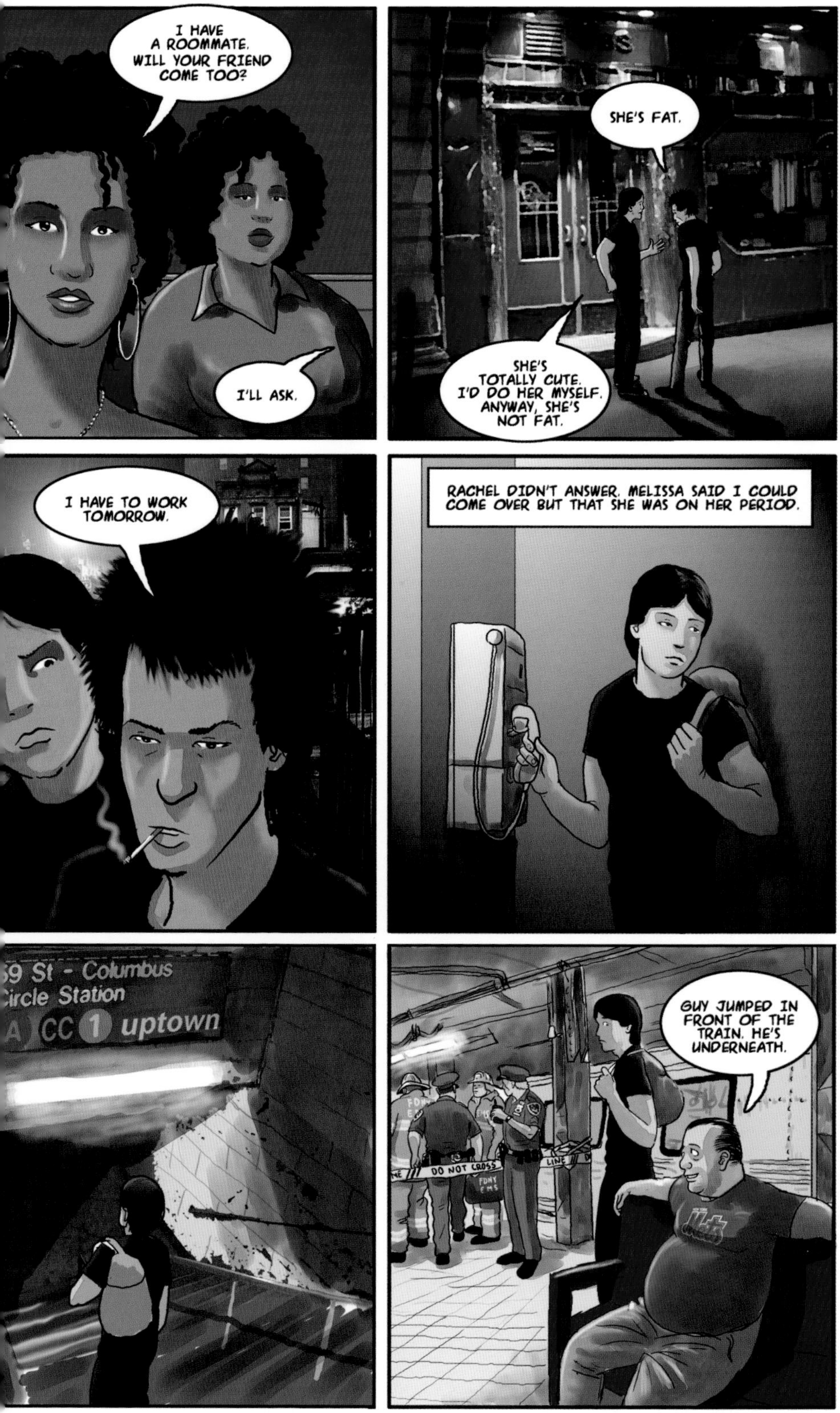
I HAVE A ROOMMATE. WILL YOUR FRIEND COME TOO?
I'LL ASK.
SHE'S FAT.
SHE'S TOTALLY CUTE. I'D DO HER MYSELF. ANYWAY, SHE'S NOT FAT.
I HAVE TO WORK TOMORROW.
RACHEL DIDN'T ANSWER. MELISSA SAID I COULD COME OVER BUT THAT SHE WAS ON HER PERIOD.
59 St - Columbus Circle Station
A CC 1 uptown
DO NOT CROSS
FDNY EMS
GUY JUMPED IN FRONT OF THE TRAIN. HE'S UNDERNEATH.

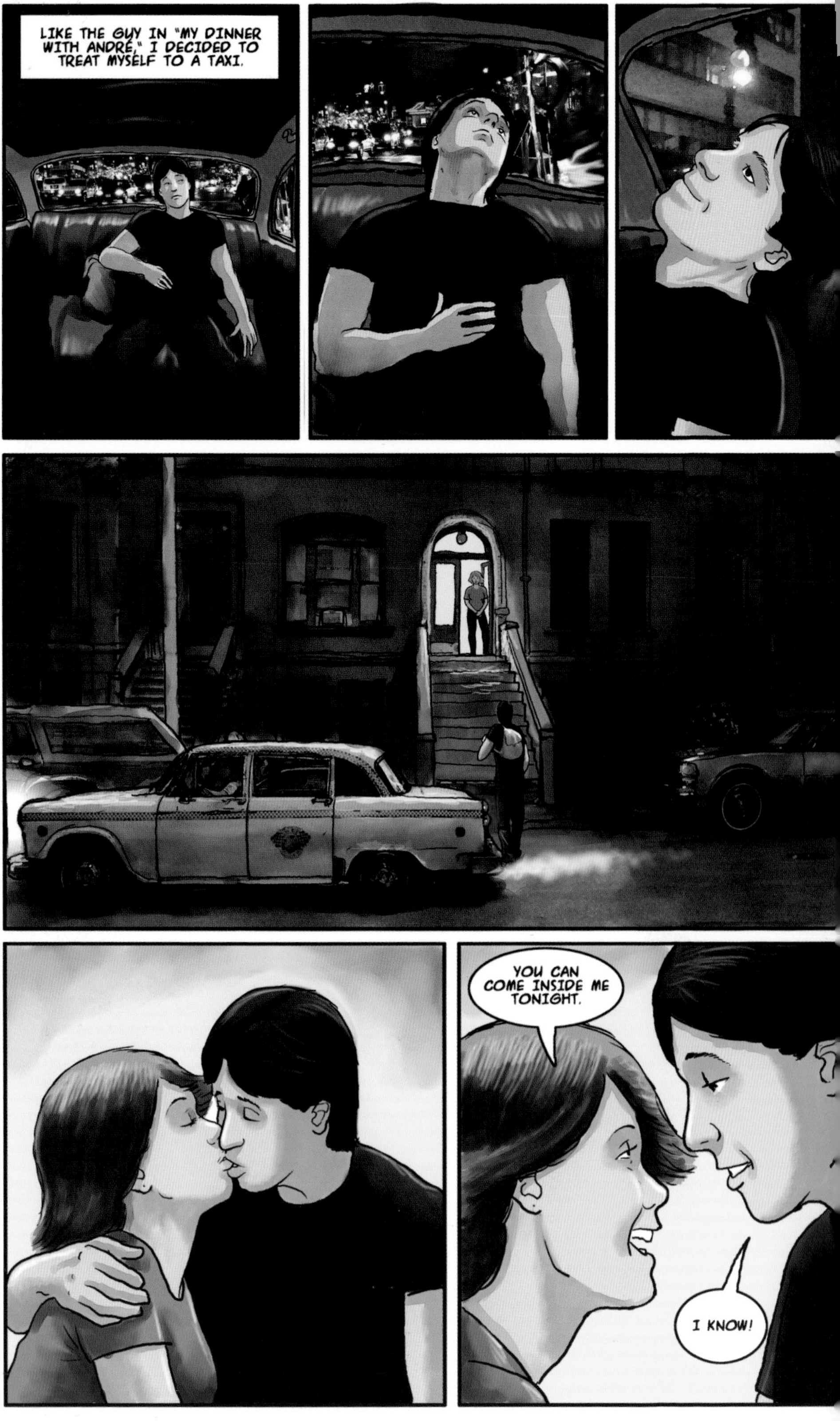

LIKE THE GUY IN "MY DINNER WITH ANDRÉ," I DECIDED TO TREAT MYSELF TO A TAXI.
YOU CAN COME INSIDE ME TONIGHT.
I KNOW!

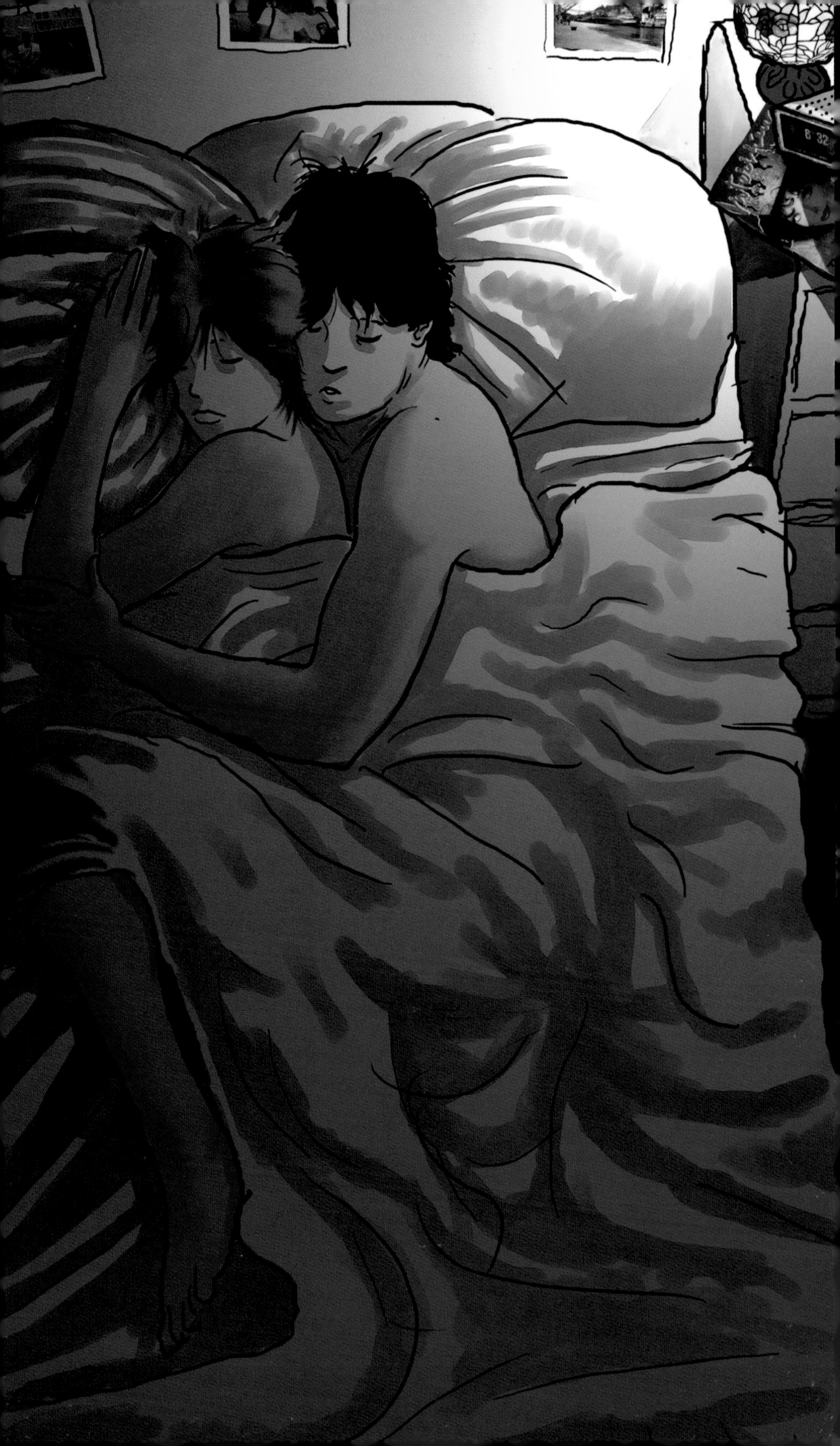

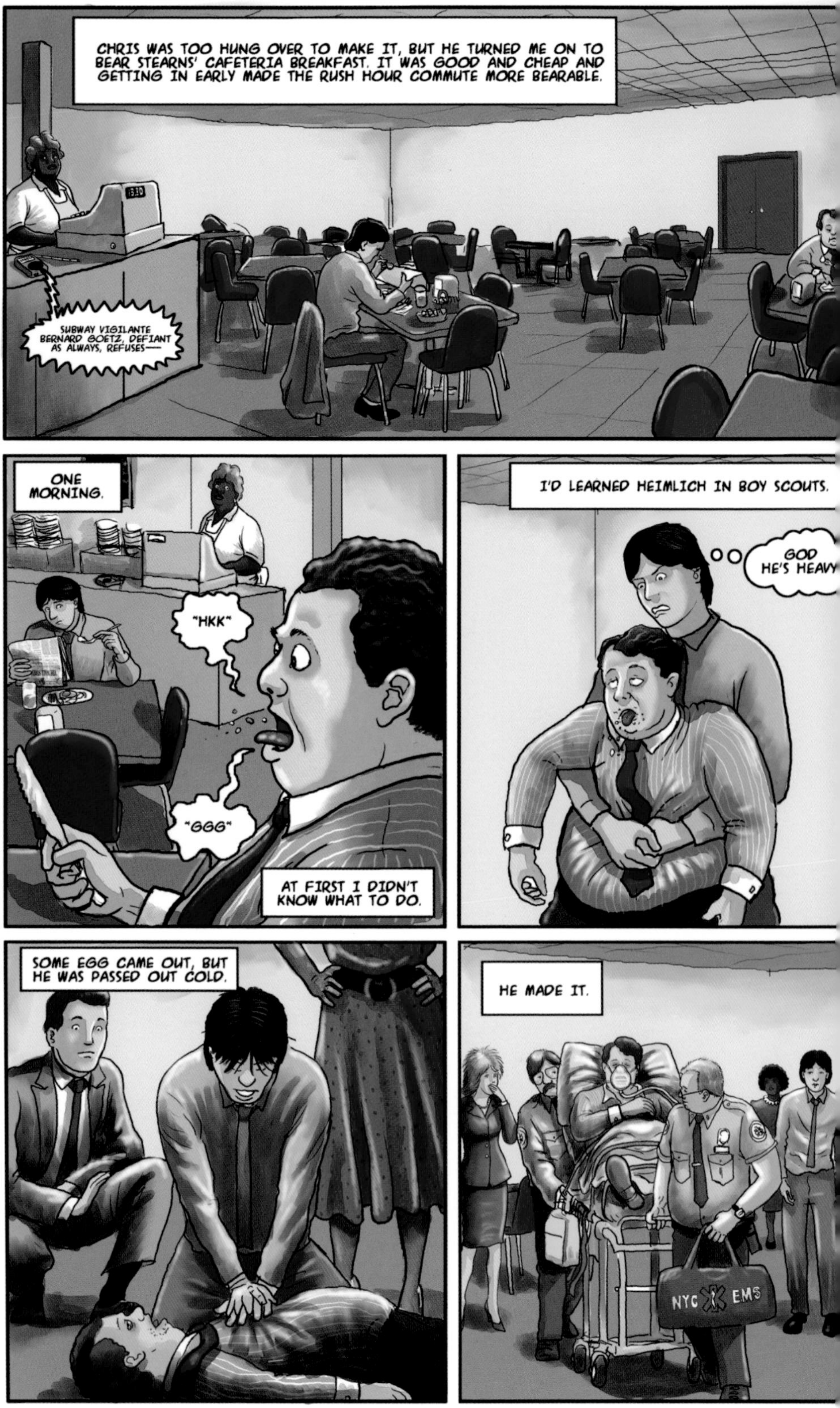
CHRIS WAS TOO HUNG OVER TO MAKE IT, BUT HE TURNED ME ON TO BEAR STEARNS' CAFETERIA BREAKFAST. IT WAS GOOD AND CHEAP AND GETTING IN EARLY MADE THE RUSH HOUR COMMUTE MORE BEARABLE.
SUBWAY VIGILANTE BERNARD GOETZ, DEFIANT AS ALWAYS, REFUSES—
ONE MORNING.
"HKK"
"GGG"
AT FIRST I DIDN'T KNOW WHAT TO DO.
I'D LEARNED HEIMLICH IN BOY SCOUTS.
GOD HE'S HEAVY
SOME EGG CAME OUT, BUT HE WAS PASSED OUT COLD.
HE MADE IT.
NYC EMS

DAYS LATER, THE GUY WAS BACK ... RK. HE FOUND ME AT MY DESK.

DON'T FUCK ME ...HIS. YOU SURE ABOUT AT BLOCK TRADE?

ARE YOU TED RALL?

HEY, YOU'RE BACK! ARE YOU OK?

THANKS FOR SAVING MY LIFE.

THAT'S ALL HE SAID.

WHAT IS IT?

OPEN IT!

$2000.

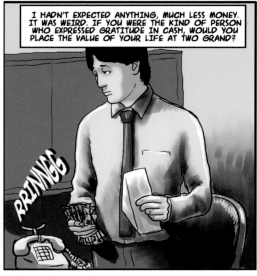

I HADN'T EXPECTED ANYTHING, MUCH LESS MONEY. IT WAS WEIRD. IF YOU WERE THE KIND OF PERSON WHO EXPRESSED GRATITUDE IN CASH, WOULD YOU PLACE THE VALUE OF YOUR LIFE AT TWO GRAND?

RRINNGG

THOUGHT ABOUT RETURNING IT. BUT THEN:

EARANCE ER. TALK.

YO. THE C OF O CAME THROUGH. ME AT THE MANAGEMENT COMPANY. 5:30, 37 T AVENUE. FIRST, LAST AND ONE EXTRA MONTH :AUSE WE DON'T HAVE CREDIT. $1275 EACH.

WHEN?

SEPTEMBER 15TH.

117

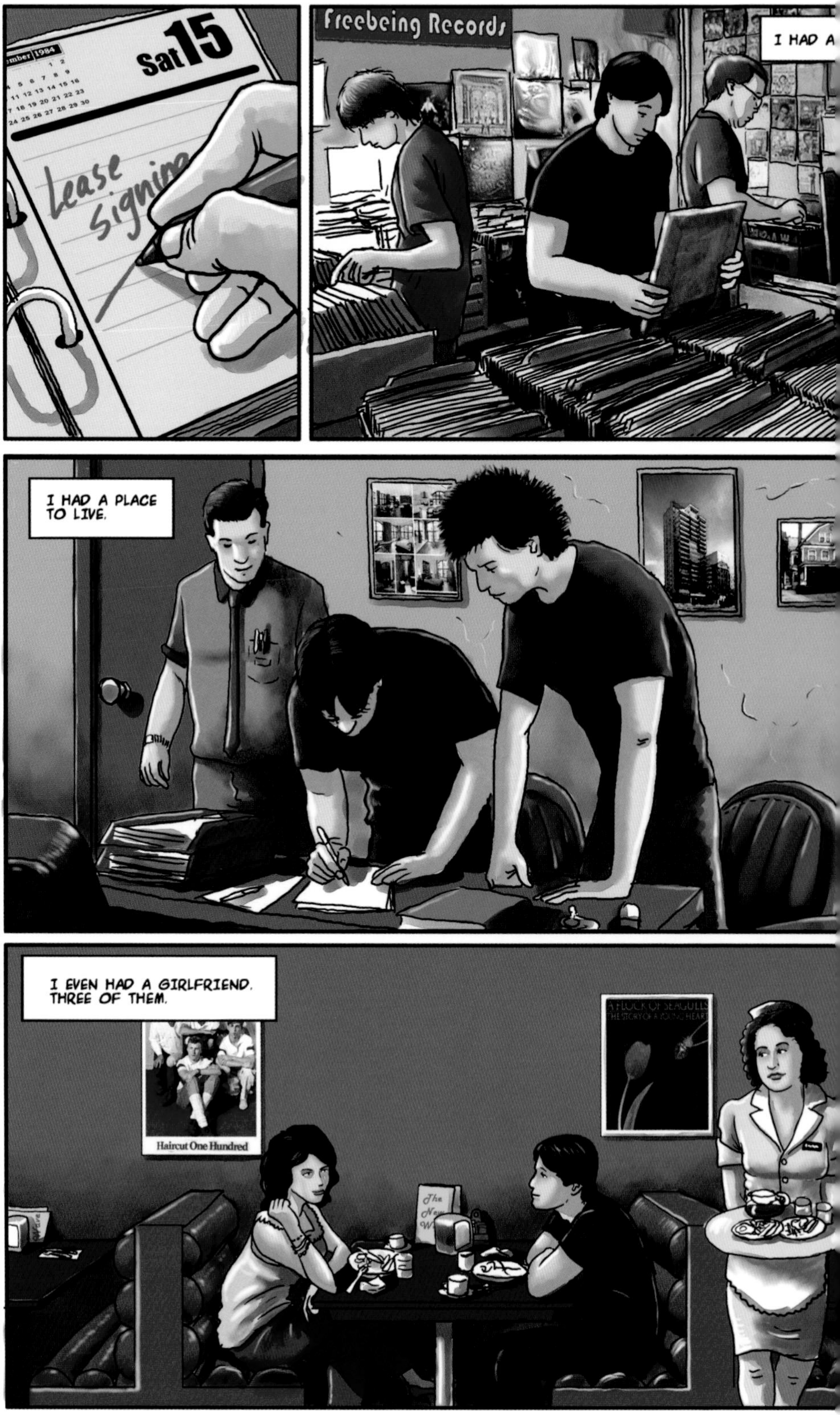
Sat 15
Lease signin
Freebeing Records
I HAD A
I HAD A PLACE TO LIVE.
I EVEN HAD A GIRLFRIEND. THREE OF THEM.
Haircut One Hundred
A FLOCK OF SEAGULLS
THE STORY OF A YOUNG HEART

…EY WERE AWESOME. WHAT I …ON'T FIGURE OUT WAS WHAT …Y SAW IN ME. I STILL CAN'T.

…THE SMART ONE. REDESIGNED …C FLOW IN THE WEST VILLAGE …HE CITY. READ DERRIDA. RE- …NIGHTS: MONDAYS, WEDNES- …D THURSDAYS. AWAY ON WEEK- …ROBABLY TO VISIT A BOYFRIEND.

MELISSA: THE SEXY ONE. INTO HAVING SEX IN PUBLIC SPACES; SUGGESTED THREESOMES WITH HER GIRLFRIENDS. COULDN'T COOK FOR SHIT. (SUSPECTING HER OFFER TO BE A LOYALTY TEST, I REFUSE.) REGULAR NIGHTS: TUESDAYS AND SUNDAYS.

RACHEL: "THE FUN ONE. PARALEGAL. OWNED A CAR. INTO FLIPPER, THE BIG BOYS AND REAGAN YOUTH. LOVED TRASHY FILMS. WEEKENDS.

SHITTIEST WHITE WINE YOU'VE GOT!

…ACHEL HELPED ME …MOVE MY STUFF.

LOOKS LIKE SOMEONE HAS BEEN SLEEPING HERE.

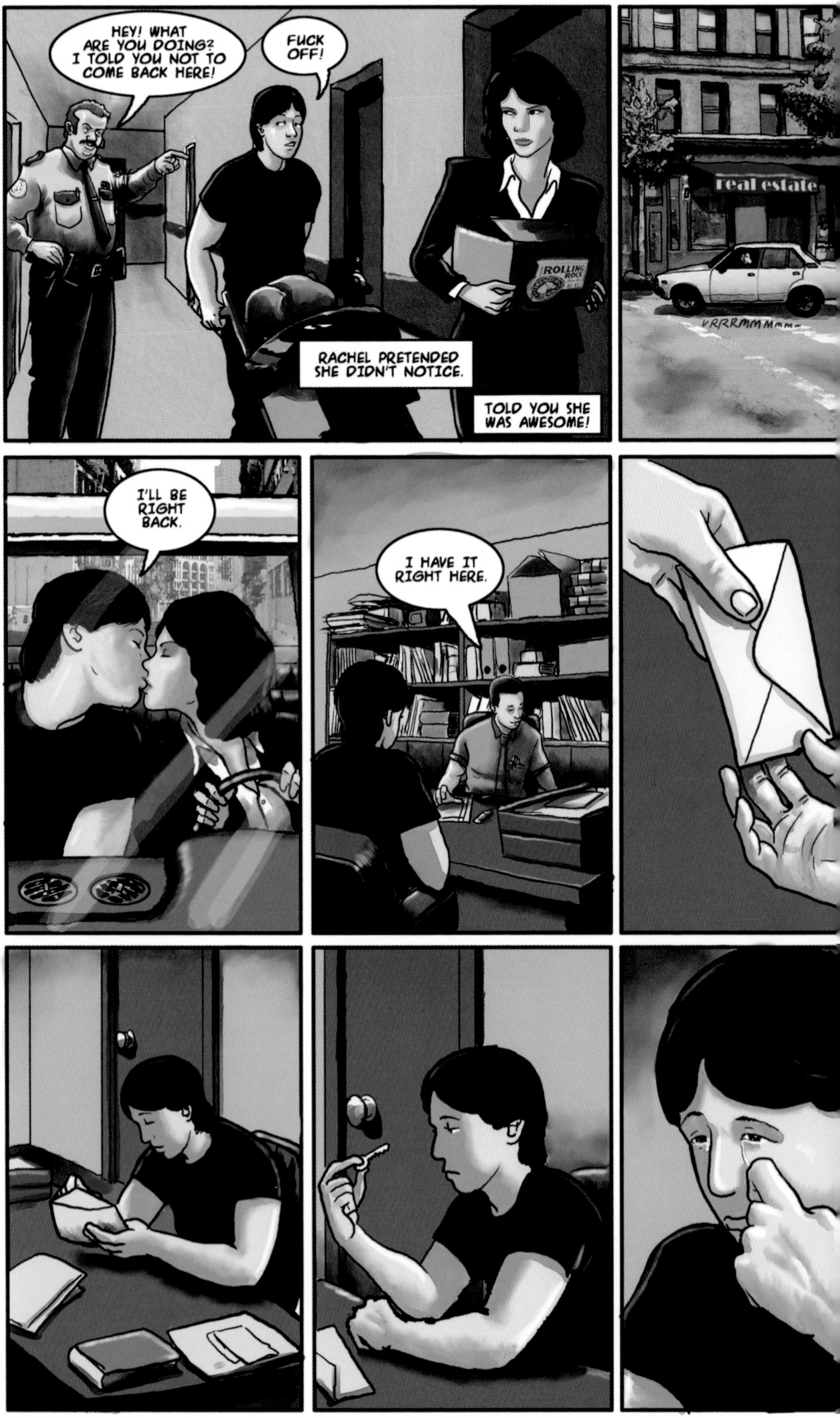
HEY! WHAT ARE YOU DOING? I TOLD YOU NOT TO COME BACK HERE!
FUCK OFF!
RACHEL PRETENDED SHE DIDN'T NOTICE.
TOLD YOU SHE WAS AWESOME!
real estate
VRRRMMMMMM
I'LL BE RIGHT BACK.
I HAVE IT RIGHT HERE.

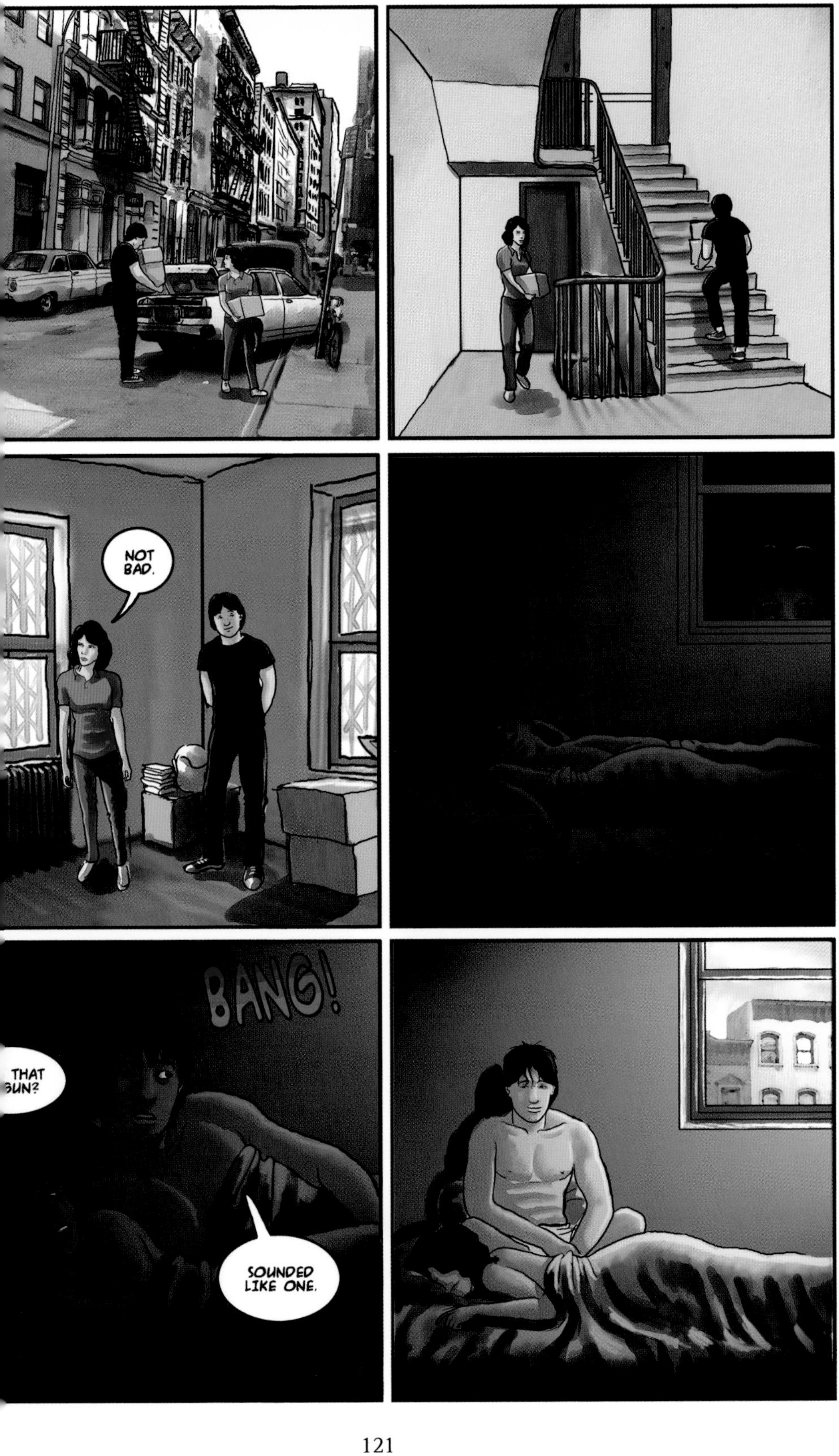
NOT BAD.
BANG!
THAT
GUN?
SOUNDED LIKE ONE.

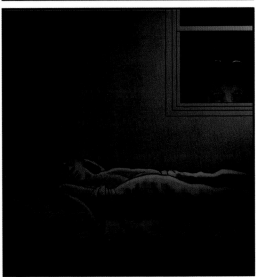

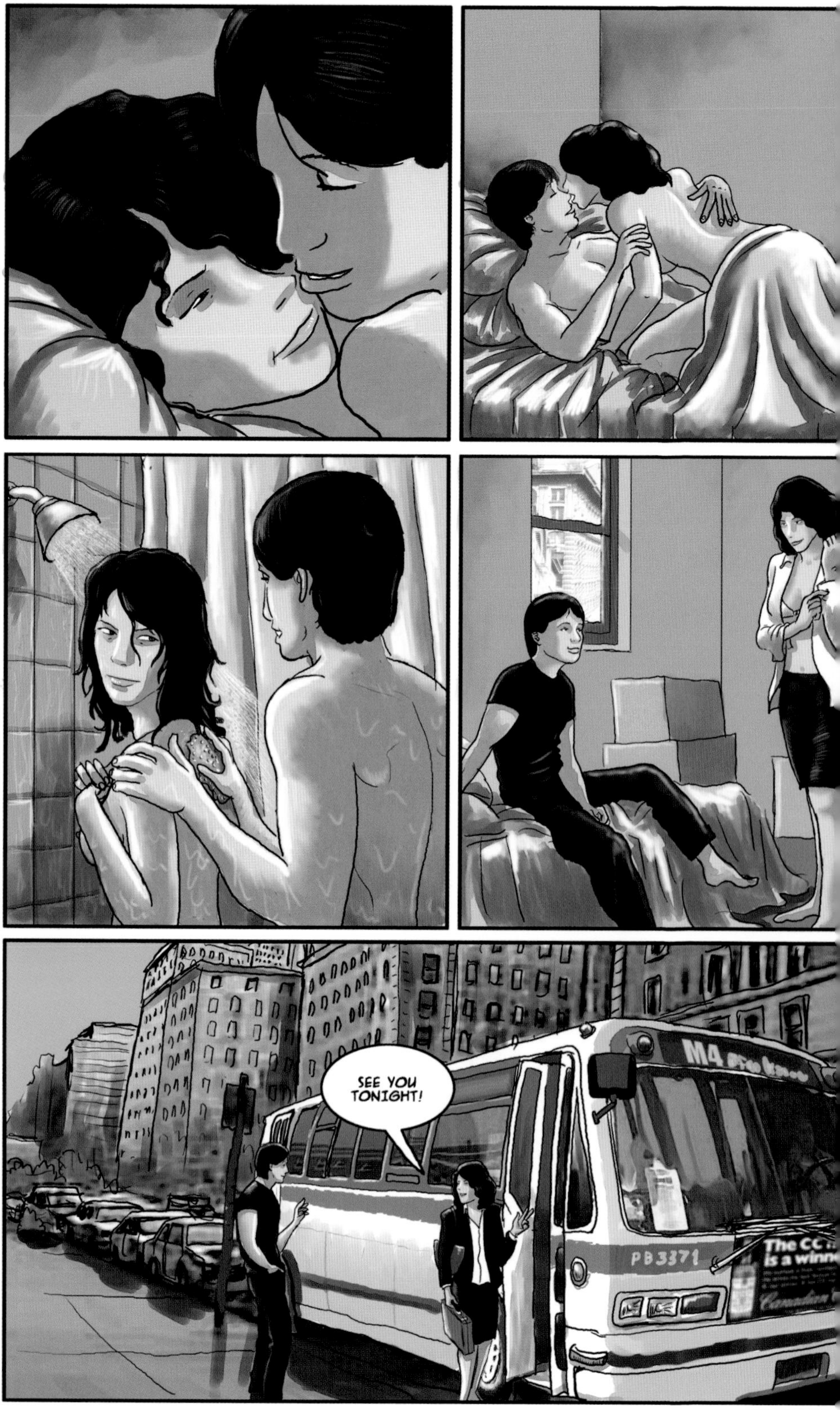
SEE YOU TONIGHT!
M4
PB 3371

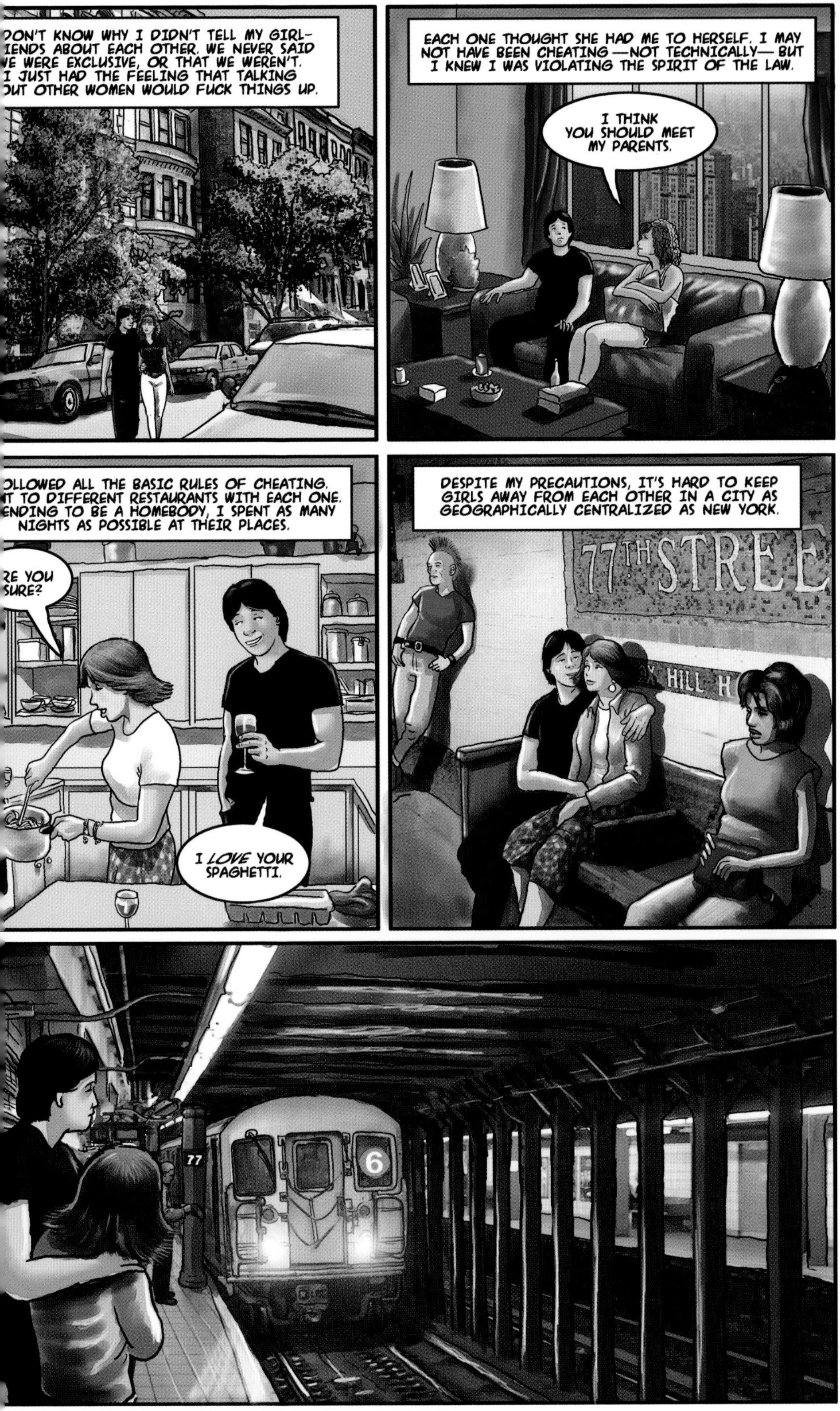
DON'T KNOW WHY I DIDN'T TELL MY GIRL-
IENDS ABOUT EACH OTHER. WE NEVER SAID
VE WERE EXCLUSIVE, OR THAT WE WEREN'T.
I JUST HAD THE FEELING THAT TALKING
OUT OTHER WOMEN WOULD FUCK THINGS UP.
EACH ONE THOUGHT SHE HAD ME TO HERSELF. I MAY NOT HAVE BEEN CHEATING —NOT TECHNICALLY— BUT I KNEW I WAS VIOLATING THE SPIRIT OF THE LAW.
I THINK YOU SHOULD MEET MY PARENTS.
OLLOWED ALL THE BASIC RULES OF CHEATING.
IT TO DIFFERENT RESTAURANTS WITH EACH ONE.
ENDING TO BE A HOMEBODY, I SPENT AS MANY
NIGHTS AS POSSIBLE AT THEIR PLACES.
RE YOU SURE?
I LOVE YOUR SPAGHETTI.
DESPITE MY PRECAUTIONS, IT'S HARD TO KEEP GIRLS AWAY FROM EACH OTHER IN A CITY AS GEOGRAPHICALLY CENTRALIZED AS NEW YORK.
77TH STREE
77
6

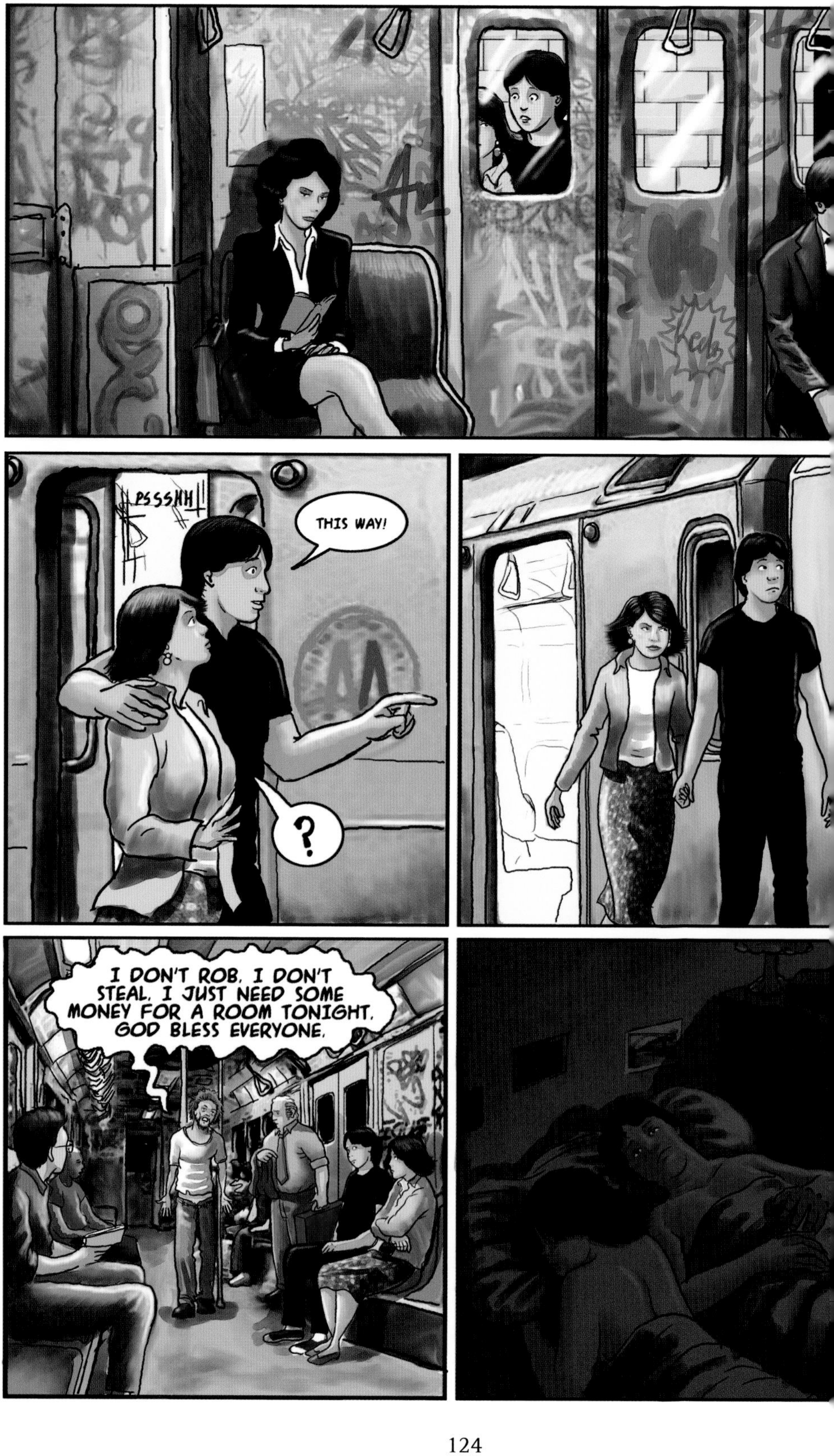
PSSSHH
THIS WAY!
?
I DON'T ROB, I DON'T STEAL, I JUST NEED SOME MONEY FOR A ROOM TONIGHT, GOD BLESS EVERYONE.

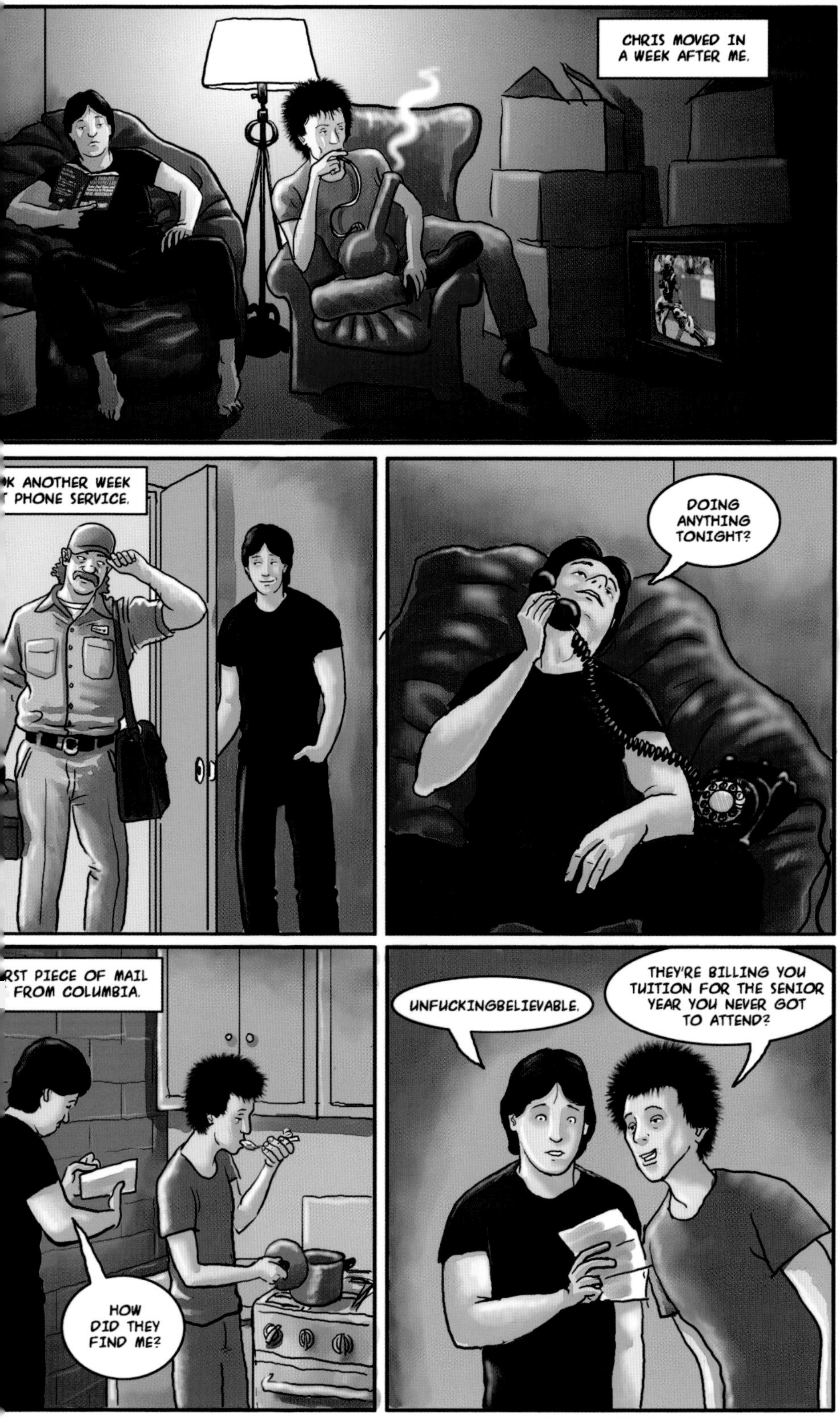
CHRIS MOVED IN A WEEK AFTER ME.
K ANOTHER WEEK
PHONE SERVICE.
DOING ANYTHING TONIGHT?
RST PIECE OF MAIL
FROM COLUMBIA.
HOW DID THEY FIND ME?
UNFUCKINGBELIEVABLE.
THEY'RE BILLING YOU TUITION FOR THE SENIOR YEAR YOU NEVER GOT TO ATTEND?

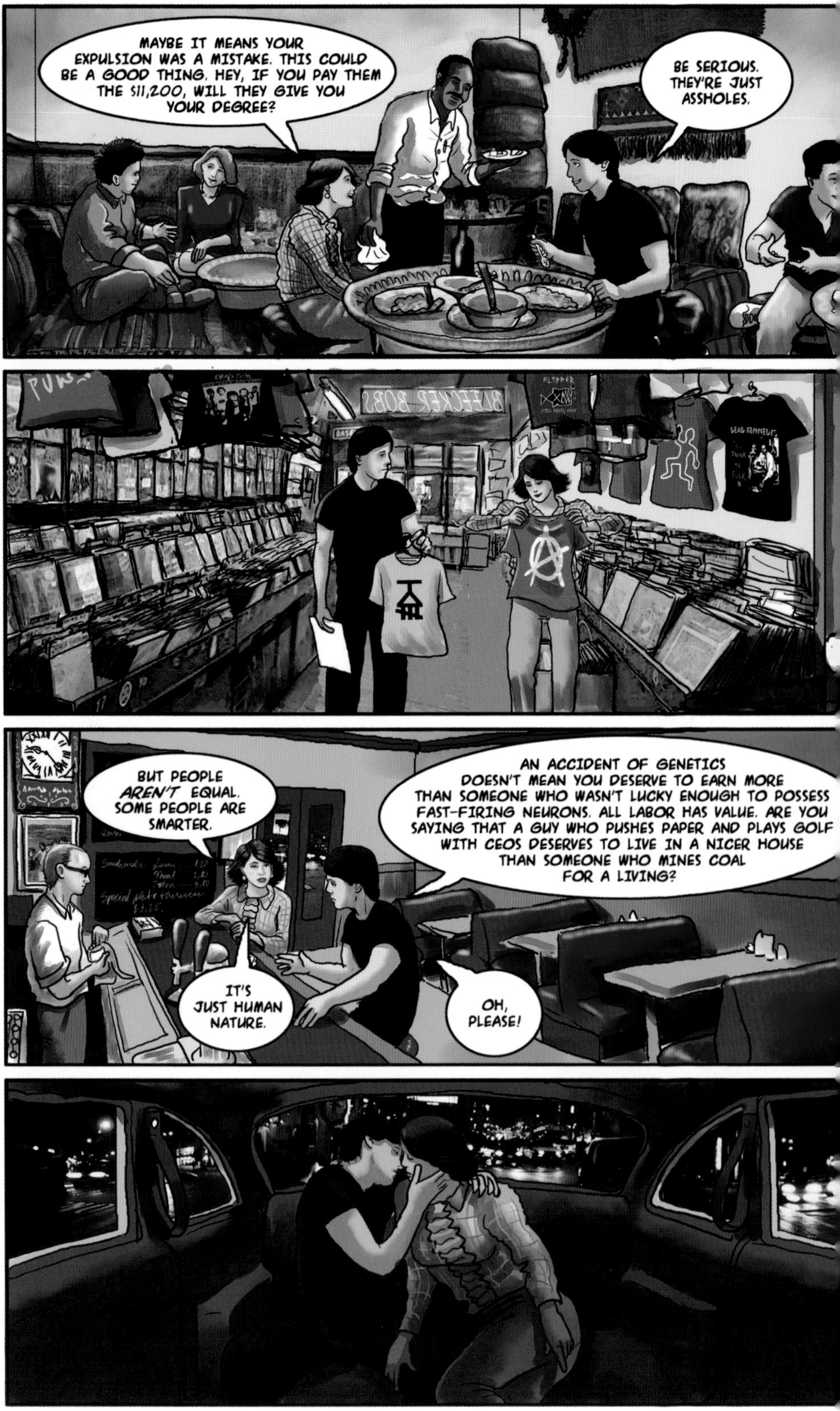
MAYBE IT MEANS YOUR EXPULSION WAS A MISTAKE. THIS COULD BE A GOOD THING. HEY, IF YOU PAY THEM THE $11,200, WILL THEY GIVE YOU YOUR DEGREE?
BE SERIOUS. THEY'RE JUST ASSHOLES.
BLEECKER BOBS
DEAD KENNEDYS
BUT PEOPLE *AREN'T* EQUAL. SOME PEOPLE ARE SMARTER.
IT'S JUST HUMAN NATURE.
AN ACCIDENT OF GENETICS DOESN'T MEAN YOU DESERVE TO EARN MORE THAN SOMEONE WHO WASN'T LUCKY ENOUGH TO POSSESS FAST-FIRING NEURONS. ALL LABOR HAS VALUE. ARE YOU SAYING THAT A GUY WHO PUSHES PAPER AND PLAYS GOLF WITH CEOS DESERVES TO LIVE IN A NICER HOUSE THAN SOMEONE WHO MINES COAL FOR A LIVING?
OH, PLEASE!

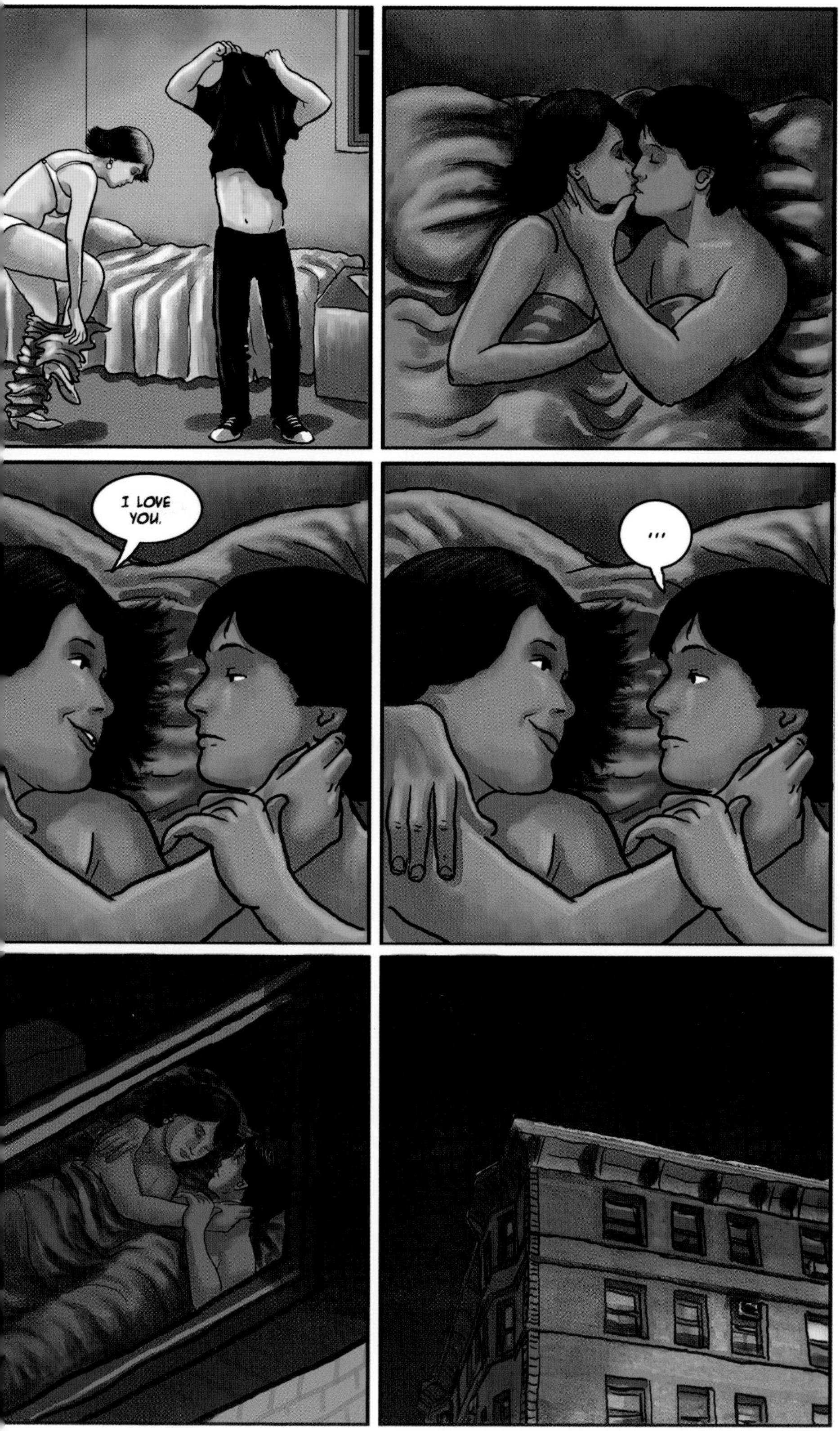
I LOVE YOU.
...

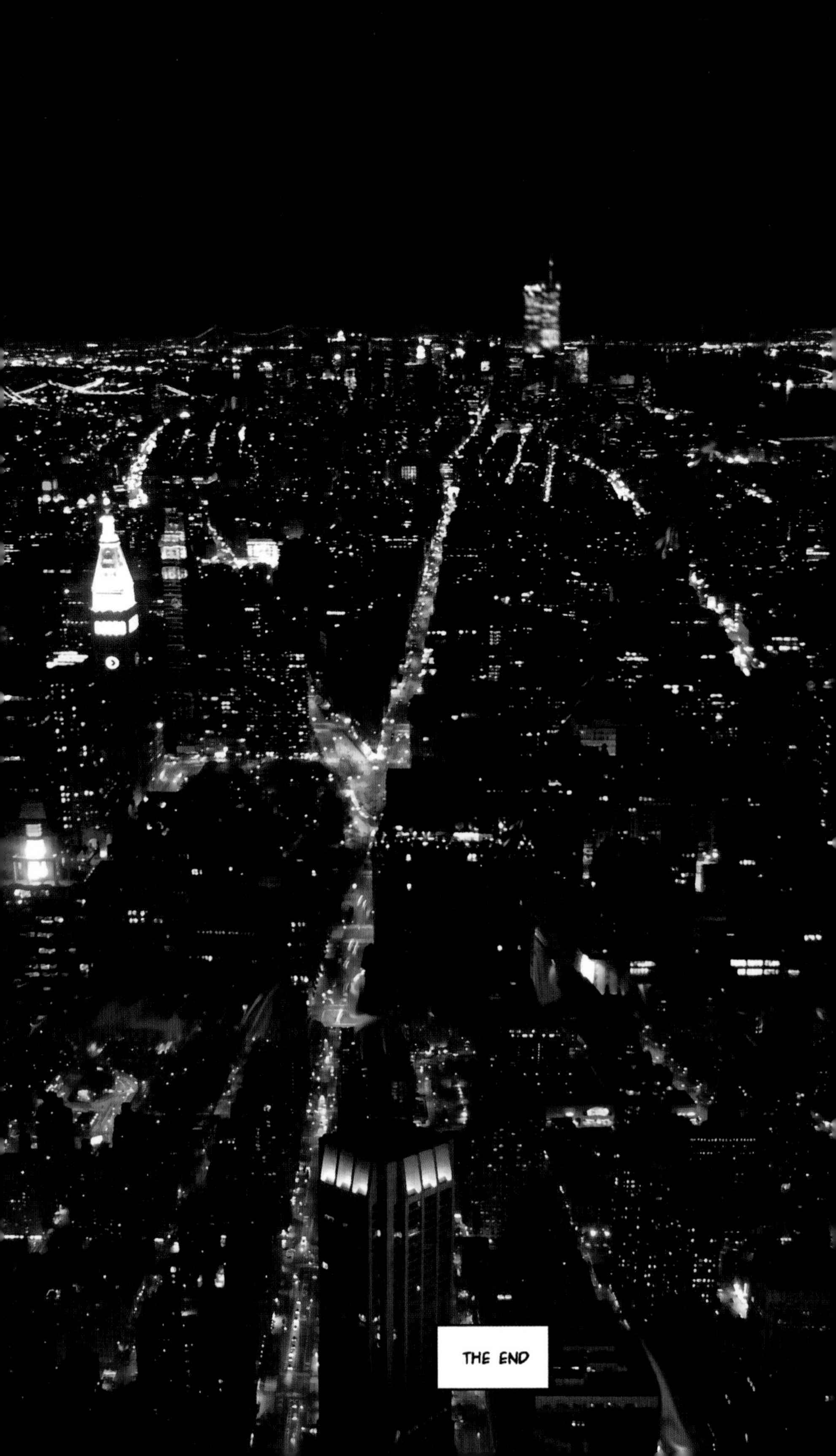
THE END

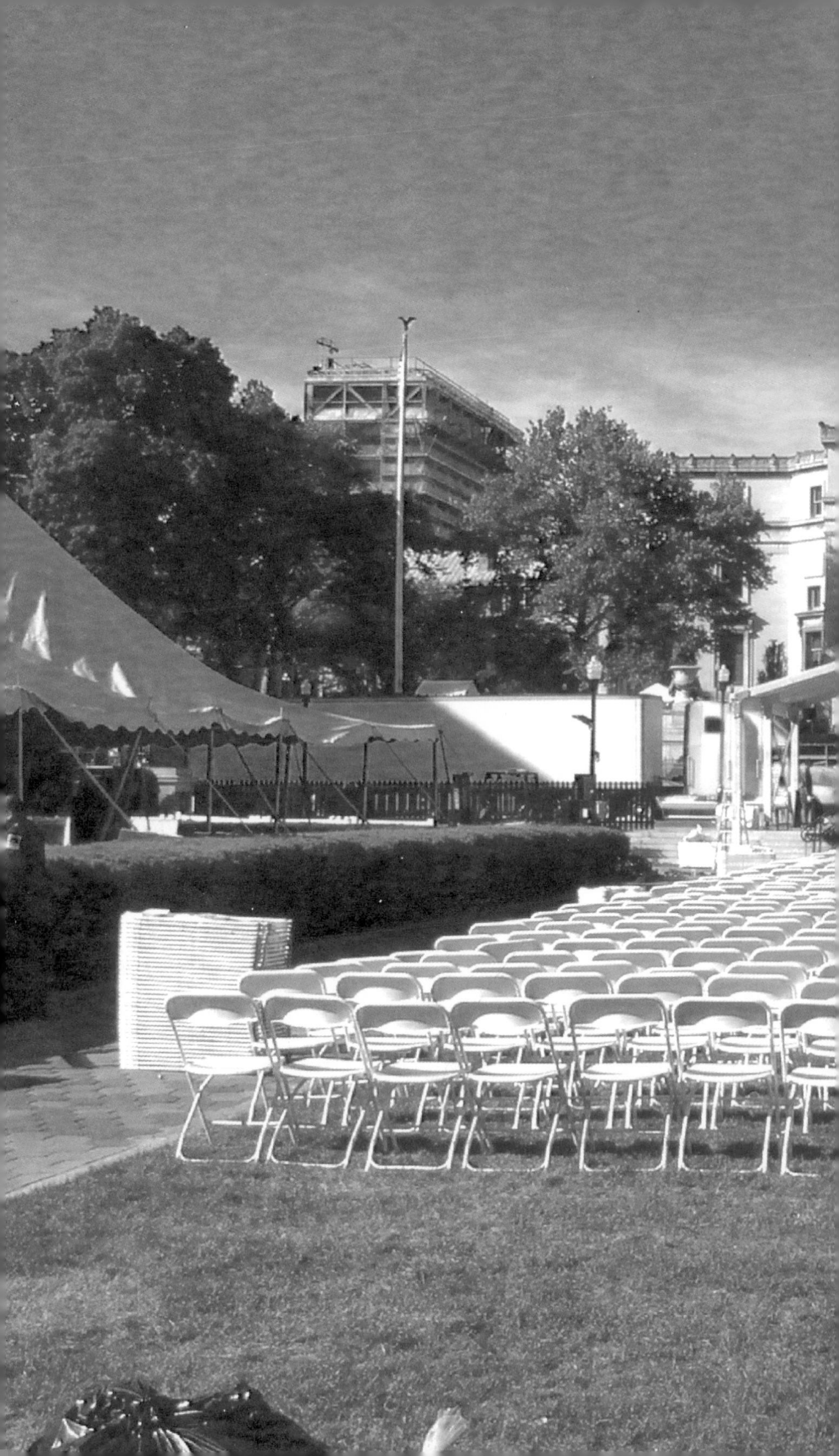